My Farming Life

My Farming Life

Tales from a shepherdess
on a remote Northumberland farm

EMMA GRAY
with Barbara Fox

sphere

SPHERE

First published in Great Britain in 2021 by Sphere

1 3 5 7 9 10 8 6 4 2

A CIP catalogue record for this book
is available from the British Library.

Hardback ISBN 978-0-7515-8202-4

Typeset in Palatino by M Rules
Printed and bound in Great Britain by Clays Ltd, Elcograf S.p.A.

Papers used by Sphere are from well-managed forests
and other responsible sources.

Sphere
An imprint of
Little, Brown Book Group
Carmelite House
50 Victoria Embankment
London EC4Y 0DZ

An Hachette UK Company
www.hachette.co.uk

www.littlebrown.co.uk

To Ewan

PART ONE

Down On My Luck

Prologue

I huddled deeper into the grubby jacket I had found in the back of Dan's van. It wasn't the most flattering or savoury thing to pull on, but as it was freezing outside and not much warmer in the van, I hardly cared.

I shivered. Is the heating not working, I wondered, as I twiddled irritably with the controls on the dashboard. My body felt cold and achy, a consequence of celebrating the new year a little too enthusiastically. Dan grunted non-committally in the driver's seat. His jaw tightened the way it always did when he was annoyed, and I noticed how he stiffly stared at the road ahead.

Don't bother being civil, I thought, as the van ate up the frosty early-morning miles.

We had spent New Year's Eve in the pub in Alston, the small Cumbria town where my boyfriend's family farmed. People in these remote communities know how to celebrate, and Dan's friends were no exception. Everyone knows everyone else, and they are all as generous as each other when it comes to buying the drinks.

Towards the end of the evening, Dan and I had had a spectacular argument. I racked my brain to remember what it had been about; although I could remember the fight, the reason behind it eluded me. But that came as no surprise. We were always quick to fire and quick to forget. This time, though, it felt different. I had been able to sense the bubbling animosity building since waking up in the morning. Dan acted as if he could hardly bear to look at me, and my attempts at conversation had been thwarted. As I curled my legs under myself dejectedly, I resigned myself to a journey home in a hung-over silence.

It was the first of January. A new start; a fresh sheet. This was not the way I had imagined 2012 beginning. It would be my third year as tenant at Fallowlees, a farm near Rothbury in Northumberland, and it was supposed to be a good year. I had a partner by my side now, for a start. We had been together long enough for him to figure in my plans for the future.

A wave of nausea swept over me. Do not be sick, I told myself. That would hardly help the already strained atmosphere. I cranked the window open a fraction and a blast of bracing Northumberland air shook up the stale interior. Dan shifted and I saw his jaw tighten once more.

'I can close it if it gets too cold.'

He grunted again.

'What is it?'

No reply.

I couldn't spend the rest of the journey like this. 'Dan, what is wrong?'

And in desperation, 'Please, speak to me!'

Finally he turned to face me. I had expected him to look angry. Instead, I was shocked to see sadness etched in his features.

We locked eyes for a fraction of a second before he turned back to the road.

'I'm sorry, Emma, but I think we are finished.'

1

Bill

Fallowlees sits defiantly against the Northumberland weather, just as she has done for hundreds of years. She is the last stand against the march of the evergreen conifers, as the forest has slowly swallowed up all of the other farms. Modern society has left her well alone, a relic of the past: there is no telephone line, no mains electricity, gas or water. She has barely changed from when she was built, probably in the latter half of the eighteenth century.

It is always a relief when I turn the final corner on the shingle track home through Harwood Forest and see Fallowlees Farm between the parted trees. *Home.* Securing the tenancy on the farm was the best thing that ever happened to me.

And today felt like the worst. The unexpected dumping had left me feeling fragile, vulnerable. I thought about the book I'd written, all fresh from the printers, neatly finished with the girl getting her prince and living happily ever after. The countryside would be laughing at me now, I thought, and blushed with shame.

I could hear them all sniggering. 'She couldn't even keep a hold of her chap till the ink dried!'

Why, oh why did I put it all down in black and white?

In truth, I knew exactly why; and I would do it all again. I wouldn't be the first person to throw herself head first into a relationship thinking it would last for ever. And I wouldn't be the first to want to tell the world how happy I was. Nor would I be the last.

It was hard for me to think rationally about work with everything going on in my head, but I knew I had only one day to get my ducks in a row at Fallowlees before a four-week lambing stint began the next night. I had been looking forward to putting my back into lambing, earning some proper money. Now January stretched out in front of me like a prison sentence. Twelve-hour shifts, no going out, no seeing other people – just a long, lonely slog in the darkest, dreariest month of the year.

In fact, I was likely to remain alone for some time, as I had, in my wisdom, booked myself another lambing for March before dealing with my own at Fallowlees in April.

Work is a cure for everything, my dad would say, and to some extent I have always believed him. Directing whatever negative energy you are feeling into doing something useful can really help. With that in mind, I had borrowed a telehandler from a neighbour so that I could clear out one of the byres near the house. A telehandler is a bit like a tractor and a forklift truck rolled into one. More manoeuvrable than the former, it has a long boom that can be fitted with different attachments, and can be used to perform a wide variety of lifting, loading and emptying jobs. The byre had been full of junk – broken fence posts, carpet remnants, old lawnmowers – since I arrived at the farm. It seemed silly to sit around moping all day, knowing it would be my last opportunity for several months to get this job out of the way, and I had to return the telehandler to its owners the next day. So, with a sense of despair and hovering loneliness, I made a start on the day's task of emptying the contents of the byre into the telehandler's enormous front bucket.

I was twenty-three when I first saw Fallowlees. I was living in a cottage on my own, looking after nine hundred sheep on a farm about twenty miles north-west of Newcastle, when someone told me about the isolated National Trust farm that needed a new tenant. I knew very little about it, but once it was in my mind I found I couldn't stop thinking about it. A voice in my head told me that this might be the place and the opportunity for me, while at the same time another, more insistent voice told me not to build my hopes up. I was definitely too young, as well as painfully single. Would someone like me even get a look-in? I sent away for the particulars all the same.

When the fat envelope landed on my doormat a few days later, little did I know that Fallowlees was my future. The papers included just a single photo of the farm steading, taken from the lowest part of the farm on a summer's day. How I studied that photo! The stone farmhouse, the handful of outbuildings and the field – framed by a drystone wall – were bathed in a pale golden light. I think I started to fall in love with her from that moment. Even when I read about the lack of amenities, my enthusiasm didn't wane.

My parents – who run the family farm in Hawick in the Scottish Borders where I grew up – accompanied me to the viewing day, when I fell for it even harder. The farm was, in short, my dream made real. At one hundred and twenty acres, it wasn't a big farm, but it was big enough for me. In the fields I saw a flock of my own, as well as an ideal training ground for my dogs; in the barns and outbuildings I saw kennels for future champions. My vision for the future was all here, wrapped up snugly in this centuries-old property.

Seeing the competition I was up against, however, felt like reality smacking me in the face. If I had expected the isolation of Fallowlees to put people off, I had been mistaken. Despite the fact that we had left the road and driven up a four-mile, badly maintained forestry track to reach it, there were cars and people everywhere. I don't know which one of us was more surprised to see this – Dad, Mum or me. Older, more experienced-looking farmers were wandering around inspecting the different buildings; men and women with children in tow walked in and out of the farmhouse, looking as if they already belonged. People who wanted the place as badly as I did. People who looked somehow more deserving of it than me.

The application process that followed was daunting. I had to submit a business plan and work out cash flows and profit and loss accounts. I was out of my comfort zone, and wondered more than once if it was worth the effort. It caused frustration as well as the odd tear. But it got me an interview.

Nerve-racking though it was to face the panel, that was the easy part. Answering questions about farming was my bread and butter. After that, I just had to convince them to put their faith in me, a single young woman, and to banish any doubts they might have had about my living there on my own. If I say so myself, I was rather proud of the little speech I gave.

They must have seen something they liked, for a few days later I learned that the tenancy was mine if I wanted it.

Two years had passed since that day in January 2010 when I had moved into Fallowlees with a suitcase and my dogs. Overnight I had found myself responsible for a farm of my own, as well as continuing with my other shepherding work, a forty-five-minute commute away. It had been a steep learning curve at times, but I had come a long way by having to just get on with things by myself, with no one else to turn to. It was amazing what you could do when you had to.

Money had been a problem, and had forced me to make some difficult decisions. The most difficult had been selling Fly, my favourite dog. Loyal and loving Fly. It was almost too painful to remember her.

The byre clear-up operation was slow-going at first, but once I started making some visible progress, I began to gain a sense of satisfaction from the rhythm of the job. I should have done this earlier, I thought, as I saw all the extra space opening out in front of me. Backwards and forwards I went with the telehandler, to and from the byre. But no matter how hard I tried, I couldn't stop my mind wandering back to Dan and the break-up. Should I have seen it coming? Were there any signs

I'd failed to read? I thought back to that fun, crazy day we met at the Kelso tup sale sixteen months ago, which ended with a game of cabbage rugby! Things had moved pretty quickly – had it all been too quick? Dan was a farmer's son, so we had a lot in common right from the start, and shared a passion for sheep. He had his own job shepherding nearby. Over the past few months we had even pooled our resources and begun to build up a flock between us. It was meant to be for ever.

My brain just wouldn't switch off. Round and round it whirred, looking for clues and answers to what had gone wrong, driving me mad, then starting all over again.

The dogs, picking up on my feelings, lurked about the yard. I had three main dogs in my life, though I was always look-ing out for promising new pups. Roy was my best work and trial dog. Handsome and intelligent, he was in his prime. He was also the Casanova of my pack, never happier than when surrounded by females! Alfie, his second in command and six months younger, was a jolly dog with a heart of gold, who, though twice Roy's size, always deferred to Roy. He was also super-obedient and a great work dog.

Oldest of the three was dear old Bill, a massive, woolly mammoth of a collie. His eyes had a silver sheen and he was totally deaf, but the sight of the telehandler today had perked him up. When he was a young, fit dog and I used the telehandler regularly, driving it laden with silage bales to feed sheep and cows miles away, he would run alongside, barking out his joy and flagging his tail, defending the feeders aggressively and noisily against any livestock who dared to venture too close while I filled them, allowing me to drop the bales of silage into them without trapping any greedy heads in the process.

I got a lot of shepherding work thanks to Bill's reputation. He could put a thousand ewes through a dipper (to rid them of parasites) and clear a hill in ten minutes flat. Not a trial dog, perhaps, but honest and brave.

'Remember those days, Bill? You do, don't you!'

I had forgotten until now how much he had loved that job, and it was a delight to see the youngster in him getting excited again. He stuck near me all day, woofing his enthusiasm and paddling his arthritic paws whenever I turned on the ignition.

That was one consolation. No matter what happened, the dogs were always there for me, steadfast in their loyalty.

'Shame I can't get a man like you!' I told Bill. Not that he could hear me.

January days are short, and it was growing dark before I knew it. I chucked the last lot of wood into the bucket and fired up the machine. I'll take it round the back to burn – a nice fire will cheer everything up, I thought, as I drove up the road.

Maybe I was destined to be single. It wasn't going to be easy to meet someone new. I had the baggage of a farm and a heap of dogs and sheep, as well as living miles from anywhere. I knew that the distance from so-called 'civilisation' scared a lot of people, who tended to panic if they couldn't get to a shop in a few minutes or pick up the phone for a takeaway. But I wasn't going to leave here for anyone.

Maybe I was a lost cause.

All these thoughts were jostling into each other in the turmoil that was my mind.

As I prepared to make a right turn into the field, I felt the whole front right-hand side of the telehandler lift up, move over something and thump back down.

A thick wave of dread swept through me.

No! Please, not Bill.

But I already knew.

I jumped down and flew round to the tyre. There was Bill, lying prone behind the wheel.

'No! No! No!' I was screaming, even though there was no one to hear me.

'Bill! Bill! Bill!'

He was motionless; he made no sound but his eyes flickered. He was alive.

I scooped him up and ran.

2

Delphi

'So that's about it,' said Ian the shepherd, finishing the tour he was giving me of the lambing shed. 'I'm sure you'll manage OK.'

I mustn't have said much, and he gave me a sidelong look. 'Are you all right?'

I had turned up a bit broken to my lambing job. I hadn't said anything about Bill as I wasn't sure I could trust myself. It was still so raw. I'd been working for Ian at the farm down the road on a part-time basis for as long as I'd been at Fallowlees, and he knew me well enough to be able to tell that something was wrong – not that it was difficult to miss my swollen, bloodshot eyes.

'I ran over Bill yesterday,' I choked. 'I had to have him put down.'

There was a moment's pause, then, much to my surprise, Ian put an arm around me, kind of awkwardly, and gave me a squeeze. Shepherds are not typically demonstrative creatures.

The human contact was more than I could cope with and fresh tears sprang to my eyes.

'I'm so sorry,' he said. 'It's hard to lose a mate like Bill. No one knows what it's like to lose a working dog, and Bill was a special one.'

It's true, the relationship between a working dog and its owner is different to anything I've experienced: you rely on each other in a way that doesn't exist anywhere else. It's a rare kind of partnership and the bond forged is very powerful. I had rescued Bill after finding him chained to an old kennel on a farm. The farmer had a reputation for tying dogs he deemed useless to a heavy block and drowning them in the sheep dipper. He was happy for me to take Bill off his hands.

'Mind,' the farmer had said as a parting shot as I led Bill away, 'he'll never make a work dog in a million years.'

It took less than a month to prove him wrong. I'd left college and was flat out with contracting work, and before I knew it Bill and I were easily getting to grips with huge numbers of sheep. After my move to Fallowlees he was my right-hand man, and we'd often arrive home after dark, exhausted and dirty but satisfied at a job well done. He passed the reins to Roy and Alfie as he got older, and more recently spent any left-over energy arthritically patrolling the molehills in and around Fallowlees. This mainly involved enlarging the mess the moles had already created. He never caught one, barring the one he presented to me still enclosed in its trap!

Losing a workmate in their twilight years was bad enough, but actually being responsible for it was heart-wrenching. I knew only too well that if I hadn't been indulging in self-pity

I might have noticed Bill before I started turning the corner. I kept thinking how overjoyed he had been to run alongside the telehandler again and it made my heart tighten and twist. A dog of mine had suffered a similar accident when I was a girl. Dad had failed to see Bess, my best friend and my pride and joy, while operating a telehandler. I was grief-stricken. But that story had a happy ending as, despite her serious injuries, Bess had surprised us all by pulling through and going on to live a long and fruitful life.

There's nothing I can do, the vet had said as I turned up with Bill. He's had a good life, it's time to let him go. I took him home and buried him under the sycamore trees. Roy and Alfie watched on patiently as I dug his grave. I think digging a dog's grave is a rite of passage: it gives you pause to reflect on all the times you had together, and it is the final act in the play of the life you shared, before the curtain falls.

Ian let go of me. We both coughed and looked at the ground self-consciously.

'I'll leave you to it, then,' he said.

I took a proper look round at what was going to be my home for the next month. A lambing shed full of pedigree Suffolks and Texels, with a smattering of Ian's Leicesters for good measure.

Suffolks are big-boned, heavy sheep with strong dark heads and long floppy ears. They are noted for their large appetite and docile nature. Texels are white-faced sheep, often structured like a pig, with a beefy bum and a short muzzle.

The Leicesters were Ian's 'pack' sheep – these are sheep

that a paid shepherd is allowed to keep for free at the farmer's expense, as a kind of bonus. If a shepherd is good, the number of his pack will often increase year on year. Ian had twelve Leicesters – tall, elegant creatures, with long necks, bodies and ears. They have very fine wool and the gentlest nature of all sheep.

My own flock at Fallowlees was a mishmash of all sorts of breeds, mostly Blackfaces, well-suited to the rough ground, but I had also collected a few dodgy characters over the years. One of these was Peggy, a stunning Texel I found in a pen waiting to be shot when I turned up to work on a farm one day. Her crime? A broken leg. I saved the farmer the bullet, took her home and set her leg. She was quite a character, often finding her way into the yard to share Bill's dog food. My pride and joy, however, was the twenty-strong flock of (almost) pedigree Texels I had bought, despite knowing deep down that they wouldn't suit the ground. I think I was trying to show Dan what a hotshot I was by buying these really good sheep. So far they had managed fine, but I treated them with kid gloves, even more so now they were all in lamb.

I had also recently added a horse to the menagerie – not the shaggy, cobby type of pony I ought to have bought for myself, but a broken-down racehorse, a thoroughbred bay. What was it about me and other people's reject animals? It seemed to have become a bit of a habit.

Delphinia – Delphi for short – was thin-skinned and had a history of teeth problems. Looking up her race record, I saw she had either fallen or failed to finish most of her races. Added to that, she was a wind-sucker. Wind-sucking is something of a vice in horses. It is a behavioural condition where a horse swallows air as it bites an object, such as the paddock fence, accompanied by a gulping noise. It isn't uncommon in race-horses and may be the result of stress, or boredom, or even just copied from other horses with the same affliction.

Delphi was the most unsuitable horse I could have found.

She was also in foal.

But she was just so beautiful! Right from the minute I saw her, all sixteen hands of her, I knew she was coming home with me. I bought her for the price of her wardrobe (her rugs, saddle, bridle, and so on) – cheaper than meat money, I was told later. She had the sweetest nature of any horse I'd ever met. She simply didn't have the killer instinct for the racetrack.

Since I didn't have any cows, I kept her in the big cattle shed, bedded deeply in straw, wearing three rugs and an old duvet. Although I bought her on impulse, I didn't regret it for a second.

I had been watching her growing gradually rounder. I didn't know exactly when she was due, but her previous owner guessed it would be some time in the early spring. I read up on pregnant horses and the literature told me to watch for wax on her teats as a sign of impending labour.

I realised quite quickly that night shift was going to be a grind. I was used to the fast pace of a busy lambing shed, popping out lambs all over the place. But the pedigrees weren't going to fall into that category. There were just one hundred ewes, their deliveries spread out over nearly a month. It's hard to keep concentration levels up over such a long shift when there isn't much going on, and that's when mistakes are made. Mistakes with valuable pedigrees are unacceptable.

One of Ian's pack sheep quickly gave me something to worry about, popping out four lambs in quick succession, none of which were particularly thrifty. I spent most of that first night coaxing them to feed and nurturing them as best I could.

I was proud to present the new crew to Ian as he came to take over in the morning.

'Grand,' he said, clearly delighted by the now healthy-looking lambs, all four of them tups (males). Relieved they had made it, and pleased to hand over the reins, I gave Ian a quick tour of the rest of the sheep, very much like a handover on a hospital ward when the day staff take over from the night shift. Then I got in my car, ready to leave.

I was about to turn on the engine when I heard Ian shout out. It didn't sound good. I dashed back to the shed, only to see him holding two of the Leicester quads, stone dead.

'She's only gone and bloody lain on them!'

Ovine infanticide – it's not uncommon, especially in multiple births.

Although saddened, as well as annoyed that my night's work had gone to waste, I was also relieved it hadn't happened on my watch. That's sheep for you, I thought.

At home I let the dogs out and fed and checked my own flock, before wearily making it over the threshold. The heating was on and my bed was beckoning. It took me a few seconds to realise that Dan had been in to collect his things while I was at work.

It felt like a final kick in the teeth.

When I got into bed I was so miserable that, exhausted though I was, I couldn't get to sleep. I turned this way and that, adjusted my pillow, but it was no good. Daylight streamed through the curtains as my body clock fought against the change in schedule. Putting the light back on, I flicked through a little booklet I'd won in the new year's raffle at the pub. It was a collection of Border collie memories and stories. On the last page was a poem. I swear I felt my heart break as I read it.

A Dog's Prayer

If it should be that I grow weak,
And pain should keep me from my sleep
Then you must do what must be done,
for this last battle cannot be won.

You will be sad, I understand;
Don't let your grief then stay your hand,
For this day more than all the rest,
Your love for me must stand the test.

We've had so many happy years,
What is to come can hold no fears,
You'd not want me to suffer so,
The time has come, please let me go.

Take me where my need they'll tend,
And please stay with me until the end,

Hold me firm and speak to me,
Until my eyes no longer see.

I know in time that you will see,
The kindness that you did for me,
Although my tail its last has waved,
From pain and suffering I've been saved.

Please do not grieve, it must be you,
Who has this painful thing to do,
We've been so close, we two, these years,
Don't let your heart hold back its tears.

Writer Unknown

3

Coquet

After the long nights of the pedigree lambing in January, I had little respite before heading to my next job, which was also a night shift.

The second lambing was much more my style: twelve hundred ewes, all inside, meant that my twelve-hour shift was busy and gave me little time to contemplate how lonely and isolated I had become. I hadn't seen anyone other than at my lambing handover since the beginning of the year, and working in permanent darkness had done little to raise my spirits after the fiasco of January.

By the middle of March, everything had become a bit of a grind. I was struggling to sleep during the day and becoming very tired on my shift. I was looking forward to getting back into a more natural routine.

One day, I thought, I would give up this contracting work and concentrate on my own farm. (But Fallowlees wasn't big enough to provide a proper living so I would need more land – and how was I going to afford that?) One day I would train champion sheepdogs. (But that took time – and time was a cost I had to account for too.) I had a hazy picture in my head of someone beside me, sharing the joys and the struggles in this future existence. (But how was I going to meet that person? Chance would be a fine thing!) I was too much of a dreamer, that was my trouble. In twenty years' time I'd probably still be here, on my own – the strange lady with the dogs; Heaven help me!

I was looking forward to lambing my own flock of one hundred ewes, particularly the (nearly) pedigree Texels. Each night as I returned home after night shift and before I left for the next one, I would feed my girls and enjoy just watching them. They looked outstanding – fat and healthy. I also couldn't wait to see the Mule lambs, my favourite sheep. Mules are the cross produced from the mating of a Bluefaced Leicester ram and a pure-bred hill ewe – in my case, the Blackies (Blackfaces). I might have been lambing sheep for a long time, but lambing your own is something different, special, and I couldn't wait.

I had a short window between the end of my second night shift and the beginning of my own lambing. I used this time to catch up on all the paperwork I had been letting slide for the past few months. It had been weighing on my mind, and although lambing was the perfect excuse to ignore it, I knew I couldn't leave it much longer.

I really dislike paperwork, but, frustratingly, farming seems to generate such a lot of it. Bills especially.

So it was with a mixture of emotions that I headed off to see my accountant one dreary day at the end of March. On the one hand, I was happy to be out and about in daylight. But on the other, I wasn't really looking forward to the fluorescent office lights or the disapproving look of my accountant under them as he eyed my badly organised heaps of receipts and my mangled paperwork.

My accountant was based in Berwick, nearly two hours' drive away. I was going to be away for most of the day.

All was well at the farm when I left. The sheep were fat and in good order, the Texels in the front field with Delphi the horse on the best grass, and the Blackies, which are hardier beasts, on the higher part of the farm where the grass is rougher.

Delphi looked huge! I felt sure she could go any day now. I regularly checked her for waxy teats but had seen no sign of this yet. The foal is going to be too big to get out if she cooks it any longer, I thought.

It was nice to be wearing normal clothes, and I left the house feeling quite respectable, and pleased I was finally going to get this job out of the way. Despite its inconvenience, I enjoyed the drive, and it was always a pleasure to get that first glimpse of Berwick nestled within its hefty walls. Seeing people going about their business there helped me to realise that the world was in good working order, even if I didn't get to see it these days.

My accountant greeted me with a handshake and asked me to sit down.

'So, how are things, Emma?'

'Great. Fine, thanks.' As I presented him with all my

documentation, I couldn't help thinking that what he was about to read would belie my bullish reply.

Was it my imagination, or did he seem to sigh a lot as he went through it all, asking me questions along the way?

'A horse now, too?' He raised an eyebrow.

'Oh yes, she's a shepherding pony. Tough little thing. Essential for the farm.'

I gave him my most winning smile as I thought of beautiful, pampered Delphi, all long delicate legs, and hoped he couldn't tell I was lying.

He was looking at all my receipts now, showing the purchase of farm equipment, sheep, silage ... I could sense him working up to something.

He coughed. 'Well,' he began, putting everything into a tidy pile, 'you have a good, saleable service to offer in your contracting, and that's where you make your money. The farm is – how shall I put it? – a drain on your business.' He paused for a second, and patted the pile of papers. 'Now, Emma, if you were to ... '

I cut him short.

'I realise that, honestly I do, and I'm working really hard to make the farm pay its way. But I've only been doing this a couple of years, and businesses can take a long time to establish. It's early days, really.'

I knew I was babbling, but I would defend my farm and every creature on it to the hilt. Why, if I decided to buy a unicorn I would have a good reason for my decision!

I smiled again. 'I'll get there in the end. I'm an optimist.'

I suspected as I left his office that optimism and accounting didn't really go hand in hand, and that optimism had been the ruin of many a business.

I was in a more cheerful mood as I drove home. The job was done – until the next time, anyway.

I can see Fallowlees a mile from home. There is a moment when I'm on the highest part of the road where the gap in the trees frames her like a beautiful picture. But on this occasion, the picture wasn't quite right. I could tell there was something wrong. Normally the sheep in the front field would be evenly distributed, like a polka-dot pattern on green material; this afternoon they were clustered in little white mobs in the corners. There was no sign of Delphi.

When I got out of the car I was shocked by what confronted me. There was wool all over the ground in the front field, and the sheep stood, dirty and traumatised, on churned-up clumps of earth. Many of them were bleeding from wounds on their faces and necks. I still couldn't see Delphi anywhere.

I knew instantly it had been a dog attack. A public footpath runs alongside the field, making it easy for a dog off its lead to get in. Sometimes I saw dogs off-lead in the forest, the owners assuming there was no livestock around until stumbling upon the sheepy little oasis of Fallowlees. Perhaps one of these dogs had set off after a deer and happened upon the sheep? There were all sorts of possible scenarios. What I did know, I thought grimly, was that the owner of the dog or dogs that had carried out this attack would know what had happened. The dogs could not have done this without getting covered in blood themselves.

It couldn't have come at a worse time. So close to lambing,

the strain on the ewes' bodies was already great. Sheep are also very vulnerable to stress and I could see how badly this had affected them.

I quickly assessed the damage. Six sheep were missing, as well as Delphi.

I was frantic as I ran round the field trying to locate them. In the bottom corner I saw that the gate had been smashed and was lying in splinters on the ground. Beyond it, under the trees in the next field, stood Delphi with my missing ewes. I was breathless when I reached them. I saw to my relief that they were all unhurt. I wondered how they had got to safety. Had Delphi destroyed the gate, or could the panicking sheep have done it? Did the dogs fail to spot them making their escape and spare them the attack, or did Delphi defend herself and her little flock against the assault? I would never know, but at least they were safe.

I went to soothe Delphi and check her over. She seemed none the worse for wear. A quick look at her developing udder revealed, yep, waxy teats. Impeccable timing.

I gathered up the Texel ewes as best I could with Roy and Alfie. (I always wonder if they were distressed as, confined to their kennels, they heard the sounds of the carnage that was taking place but were unable to help.) The wily Blackies on the higher part of the farm had completely escaped the notice of the dogs and were grazing nonchalantly, as I had left them.

When I had them all inside, I surveyed their injuries. Thank goodness for their big thick fleeces, which had protected them like woolly armour from the worst of the attack. A few of them had bites to their legs, and several had lost great chunks of fleece. The ewe who had suffered the most had severe facial injuries and had lost the whole of her top lip.

I rang the vet to ask for his advice. He warned me that with them being so heavy in lamb, there might be worse to come.

I injected the worst-bitten with antibiotics and gave sugary water drench to those who looked flat and exhausted. All of them came to feed, which I took as a good sign, as a really sick sheep would not want to eat.

It was a deeply upsetting experience for me. I could hardly believe I had been so unlucky – my one day off from the farm in months, and disaster had struck. After such a bad start to the year, I had thought I was due a change in my fortunes. Surely I deserved it! I can usually find a bright spot to focus on, but at that moment I felt very low. I hoped that my run of bad luck wouldn't extend to Delphi's foaling.

I checked regularly on Delphi throughout the night, setting my alarm every two hours. I would love to say I was there for the birth, but she foaled first thing in the morning, when I was having a nap. Foaling, it turns out, is a far faster affair than lambing or calving.

She gave birth to the most strikingly marked little colt. I named him Coquet, after the valley and river where I enjoyed shepherding most. Coquet had also been the name of a horse my mother rode when she was young. My sisters and I had grown up hearing about this magnificent creature, and the name just seemed to suit the new arrival.

Coquet was exactly as I had imagined: dark bay like his mum, with four knee-length socks, a white face blaze and two thick white flashes on his withers and rump. Delphi was a natural mother and adored him right from the outset.

Karma, of course, was at work, as during the night one of my Texels died, the stress of the attack being just too much. It wasn't entirely unexpected, but I hoped now that the rest of them would be OK. The ewe missing a top lip seemed to have rallied, though the poor thing looked a fright. Otherwise they were quite the picture – a racehorse, her gypsy-coloured foal and a heap of pregnant Texel ewes all sharing the same shed space, munching happily on their hay.

Time for some good things to happen.

4

Big Daddy

It came as no surprise when the Texels didn't have a good lambing that April. A number of the lambs had died inside the ewes, the stress and violence of the dog-worrying having been too much. This made the births more difficult as the birthing fluids just aren't the same when the offspring are stillborn. However, Peter, the farmer at my previous lambing, gave me a stock of 'pet lambs' as a kind of bonus to replace the ones I had lost.

Lambs become pet lambs when they are orphaned or, more commonly, when a ewe gives birth to more lambs than she can happily rear herself – for example, a ewe having three lambs, or producing milk on only one side of her udder. In these cases a farmer would take one of the lambs away and rear it on the bottle. Most commercial sheep producers don't like pet lambs: they are difficult to rear on artificial milk and are more susceptible to ailments, so Peter was happy for me to take them off his hands.

In an ideal world, each ewe in my care would rear two lambs, one for each teat. If a ewe gave birth to a dead lamb, a pet lamb could be the answer for both farmer and ewe. I would take one of the pet lambs and soak it in the birth juices of the dead lamb. Then I would tie the pet lamb's legs so that it would appear to be newborn, struggling to stand for the first time. A ewe's hormones are so overwhelming at this time that she wants a baby to fall in love with and will hopefully accept this impostor as her own. This technique generally saves a lot of heartbreak. There can be no worse sight than a ewe looking for her dead lamb – and they do. All of their instincts are crying out for something to love, and if I can give them that something, they are none the wiser that it is not their own, and everyone is happy.

Fortunately, only the ewes who had been most worried by the dog attack lost their lambs; most of my other girls rallied and gave birth with no problem. Even Lippy had a single ewe lamb, who gave not a hoot about her mother's disfigured face. And of course those tough old Blackies gave birth on their own, out in the open, with very little intervention from me.

I had tried to make the best out of a bad situation, but I was so shaken by the dog-worrying that I wasn't keen to leave the farm. This, coupled with the solitude of months of lambing, meant I hadn't seen a friend or gone out for a drink – not even a coffee – since the previous year.

I found myself living on bowls of cereal – fast, easy and requiring zero creativity. I knew it wasn't healthy, I knew I was in a mess, but I also knew that summer was round the corner and I was hopeful I could shake off my apathy when I needed to.

Fortunately my contracting work came along and got me out and about again. The demand for contract shepherding is usually at its greatest directly after lambing, and this year was no exception. The arrival of May found me travelling to a different farm each day. I was often employed by farmers who didn't have sheepdogs, pleased to have me bridge the gap in their workforce. I would do whatever jobs needed doing, which at this time of year included gathering ewes and lambs for the first time, clipping all the muck off the ewes' tails, dosing lambs for worms and foot-bathing them. I had around three thousand sheep between the four farms I contracted for and I was never short of work.

This year I had also picked up a contract from my old college, Kirkley Hall, where I had spent an enjoyable year as a fresh-faced seventeen-year-old studying sheep management, with Bill by my side. They had asked me to look after the sheep on their massive hill farm, Carlcroft, as Geoff, the shepherd there, hadn't been well. It was possibly the nicest work I'd had since starting up my contracting business.

The daily commute from the forest up the valley is as pleasant a one as you will find. The road clings to the Coquet all the way up to the foothills of the river's birth, flanked by steep hills. Proper sheep country – which makes for proper dog country.

The hills of the Hope and the Slyme are familiar to me as I lambed them during those student days. I'd heard that right up until the 1860s there used to be a Slymefoot pub, an old meeting place for drovers and smugglers, located where the Rowhope Burn meets the River Coquet. There's nothing left of it now, but it's fascinating to think of the people who have walked the ground before me.

When I reached the farm I used the quad to drive around both hills inspecting the flock. Roy, Alfie and the youngsters enjoyed running alongside the bike. They all loved the solid two hours of exercise.

Driving a quad on the hills of the Coquet in late spring must class as one of the most enjoyable things on earth. It's like the land that time forgot. You feel as if you are the only person for miles around. However, you might not be! I remember getting caught short one day after too many morning cups of tea – no facilities anywhere on the hill, of course; you have to get used to powdering your nose alfresco. I was just about to, you know, when seemingly from nowhere, a squaddie in full camouflage stirred about twenty feet away from me. I'd like to say I didn't scream, but I would be lying. And it echoed for ages! I was mortified, and he looked pretty embarrassed too. The hills are owned by the Ministry of Defence and used regularly for training. Since then I've always been a bit more guarded when it comes to calls of nature.

My favourite part of the morning was always coming across the wild goats. They have to rank as some of the most extra-ordinary creatures I have ever seen. They can usually be smelt before they are seen. The billy goats have a unique stench, like a very overripe goat's cheese left out in the sun. They are big, shaggy creatures with huge, upright curved horns, like some demon from a storybook. Most of them wear a dark grey colour, but one billy, I assume a very old one, had developed a light silver back like a gorilla. He carried the most impressive horns and seemed to be the dominant male. I guessed he was the father of the majority of the kids. I named him Big Daddy. The nannies were hardy little ladies, with much smaller horns. Since the weather had been so good, many of them had kids that year. The goats aren't protected, nor are they farmed, nor do they seem to be hunted. They just exist in the valley like they have for hundreds of years. Apparently they have been roaming the hills since Neolithic times, when they probably escaped from farms. They are said to bring good luck and ward away the devil, which would explain why they have escaped persecution for so long.

One day, on finding a little batch of billies nearby, I set Roy the challenge to go and gather them, just to see what would happen. Roy worked his socks off and brought them close enough for me to film them on my phone, a clip I still have to this day. But even tough old Roy couldn't hold the goats together for long before they split every which way and disappeared into the hills.

The terrain on the hills can be treacherous, and sticking to the quad tracks is the best and, really, the only way to operate safely. The tracks are exactly where they need to be for the shepherd to check and gather the hills effectively; they follow paths all over the hills, and have done since the invention of the quad. Constant use keeps them alive, easy to find and easy to use.

I once found a quad track going up a very steep part of the Hope. I needed to gather some sheep and it was a long way round. I figured if the track was there, it meant Geoff had made it with the bike, and therefore I could too. I put her in gear and with a never-say-die attitude, zoomed her up the hill, knowing that I couldn't stop or slacken off or all would be lost. En route I felt the bike's front tyres lighten and lift a bit. I couldn't help but think of an accident my dad had had at about my age when an old three-wheeler bike had turned over and landed on top of him while he was climbing a hill like this one. Despite his broken back, he had somehow managed to crawl back to the farmhouse, where Mum had called an ambulance. I was shaking like a leaf and my heart was pounding when I made the pinnacle. I decided Geoff was a far braver person than me, and vowed never to do that again.

I discovered later that the track was a 'down only' route.

'No one would be dumb enough to do that one uphill,' Geoff confirmed.

I remember nodding and agreeing that someone would have to be pretty stupid to try it, while biting my lip and hiding a blush.

Thanks to the combination of approaching summer and doing a job I enjoyed, I was slipping out of my despair. Life at Fallowlees was getting sweeter. The sun was shining. Coquet was a daily delight and quite the entertainer. However, he was a cheeky chap, not averse to giving the odd nip. It was around this time in early summer that I had a special visit from the crew of the television programme *Tales from Northumberland*, hosted by Robson Green. They were keen to see what life was like on such a remote farm. I took Robson, a devoted racer, to show off my own racehorse and her foal. Robson held out his hand to Coquet in the time-honoured way, hand flat, no fingers loose. Coquet gave it a sniff and looked ever so gently at Robson before biting him square in the middle of his palm. I could hardly believe it was possible! He didn't do any serious damage, thank goodness, and Robson, being a good sport, just laughed, but I swear I could see Coquet sniggering from his spot beside his placid mother. I think Coquet enjoyed being the only man on the farm. He was surrounded by women, and that's how he liked it. He was growing up thoroughly spoilt.

Northumberland County Show, the start date in my social calendar, was just around the corner. But a day at Mum and Dad's was in order first. I hadn't seen my family for ages.

5

Muirfield

There is a fever that is caught by horses, cows, sheep and farmers alike. They call it spring fever. Symptoms include a lightness of step, a feeling of motivation and an enthusiasm for life. You might even call it euphoria. Horses will buck unexpectedly, cows will kick up their heels, lambs will frolic and even weary shepherds, finally released from their lambing garb, will crack a grin!

I had spring fever. I felt that the tide was finally turning. Lambing was over and I had earned some money. The sun was out and the grass was growing. Those months of hard grafting had been good for me, I reflected, as I set off for Muirfield, Mum and Dad's farm in the Borders, on the first weekend in June. I felt as if I was finally getting Dan out of my system. Heartbreak had been followed by acceptance. There were other dividends, too: I had lost weight and toned up. I was feeling excited about the future.

It was the day before county show day, when all of the

farmers in Northumberland congregate to show off their stock in what is the first show of the season. Everyone would be shaking off their winter woes and sharing tales of the trials and tribulations of lambing as they gathered with friends in the beer tent. I was looking forward to being one of them. My farming friends would all be there and it would be the perfect opportunity to catch up. It felt like an even bigger deal for me than usual as I hadn't been anywhere since New Year's Eve. I had a lot of news to share, that was for sure. It was also the weekend of the Queen's Diamond Jubilee celebrations, and I could sense the carnival atmosphere in the air.

But always before fun comes work. I was helping my parents to gather in their 'hill' – a hundred acres of rough grazing. Bess, my first sheepdog – the one who had recovered from the accident with the telehandler – had passed away not long ago at a grand old age and my parents didn't feel the need to replace her when I could come up on the big days with my team, something I was more than happy to do. It was strange not to see Bess there. Though our relationship had changed since I left her with Mum and Dad when I went to college – I had soon been usurped by Mum as number one in her affections – she always came over to greet me and have a fuss made of her.

'Hello, stranger!' Mum gave me a hug.

It was good to see her again. I realised how much I'd missed my family these last few months.

People assume I got into farming largely thanks to Dad, who was in turn influenced by his own father, Grandpa Len. But actually, I think if it hadn't been for Mum, I might never have become a farmer. Although Mum wasn't born into a farming family, she quickly had to learn as it was foisted upon her. Like a lot of farmers' wives, she was the one holding the fort, getting on with the day-to-day jobs while Dad was doing other work away from the farm to make ends meet. As the oldest child, I was often helping her, trailing around after her, learning as I went. Seeing a woman coping like this, in what is traditionally a man's world, was a big factor, I reckon, in my decision to follow in the family profession.

'Where's Dad? I'd better say hello before I get started.'

'He'll be back later. But come and have a cup of tea first, we haven't seen you for ages. What's new? Have you been looking after yourself?'

'Oh, work, work and more work. Not much to tell.'

'Well, Caroline is inside. Go and let her know you're here.'

My sister Caroline is three years younger than me and we've always been close. I popped my head round the door to tell her we'd have a proper catch-up later and she shouted back that she'd put the kettle on ready. Then I went back outside to get on. Mum made sure I admired the new dog box fitted to the bars on the back of the quad. I had long been an advocate of having something comfortable for the dogs to ride on, and hated to see dogs crouching on the factory-basic bars. These bars also made them vulnerable to broken legs, as they could get them caught when they jumped off. After making suitable appreciative noises about the improvements, I set off on the quad, Roy and Alfie riding on the new dog box, to gather the two hundred ewes and lambs from the hill.

Ewes and lambs are tricky to move the very first time after

lambing. Sometimes a ewe would rather stand and fight the sheepdog than be moved on. Other times they like to crouch in the longer grass and rushes and try to hide. The worst scenario is if the lamb loses contact with its mother and starts to panic; the lambs don't understand the dogs as well as their mothers do, and often run in the wrong direction in confusion.

It takes a great deal of skill on the dogs' part to move the flock down to the farm in these early weeks. The dogs need to be quiet and sensible in order to coax the protective mothers in the right direction and find the ewes who are hiding, and to be patient, to try to keep the lambs trotting along with their mothers.

Roy and Alfie were both pros at this. I sent one off in each direction and gave them the odd instruction via a whistle. A toot of the bike horn was enough to set a lot of the ewes in motion – most of them knew the drill as well as the dogs.

Things were well under way, the flock heading in the right direction, and I was enjoying myself. The ground was radiating life, the clover blossom releasing a heady scent as the tyres passed over it. The grass was dry and could have done with some rain, but with not a cloud in the sky it didn't look as if it would be watered any time soon.

Towards the end of the gather I saw across the side of the old quarry a ewe and two lambs who had pushed through into a section of the farm fenced off for wildlife, no doubt tempted by the lush grass. I sent Roy slipping through the fence to out-pace them and direct them back to the main flock.

As he was wheedling the ewe out of the field, they dipped out of my view behind the quarry. Now Roy was good, but the ewe was aggressive without the protection of the flock and wanted to fight. I needed to be able to see Roy in order to guide him, so I drove the bike round the edge of the quarry to get the best vantage point.

It wasn't new to have an escapee in the wildlife field, nor was it unusual for me to drive so close to the quarry. That day, however, I was concentrating so hard on not allowing the ewe to hurt Roy that I drove slightly too high on the quarry's edge. The next thing I knew, the whole right side of the bike was tilting up into the sky. I saw a sudden view of brilliant blue above me before the heavy machine rolled on top of me, crushing my body into the ground.

I know it is a cliché to say that these things happen in slow motion, but that's exactly how it was. I could feel the bike pressing onto me, squashing me into the earth. I tasted soil in my mouth. The weight was so heavy, I couldn't breathe, I couldn't move.

Then it was off, careering down the hill, end over end.

But I still felt as though the bike was there; I could still feel its weight on top of me, flattening me. And I still couldn't breathe. I started to gasp like a floundering fish, but my lungs wouldn't inflate. Was this how it would all end for me, in a field on my family's farm? Images flashed across my mind – Fallowlees, my parents, my dogs. Would I see them all again?

I could hear myself groaning. I was still alive then. Now I had to make sure I stayed alive.

Gradually, a tiny bit at a time, I managed to suck in some air. To start with it was like breathing through a straw, tiny sips, then I managed a little more, wheezing like an old man.

Roy, having abandoned his ewe, came running over to offer me moral support.

Eventually I managed to sit myself up, but when I tried to get onto my feet I felt an excruciating pain in my back. I had obviously forgotten the agony of being winded.

I surveyed the damage to myself. Part of the bike had slashed right through my jeans and left a long, bloody mark on my thigh, but other than that I appeared to be unscathed. Apart from the pain in my back, I felt OK.

The bike, however, had come to a stop at the bottom of the slope and was in less good shape. I groaned as I noted the smashed dog box – its first outing had turned into its last! Mum was not going to be happy. Luckily the quad had landed back on its wheels and looked drivable.

I shuffled off to retrieve it. Each step was agony, but I needed to finish the gather – to let the sheep go back to the hill now would have wasted the whole morning's work. After a wretched few minutes, tears streaming down my face, I reached the bike and made to swing my leg over the saddle, but try as I might I just couldn't do it. Every time I tried to raise my leg I felt a stab of agonising pain. After a few attempts I gave up and set off to finish the gather on foot. I'd have to come back for the bike later.

Alfie had already pushed most of the ewes homeward by himself, and at my command Roy set off to give him a hand. I left them to it – they knew the drill by now.

The final two hundred yards were a struggle as I could only walk very straight-legged with my chest pushed forward. I watched as Alfie and Roy chivvied all the ewes and lambs into the pens, then went to break the news to Mum that I had not only broken her dog box and left the bike stranded, but I wasn't going to be able to help with the next job, dosing the lambs, because I was struggling to move. My breathing still felt stilted.

Tears sprang to my eyes when I tried to explain the pain. I'd expected Mum to be annoyed, but seeing the state I was in she sent me up to the house for a cup of tea, dealing with the enormous drove herself. In the kitchen Caroline took one look at me and rang the cottage hospital.

'They're sending an ambulance,' she said, putting the phone down.

'That's ridiculous!'

She shrugged. 'Wonder if they'll have to cut your clothes off?' she questioned with a grin.

'I bloody hope not! Here, help me take off these wellies, just in case. They're my favourites.'

The ambulance arrived unbelievably fast, which further embarrassed me. I was hardly an emergency. The crew agreed on this, after finding me on my feet and walking around. But protocol was protocol, and would I just lie on this stretcher please.

At the hospital the doctors wanted an X-ray and a scan.

'Honestly, there's no need. Please just give me some pain-killers and I'll be good to go.'

I was thinking of the county show the following day. The day I'd been looking forward to for so long. Nothing was going to keep me from being there.

Caroline waited with me, perusing the ancient magazines, while I was wheeled off to various rooms. I lay for ages on a trolley before a female doctor I hadn't yet seen came in and shut the door carefully behind her.

'I'm sorry to say that you've broken your T12 vertebra. It's unstable.'

I gasped. Caroline stopped, mid page-turn, and looked at me in horror.

'I'd better ring Mum,' she said.

It was the bank holiday weekend with only a skeleton staff working at the hospital. The country was celebrating and I was confined to a hospital bed, a physical and emotional wreck.

'You have been a very lucky young woman,' the doctor had said.

Lucky? I didn't feel very lucky. But it turned out that if it hadn't been for Caroline's quick thinking in getting me straight to hospital, I might never have walked again.

I couldn't get my head round what had happened. Breaking my back while doing what to me was an everyday job, a routine activity, seemed such a ridiculous way to almost cripple myself. I imagined backs were broken in high-speed car chases, or motorbike crashes, not a ten-miles-per-hour quad roll. But then I remembered that day on the Coquet hills when the bike had almost tipped, and my dad's accident all those years ago. There was no doubt about it: a small mistake could have far-reaching consequences. I cursed myself for not being more careful. Crazy how history was repeating itself. Thankfully, I could reassure myself with the knowledge that Dad had made a complete recovery.

*

Where am I?, I wondered as I opened my eyes the next day to the sound of nurses' voices and a ward being woken. I hadn't slept well, thanks to the pain in my back and the unfamiliar noises. It was a shock to remember where I was and why I was there.

My ward was full of elderly ladies having hip replacements. As the morning wore on and they each took their turn to walk past my bed, using their walking frames for support, I realised that they were more agile than I was. I tried to return their smiles but I knew I probably looked as grouchy as I felt.

To say I felt sorry for myself is an understatement. All I wanted was to be on my two feet, up and out of here, seeing my dogs again, seeing the sheep and Delphi and Coquet. Never had the most humdrum of my daily jobs held such an allure.

There were six beds in the ward and one television on the wall next to the window. I watched the Queen's Jubilee celebrations on that little screen. It was all a bit hazy as the morphine had started to take effect.

My phone pinged with messages from friends asking where I was, telling me to meet them at the bar. Telling me to get a move on. Reception was good enough to receive the messages but never good enough to reply, and it wasn't as if I could get up and move to the window for better service.

If I get out of here, I thought – *when* I get out of here – there will be no stopping me. I really will turn my life around.

I cheered up a bit when my parents, Caroline and my other sister, Elizabeth, the youngest of the family, came to visit, bearing fruit and sweets and books.

'Fallowlees is just fine,' said Caroline, who was looking after the farm in my absence.

'The dogs are missing you, though,' added Elizabeth, who was also helping out. Elizabeth was the one who took pride in knowing all of my dogs' quirks and personalities, so I knew they were in good hands. All the same, my sisters' comments brought tears of guilt and self-pity to my eyes.

Mum saw my distress. 'There's nothing you can do, so don't worry, we're taking care of things. Make the most of the rest.'

But I did worry. I was anxious about all the jobs I should be doing and places I should be going to. It wasn't easy for anyone to placate me.

Oh, I was grateful, of course I was. When you're in a situation like that you are hugely thankful for our amazing NHS. But I felt so helpless, and for possibly the first time in my life I couldn't do anything about it. It was bringing out the worst in me.

All the same, I managed a smile. 'Thank you. And please thank everyone else who's mucking in.'

I stayed in hospital for a week. They say to leave your dignity at the hospital door and pick it up on the way out, and I found this to be sound advice. Stretched out on the bed unable to move meant having to suffer the indignity of bed baths and being rolled onto those cardboard pots to wee into at regular intervals. I stopped eating the moment I arrived and didn't touch a thing throughout my entire stay. There was no way I was going to suffer the ultimate humiliation of performing that other bodily function in situ. Most of the nurses were kind and understanding, but I think my hunger strike was challenging for them. I know at least one of them was glad to see the back of me when I went home!

It wasn't a pleasant experience, but I knew I was lucky: that I would get up at the end of it all and walk away. That it could, in fact, have been so much worse.

6

Dreams

I left hospital on a sunny June day wearing a corset brace from my neck to my hips. It wasn't the sexy Victorian-style corset I had been imagining when the word 'corset' was mentioned – more of a gladiator-style bondage get-up in white plastic with painted black metal trim.

Caroline came to take me back to Mum and Dad's. She whizzed me out of hospital in a wheelchair as if she was my getaway driver.

'That was so funny, you thinking you were still going to the show when you had broken your back!' she quipped, as we careered into the car park.

'Hey, slow down! I feel like an escapee on the run!'

I managed to grin at my foolishness, though I was still sore about missing the show. It would have to wait till next year, I thought, as I eased my way carefully into the back of Caroline's car. To my surprise she hopped into the back beside me before crawling through the gap to install herself in the driver's seat.

'The front door packed in,' she told me as we drove off.

I giggled. Caroline and cars were an ongoing saga that rivalled my own often fraught relationship with them.

I had already asked Mum to contact everyone she could and let them know I wouldn't be able to work for a week or so, but it was evident now that that was going to be a much longer period. I had to stay at my parents' farm while I healed and got used to the brace, and one of the first jobs I did on my arrival was ring up and cancel all my forthcoming contractual work. I hated doing it. I felt guilty and unreliable. Even worse, it meant I had zero income until I was able to work again. I was used to getting by on very little, but this was supposed to be one of my busiest and most profitable times of the year. I had my lambing money, of course, and I could survive on that, but I'd been planning to invest it in things for the farm rather than fritter it away on just existing. I felt as if my dreams had been ripped from me.

I was a terrible patient. Frustrated and restless.

I knew I had only myself to blame. I thought of how the year had panned out up until now – breaking up with Dan, Bill's death, the dog-worrying and now this. One thing after another. Perhaps I wasn't cut out for this life after all.

Dad gave his mum a ring to tell her what had happened. Grandma Gray is the widow of Grandpa Len, the grand-father who gave me Bess when I was a thirteen-year-old girl. A farmer's wife and mother of seven – three boys and four girls – she had seen it all. Dad and his brothers Toffa and John, all of whom had gone on to be farmers, had given her plenty to worry about when they were growing up – and a fair bit in adulthood, too! I guessed that on the danger scale my accident would rank only around midway when compared to some of my uncle Toffa's exploits. Fortunately Granny took the news in her stride.

It was at times like this that I realised how important my friends and family were. Caroline stayed at Fallowlees by herself in the early days of my recovery. She looked after the farm and commuted an hour each way to her job in Newcastle as a dog groomer in her unreliable one-door SEAT Leon. It was a weight off my mind to know someone was there. I knew it must be a great effort and highly inconvenient for her, but she never once complained.

Mum and Dad went down to treat my ewes and lambs, setting up some makeshift pens in the polytunnel. They were helped by my dear friend Archie who, despite being in his seventies, was still one of the most capable shepherds around.

Archie and I met somewhere in the mists of time, when I was starting off as a young shepherdess. He'd always been there to lend a hand and give me advice when I needed it.

'Emma Gray, what have you gone and done to yourself, yer daft bugger?' said the voice at the end of the phone one day as I sat there feeling sorry for myself.

I swallowed, and tried to give a breezy reply. Underneath the bravado I knew Archie would be worried about me.

He drove up to Fallowlees for several days in a row, even though it was quite a commute for him and his car was less than suitable for the track, and gathered in all of the sheep with his ageing Border collie, Dale. Mum and Dad couldn't have managed without him as none of my dogs would work for them – sheepdogs often won't work for other people.

After a few weeks I was allowed back to Fallowlees on strict orders. I was delighted to be home. Restricted by my brace, I couldn't bend down, I couldn't pick anything up, I couldn't carry things, but I was mobile, and that was all that mattered. Caroline, Elizabeth and Mum popped down when they could to do the heavier tasks.

I quickly discovered that there was one thing I could still do without too much difficulty: train the dogs. At least the older ones, whose obedience I could rely on. And train them I did. Roy and Alfie had never been so fit.

Sometimes I would lead Delphi on long walks in the forest, with Coquet and the dogs tagging along. Coquet was the apple of my eye.

I was used to being alone, but there was a difference between my chosen isolation and having it forced upon me. I realised I was starting to live a rather sad existence. When I wasn't walking or training the dogs, I was just mooching about. On my own. I had to admit it – I was lonely.

But this lack of structure also gave me a lot of time for contemplation: time to think about where I was going and what I wanted. My dreams seemed so outrageously big, so unreachable, but I wrote them down anyway.

First on my list: I wanted to find a way I could give up my contracting. This had only been reinforced by my accident, as I now had the additional worry of the stress that looking after a large number of sheep would put on my now fragile back. Contracting is far harder work than normal farming because you have a greater number of sheep to look after. You also don't tend to get the more enjoyable parts of the job. Just the jobs no one else wants – like gathering in the sheep in freezing rain, or tailing dirty lambs in concrete pens under a burning sun.

Secondly, I wanted to be better at competing with dogs. I had already had some success at trials, but I wanted to make the big time. I wanted to be known for my dogs more than anything.

To achieve the above I also wanted more dogs – who doesn't! I wanted to be able to spend more time with them, and to provide them with state-of-the-art kennels and lots of exercise space. I also wanted to be able to generate an income from the dogs – not by training other people's, as I had done in the past, but by choosing and training the best-bred dogs I could to the highest level and selling them.

I wanted to improve the appearance of Fallowlees – to get rid of junk, to keep it tidy, to make it work better for me.

Finally, I really wanted to find someone to share it all with. The five previous months had made me realise how vulnerable I was on my own. Sometimes I scared myself by wondering what would have happened if I had had the accident at Fallowlees rather than at Mum and Dad's place, with no one to overrule me when I thought I didn't need medical help. But it wasn't just that – the fact was, I might have been used to living and working alone but I was not a recluse, not by any means. I didn't choose to live at Fallowlees to get away from people; I just accepted the solitude as part and parcel of the farm. Now I wanted someone to share this amazing life with me. And it was an amazing life! I may have had my troubles, but I was realistic enough to know that they did not define my existence. I was doing my dream job, and how many people can claim that?

How was I going to achieve any of these things, though? They were big asks.

It was around this time that I heard on the grapevine of a farm that was coming up to let. In some ways I was surprised to find my interest piqued. I had never given any thought to leaving Fallowlees. But the more I heard, the more I realised that Broomhouse might help me to fulfil some of my dreams. Like Fallowlees, Broomhouse was a National Trust farm on the Wallington Estate, close to the house and gardens of Wallington that are such a popular Northumberland tourist attraction. When I also heard that they weren't specifically looking for a farmer, but for someone who could work with the National Trust to bring more visitors to Wallington and encourage them to explore what farming is all about, I became even more interested.

Perhaps taking this step in a slightly different direction was the way forward for me, and would enable me to earn a living while also allowing me to spend time training my dogs.

7

Arthur

Broomhouse had got me thinking, that was for sure. I kept leafing through the brochure, wondering if it might be the move for me. I was still having to take it easy, and used some of the extra time I had to sort out all the paperwork I had amassed. In the stack, I came across some information about the Environmental Farming Scheme, something the Wallington Estate was keen to get its tenants involved in. It was a voluntary scheme in which farmers who were accepted were given support to carry out environmentally beneficial farming practices, a matter close to my heart. The scheme was made up of three levels, the higher level being most relevant to me: this involved making changes to agricultural land in order to provide habitats for particular species of wildlife.

Fallowlees itself hadn't changed physically since I took over the tenancy, but I had made several improvements. I had fitted new gates, and had a go at repairing some of the drystone walls. Drystone walls don't just keep your cattle where they are supposed to be, or act as windbreaks – they are a sanctuary for wildlife. Mice, voles, birds, toads, newts and insects all seek refuge in their nooks and crannies. The walls have their own microclimates: a south-facing wall provides a sunny environment favoured by warmth-loving insects and basking reptiles; a north-facing one provides refuge for lovers of cool dampness. Wild flowers can put down roots in the shallow, nutrient-poor soil that might develop in the gaps. But these benefits decline if walls are not maintained or are allowed to collapse. Fallowlees might never be a highly productive farm, but this was an area where she could outshine the others. I hoped that the scheme might enable me to get a grant and have the walls repaired by a professional. I was only too aware of my own shortcomings as a builder.

So it was that I had an expert come to the farm to evaluate whether Fallowlees had enough environmental value to be considered. Arthur Davis was the man who turned up. How could I know that meeting him would be the first step in realising my dreams?

Having a stranger on the farm felt unsettling, particularly as he was there to 'analyse'. It had been a while since I had dusted off my social skills, and in the silence of the Fallowlees kitchen, I found them a bit rusty.

After Arthur had sat down with his paperwork and accepted my offer of a coffee, I was mortified to find out I didn't have any! As he was sitting with his back to me, I hastily poured some boiling water into an ancient Nescafé jar in which some coffee was welded to the bottom after too many wet teaspoons. I gave it a rough shake, tipped it into his mug and presented it to him.

He sipped it without expression while talking me through what the higher-level scheme entailed. He was very knowledgeable. I listened and nodded and tried to ask some intelligent questions. He then took a walk by himself around Fallowlees, making notes as he went. As I was still limited in my mobility, I knew that the farm wasn't as tidy as it might have been, but hoped that Arthur might still see its potential. All the same, it felt odd, and a little bit intrusive – like someone checking to see how tidy your bedroom is. I couldn't help feeling judged, wondering if Fallowlees – and myself, by extension – was up to scratch.

I've always been careful to farm extensively – farming with little input of labour or investment relative to the land being farmed – as it's really the only way to manage an upland farm, where levels of agricultural productivity are low. I know of farmers on short-term leases who have to take what they can get while they can, exhausting the ground in the process. But I knew I was at Fallowlees for the long term – well, I had thought I was until Broomhouse started putting ideas in my head! – and I was happy to go with the pace of nature and work with what suited the farm. Consequently, I felt that what I was doing already suited the wildlife, or at least I hoped it did.

'Your farm looks like a good candidate for the scheme,' Arthur announced.

Phew.

'Your best option would be to create more habitat for ground-nesting birds – you already have some lapwings and curlews, and it wouldn't surprise me if there were snipe here too.'

I nodded.

'That would involve getting some cows. You see, their grazing action and the varied growth it encourages, along with their movements treading on the rough ground, help to create the right combination of bare ground and thick cover needed for the birds to nest and for the chicks to avoid predators. Is that something you could do?'

'Of course,' I replied, panicking a little. I've always been a people-pleaser and my natural instinct is to say yes.

'Yep, I can get cows, no problem,' I continued, while my mind made some frantic calculations about how much they would set me back.

We talked about it all in more detail, then, as he packed away the paperwork, Arthur caught sight of the letting particulars for Broomhouse.

'Are you thinking of moving?' he asked, pointing to the brochure.

'Yes, well, I'm going to apply.' Then with sudden inspiration, I quipped, 'You don't fancy representing me, do you?' An agricultural consultant would be the perfect person to help with my application.

Arthur smiled but shook his head. 'I'm sorry, I would love to but I'm already representing someone else.'

'Oh, OK, of course.' I tried not to sound too disappointed.

'But, you know, I do represent people who are involved in share-farming practices. It might be something for you to think about if you are serious about wanting to expand.'

I nodded. 'Yeah, that sounds interesting.' I wondered if that meant he thought I was unlikely to succeed with Broomhouse.

We shook hands. 'I'll be in touch,' he said, before driving his nice car tentatively across the crater-ridden farm road.

A few days later Arthur rang to say that he had submitted my application for the higher-level environmental scheme and that it looked promising. He also mentioned that although he couldn't advise me on Broomhouse, he knew some people who might be able to help me with my proposal.

'They have a couple of farms and do a lot for farming in the area. They know what they're talking about, and I really think you'd find them helpful if they were to look over your application. I've told them all about you.'

He gave me the telephone number of John and Rosalind Murray.

PART TWO

Bouncing Back

8

Broomhouse

I had worn the brace for six weeks. Once it was off, in the middle of July, I could officially return to work. At last! I could hardly wait! I had been told to take it easy at first, and I did try, though I dare say the doctors wouldn't have been too happy about some of the inventive ways I got round certain jobs. But I wasn't going to do anything foolish; I knew how lucky I was.

Broomhouse was consuming my thoughts more and more. The farm was to be let in November. This farm was the real jewel in Wallington's crown, an in-bye farm (not a hill or upland farm) with lots of nice parkland field running alongside Wallington Hall itself.

Fallowlees and Broomhouse might have been relatives, but they were from different branches of the family. One was the affluent family member with a good job and deep pockets; the other was the impoverished cousin struggling to get by. Broomhouse was fertile and well sheltered; she benefited from mains electricity and water, and a telephone line. Fallowlees consisted of poor upland grazing and was exposed to all weathers, while a generator provided electricity. Broomhouse was only ten minutes' drive from the village shop in Kirkwhelpington. At Fallowlees it took me fifteen minutes just to get to the bottom of the forestry track and onto a proper road!

I couldn't help thinking that all of the above meant that Broomhouse would make it far easier for me to meet (and keep?) the man of my dreams than Fallowlees.

It was also way beyond the reach of any farm I could imagine running for so many reasons, but I thought I might have a trump card to play. The National Trust didn't so much want a farmer as someone to entertain and inform the public – someone to help increase the footfall to Wallington itself, to bring farming closer to the community and to strengthen the connection between food and farming. A people person.

This was where I thought I could shine in a way that old-fashioned farmers might struggle. I was a sociable person. I especially loved talking and showing off my passion for dogs and farming.

It was probably an unachievable dream, but I had to give it my best shot. I would be a wild card, and sometimes even wild cards succeed.

The viewing day for Broomhouse was bright and sunny. Interest in the farm had been so great that Anna Shiel, the National Trust agent, and Paul Hewitt, the countryside manager, had staggered arrivals so that they could meet everybody. But you'd hardly have guessed it as there were cars everywhere.

Viewing a farm is a funny experience for all involved. Farmers who are normally friendly and gossipy become gruff and non-communicative on spotting a fellow farmer on a viewing day. People will pretend not to see you, and I'm sure I do the same. No one wants anyone else to know that they might be tendering for a farm. But when a fertile and productive farm like Broomhouse becomes available, well, anyone with the slightest interest wants to see it for themselves, and it's impossible not to bump into people you know. And yet, when you do meet, if you really can't avoid it, the pretence continues, and the conversation skirts around the elephant in the room. Perhaps it is simply that none of us wants to show our hand. Perhaps we are scared of looking foolish should our own proposal fail to succeed. Whatever the reason, everyone is kind of stilted and embarrassed. Even those who seem assured on the surface can't hide a hint of their inner turmoil. How much is the farm worth to them? Could they move there? Do they *want* to move there? Could they afford to offer more than the rest? Bids are confidential, and although agents often say it's the candidate that matters, it is their job to fund the estate and therefore in their interest to prove themselves by securing a high rent.

I felt enormously sheepish – if you'll excuse the pun – turning up on my own in my battered pickup. I had made an effort to dress well, to present what I hoped was the right image to the agents. But standing there alone, clutching the farm particulars in a clammy hand, I felt self-conscious and out of my depth. I was the only single person there among several family groups, many of them accompanied by their agricultural advisers. Everyone was dressed in cords or chinos with a Schoffel gilet. They looked as if they had stepped out of the pages of *Horse & Hound* magazine. I was like Bridget Jones turning up to a party without knowing the dress code.

Broomhouse didn't disappoint in the flesh. It was a truly beautiful farm. With more than twice the acreage of Fallowlees, and a mix of arable and grassland, I could see the extra opportunities it offered. The ground seemed to be made of milk and honey; rich and fertile, any type of animal would thrive on it. And the farmhouse looked a lot more comfortable than Fallowlees, less raw and rugged. Well, that wasn't terribly hard! I suppose I fell in love with it a bit – perhaps not in that head-over-heels way I had fallen for Fallowlees when I first saw her, but a love resulting from having an older, wiser head on my shoulders. Life would certainly be easier here in the lowlands.

Once I got home I was quick to get to work on my proposal for the farm. I had big plans and needed plenty of time to think them through properly and get them on paper before the deadline.

The core of my plan was a sheepdog centre; this seemed particularly appropriate when the father of the modern Border collie, a dog called Old Hemp, had been born in the village of West Woodburn, a stone's throw from the Wallington Estate. I wanted to give dog and duck displays (my displays with Indian Runner ducks, which the dogs herded like sheep, had been popular in the past). I could offer lessons in dog training and give the public access to lambing. I pictured tractor and trailer rides so that visitors could see parts of the farm they couldn't on foot. I imagined sheepdog trials on the large parkland in front of Wallington Hall. I made it very clear that I was happy to work with the Trust at every stage, that I would listen to what they thought would work and that it would be very much a two-way process.

I really felt inspired by my plans. I even dared to feel a little optimistic.

Not long after, I heard on the grapevine that I was one of the favourites for the farm. I was surprised, but secretly rejoiced in the gossip. It invigorated me. I looked at the business plan again and made some improvements.

One Friday evening I had a call from Arthur. He asked how the application was going and I replied that I was pleased with it, on the whole, but that I was struggling with a few figures.

'Remember those people I mentioned?' he said. 'John and Rosalind Murray are actually my in-laws. I think you'd find them really helpful. Perhaps you should meet them.'

A couple of days later I found myself driving along the red tarmac road that swept steeply up a hill above the market town of Rothbury, with butterflies in my stomach.

I knew the Murray name. Everyone did. They were farming royalty in these parts, and they helped to run an evangelical church in the nearby village of Thropton.

Cartington Farm, the Murray home, was daunting and, well, unexpected. I had never come across a farmhouse quite like it. Perched on the highest hill in Rothbury, surrounded by large and well-manicured gardens, it sat in dignified splendour. It was less of a farmhouse, more a stately home. It was over-looked by a rather magnificent ruined castle.

But in the end, the meeting wasn't nearly as intimidating as I had anticipated.

A lady gave me a warm and generous welcome at the door, ushering me through the high-ceilinged porch. This was Rosalind Murray. Rosalind gave off a sense of attentiveness and a lively energy. I imagined she was the sort of person who would always be busy. The hall I found myself in, though impressive in size, felt homely, thanks in part to the photos and news cuttings that were pinned to boards flanking either side of it. I was just admiring the cuttings, including one showing a man receiving an MBE from the Queen at Buckingham Palace for services to the community and education, when the man in question emerged from the end of the hall.

John Murray shook my hand firmly. Right from the outset I knew I was going to like this family.

They ushered me into a conservatory, where I gasped at the view of the Coquet Valley spread out in front of me.

'This must be one of the best views in Northumberland!' I exclaimed, and the Murrays agreed that they were very fortunate.

I could have sat there all day, just looking, watching the comings and goings in the valley below.

Rosalind poured tea from an elegant pot and pushed delicious cakes on me. Never one to turn down a piece of home baking, I was more than willing to indulge.

Of course, I thought to myself, once I had settled in my chair, I ought to have known there was no need to get stressed about the company, for despite the grandeur, John and Rosalind were farmers like me, and farming is the best leveller. Be you lord or labourer, if you have farmed you have lots of common ground. Sheep, in particular, have little regard for your station in life – they will do something dumb or reckless regardless.

After a while we came to the real reason I was there: Broomhouse. John and Rosalind both had some ideas about my proposal, and I found talking it through with other people helped me to see some things more clearly, as well as giving me new ideas to think about. The afternoon slipped away quickly and enjoyably. When I got up to leave I felt reinvigorated, and John and Rosalind gave me their vote of confidence.

A few weeks later I hand-delivered a bound copy of my vision to the National Trust office, complete with glossy photographs, carefully worked-out spreadsheets and gross margins for the first three years. I had struggled with my proposal for Fallowlees, and this one was even more detailed, but I had more of a business head on my shoulders now. I don't mind admitting that I was very proud of this proposal. And optimistic, too. Seven candidates would be selected to go through to the interview stage. I had to be one of them.

9

Mr Tumnus

I always was a bit of a dreamer. Every report card I brought home, from the start of my schooldays to the last, said pretty much the same thing: 'Could do so much better if she stopped dreaming and applied herself.'

But I love to dream! My lifestyle gives me such a lot of time for contemplation that to this day, even when I am working, I can just zone out and switch into automatic mode. It helps kill some of the monotony of my job.

And contract shepherding can be monotonous. I don't dislike any of the jobs it entails per se, but when you find yourself doing each one of them hundreds of times over – whether it be dosing, shearing or foot-trimming – the novelty can start to wear off.

But after a long period of imposed rest, I was back at work which, oddly, seemed like freedom after the time out. I had felt very guilty about letting down my contracts, and I was now working double time to catch up.

Thankfully my favourite contract was waiting for me, the one with Kirkley Hall. They had arranged for Michael, a student, to cover for me when I was bedridden. We would discover we shared a similar outlook on life and would go on to become great friends.

I had wondered how it might feel to get on a quad bike again. But actually, it was fine. It felt good to be in the driver's seat once more. I was just happy to be back.

When I arrived Michael told me about a large wet hole on the track where he had got the bike stuck twice. Quads are amazing things – they go almost everywhere, and it takes a lot to get them stuck, but it does occasionally happen. This particular track had been well used for many years but for some reason had become washed away. I scoffed at Michael for letting it happen twice and not learning his lesson the first time.

By the time I left the farm in the autumn, I had made the walk of shame from that particular wet spot back to the farm steading three times. Michael took great glee in my discomfort when he found out.

After the long hours spent at the kitchen table preparing my application, it was good for my own mind and soul, as well as for the dogs, to spend a few hours cruising the hills I loved so much. It was a cracking summer and the ground was bursting with life. Rabbits pricked up their ears and scarpered when they heard me coming, and birds on the wing called out to each other.

I was just rounding the top of the Hope, a long way from the farm steading, the dogs jogging casually alongside, when I heard a terrible scream. It was truly horrifying, like a person – a small child even – caught in a trap. The dogs, hackles raised, like true protectors jumped on the bike and hid behind me, growling unsteadily.

Again it came, a heart-rending wail. There's a kind of dread that seeps into you when you hear a sound like that. Part of me just didn't want to know what it was – wanted to close my ears and head in the other direction – but the other part of me knew I couldn't ignore it. Imagine if it was an abandoned baby, or a walker who had met with an accident? Unlikely, perhaps, but the papers are full of all sorts of strange occurrences and I could rule nothing out.

I continued along the valley, listening for the sound. I could smell the billy goats nearby, and as I rounded the corner into the plantation, I saw some of the large males gathered. They were vigorously assaulting something with their horns, and it was the creature on the receiving end of this attack that was emitting the awful noise.

There in the midst of them stood a little black and white goat, trembling and panting. He clearly didn't belong to this herd of wild goats, but had decided he wanted to join them. He just wouldn't leave the other goats alone. When the wild goats thought he had had enough of a beating from their curled horns, they would turn to leave. But every time that happened, the little black and white goat, battered though he was, would pick himself up and follow them, panting and bleating pathetically. The billies would go a short way then turn round and start attacking him again. He was a dogged little chap, that was for sure.

As soon as they saw me the wild goats ran off like deer. This little goat must have been someone's pet once, as he trundled over to the bike, showing no fear of me.

His neck was bald where he had previously worn a collar, and his ear tags had been cut out to hide anything that might have identified his owner. It was clear he had been dumped. Perhaps it had been carried out with decent intentions – perhaps his owner had thought he would be accepted into the wild goat community. But it was obvious that that wasn't going to happen.

He was a cute little fellow and appeared to be well fed, with a bit of a pot belly. He had stunted horns, not the impressive, scimitar-like ones that some of the wild goats had – his were more akin to upside-down ice cream cones. He seemed pleased to see me, and was unperturbed by the dogs. I tied a bit of orange baler twine round his neck and, still on the bike, proceeded to lead him back down to the steading. The dogs, thoroughly disgusted by this interloper, trotted along behind.

Back in the steading I had a predicament. I couldn't put the goat in the back of the pickup with the dogs as one of the parties would end up having a rough time. But I could hardly put him in the back seat. Or could I?

Of course I could. The goat hopped in as if he had been travelling in cars his whole life. I tied his makeshift collar to the Jesus handle and set off, hoping to hell I wouldn't meet a police car.

Just out for a drive with a battered, overweight, abandoned goat, Officer!

Back at Fallowlees, I wondered what on earth I was going to do with him. For one thing, I didn't need a goat. But this plucky little character was a real sweetheart. I put a dog collar on him and attached him to a dog tie-out stake on the lawn in front of the house while I decided on my next step.

I've done it again, I thought. I've adopted another hopeless case! This wasn't just a habit, it was an addiction. I'm sure a shrink would have had a field day with me. 'Do you feel rejected yourself, Miss Gray? Are you a loner, isolated, in need of love?'

I already knew what I was going to call my latest addition: it had to be Mr Tumnus.

Ten minutes later, Mr Tumnus was hot-footing it across the lawn trailing the stake behind him. He gave a bleat of recognition as he saw Delphi and Coquet in the front field. The gate wasn't an issue as he made a surprising jump for one so portly and cantered across to join them, the stake clanging off the metal five-bar gate.

He ran straight up to Delphi, bleating with joy. She sniffed him appreciatively with her gentle nose before going back to grazing. For Mr Tumnus it was love at first sight, and from that moment on he was never far from her side.

His welcome from her son was less enthusiastic. Coquet instantly viewed Mr Tumnus as a rival. He was furious, and chased the new addition round and round his mother with angry squeals, bites and kicks that only just missed their target. Mr Tumnus was untroubled, settling eventually for the safety of a spot under Delphi's belly. He had found his place in the world and the love of his life all in one go!

And so I had yet another addition to my farm. Mr Tumnus, like the faun in the Narnia books by C. S. Lewis, would prove to be as big a character as his namesake.

10

Penny

Every day I hoped I might hear about Broomhouse. Perhaps I hadn't made it after all, I thought, as no letter or phone call was forthcoming. Yet I had enough confidence in my proposal to feel I should at least make the interview stage. As I waited for news, I carried on with my plans for the higher-level environmental scheme. I knew from my conversation with Arthur that cattle were the next step for Fallowlees if I wanted to be accepted for the scheme. In order to function well, every good livestock farm needs a mix of cattle and sheep to complement each other and keep the grazing right. The cattle eat the brash and less palatable grasses and make way for the sweeter grass to come through for the sheep. Their trampling action also helps to clear the ground of rushes and bracken.

The most cost-effective way to begin a herd at Fallowlees, I reasoned, would be to buy the cattle at their cheapest, in other words, as newborns. But then I would be faced with the problem of how to rear them. Pet calves, like pet lambs, don't thrive on artificial milk. And if I were to go down that route, I would have the added bother of being tied to regular bottle-feeding, something made difficult by my daily contract work. The real crunch, however, was that I really didn't have the funds for cattle, newborns or not. Those six weeks of not working had played havoc with my bank account. I would just have to wait.

Then one day a location scout for ITV's detective drama, *Vera*, appeared at the door like a fairy godmother. He had been briefed to find a remote farmhouse in a bleak location.

Music to my ears!

ITV had filmed an episode of *Vera* at Redpath, a derelict house on my land, a few years earlier. Knowing the state of Redpath inside and out, I had thought it was a joke at first, but had been assured that the farmhouse was just what they were looking for. They had decorated the whole interior and it had been unrecognisable when the programme aired. This time they wanted to use Fallowlees, and I knew they paid well. What a stroke of luck!

OK to redecorate? he asked.

Yes!

Set up a canteen marquee?

Yes!

Use your house for a week?

Yes!

Borrow your car?

Yes!

In fact, yes, yes, yes – to everything!

The funds had no sooner hit my account than I used half the sum to buy my first generation of cattle for Fallowlees. If I was successful in my bid for Broomhouse, well, the cows would come with me.

Early one morning, I drove into a deserted car park at Hexham Mart. Although dawn had broken several hours ago, the weak sun was making little impression on the broody sky. I switched up the heating, even though I was clad in waterproofs. It had been raining solidly for three days, pretty much since the TV entourage had arrived at Fallowlees. Now it started again. I watched the windscreen wiper as it screeched back and forth.

A pickup pulled into the car park, flashed its lights and pulled up beside me.

'Emma?' the driver questioned.

The week before I had rung one of the few dairy farmers in the area to see if there was any chance of buying some baby calves from him. We had struck a deal for four cross-bred heifers. In the cold light of day, the spindly calves in his vehicle didn't look as if they were worth the money we had agreed. I quashed a brief flash of regret that I had already made the deal, and reassured myself that nothing looks its best on such a cheerless day. I handed over the cheque; a deal was a deal, after all.

The calves were all about three days old. They looked kind of scrawny, offspring of long-legged dairy cows mated with the meaty, overdeveloped Belgian Blue. They were mostly patchy, apart from one, whose coat was an unusually brilliant white, who instantly became my favourite. They were dairy calves and they smelt like it; the scent of warm milk on the turn, kind of cheesy, isn't unpleasant but it's not exactly delicious either.

Between us we managed to transfer the calves from his vehicle into mine. I had deeply bedded the pickup with straw, in readiness.

At Fallowlees the calves were unruffled as I carried them from the pickup and deposited them in the shed. I always find baby animals have a kind of indifference to being handled in the very early days – they don't seem to have developed that fear or survival instinct they will have after a few days have passed. They looked pretty wretched as they huddled together in the shed, butting each other in their search for milk.

Plan A executed.

Now for Plan B.

Penny was a pedigree Jersey cow in full milk, and probably the most beautiful cow I'd ever seen. Had she been a person she would have been a sought-after model. Her eyes were huge, fringed with lustrous black lashes and lined with permanent kohl. She was a deep tan colour with brown points on her knees and nose. She carried a perfect full udder with excellent teat placement.

My plan was to use Penny to multi-suckle the calves. She would have more than enough milk to accommodate all four of them. I felt that the combination of being fed the way nature intended, as well as a mother's love, would mean they would grow into strong adults. I had chosen heifers so that in a few years they would become the foundation cows for the Fallowlees herd.

So, OK, I came up with this plan after a glass (or two) of wine, but I really thought the idea had legs. But for the plan to work, both A and B had to come together.

Would Penny take to the calves? I needed her to mother them as if they were her own. It was possible she would reject them outright. The more I thought about it, the more it seemed crackers to think a cow who had never reared her own calf would suddenly want to rear not one calf, but four. And foisted on her out of the blue, at that. I was also very aware of the fact that Fallowlees was far from ideal territory for a dairy cow. They thrive in the milk-and-honey grazing of the lowlands, not the adder-and-tick country of Fallowlees.

I drove round the back field to the shed with newly purchased Penny in a borrowed horsebox. I had to drive carefully, weaving between random police cars and buses the TV crew had left all over the field.

The ground was slippery and the pickup slid dangerously close to the guy ropes on the canteen marquee as I inched my way closer to the cattle shed.

It was with some trepidation that I lowered the ramp and let caramel-coloured Penny step blinking into the shed to meet her new children.

I needn't have worried. Penny took to motherhood instantly. The four calves, with a delighted moo and a skip, gathered round her. They knew instinctively how to be calves in the same way Penny knew how to be a mother. They butted and nudged at her udder and set to work drinking. It was wonderful to see how happy Penny was to have them. She kept sniffing and licking at them as if she couldn't believe her luck.

But I was really the lucky one – lucky to have found Penny, a born mother, with the kindest of natures. This was hammered home to me a year later when I tried the same thing with another cow who promptly rejected her adopted offspring. As someone with no thoughts of being a mother myself, I watched Penny with admiration.

I was just sitting on a bale in the corner of the shed, watching the happy family scene playing out in front of me while the rain drummed noisily on the tin roof, when I heard voices coming from outside.

'Ahh! Look at the baby cows!' a female voice cooed.

I could see a woman peeking through the hole in the door.

'Ahh, yeah, they are cute,' a male voice agreed.

'You don't think they're for veal, do you?' asked the female voice.

'Probably. You know what these farmers are like.'

I was up like a shot and bounded over to the shed door, swinging it open to reveal a young, very pierced, red-haired woman in a paramedic's uniform and a heavily built security guard.

'They aren't for veal, they're going to be kept to be cows,' I retorted to the clearly surprised pair.

They stepped back apologetically.

I softened at their embarrassed faces. 'Come inside and have a look. You'll want to get out of the rain.'

I was always happy to explain to people the fundamentals of farming work, and today I was keen to show off my new additions, too.

I was also fascinated to know what it was like for them, working on a TV show. Worlds apart from my own life. It seemed it wasn't as glamorous as I'd thought.

'The money's not bad, but we spend a lot of time just twiddling our thumbs until they need us,' said the woman.

'It gets pretty boring,' her companion agreed.

'It's nice here, but a pity about the weather,' she said.

The calves were a welcome distraction. We stood there watching them.

'What are they called?' asked the woman.

'They haven't got names yet. I've only just got them.'

'That white one's got to be Chalky,' she said.

We chatted for half an hour and I explained why I had bought the cattle, and how they were part of my environmental plan for the farm. How the calves would have Penny as a mum until they were older. I also dispelled any myths they had about veal. They in turn gave me some juicy gossip on the cast and crew.

Meanwhile the calves had drunk their fill and all four had lain down in a satisfied heap. A proper feed had done them the world of good, and they looked far more substantial than when I had first seen them in the dingy morning light. Penny stood, her contented head lowered protectively over her new charges, watching lovingly with her chocolate eyes.

'Fancy some lunch?' asked the security guard. 'The marquee food is really good.'

The three of us plodded through the ever-deepening mire to the makeshift canteen. It wasn't much drier inside. Fallowlees soil is mostly clay and doesn't take well to being tramped on by man or beast. It had rebelled by making the floor inside as greasy as an ice rink. But that didn't matter – the food was indeed exceptional. How those chefs could conjure up such delights with so few facilities I had no idea. Having loaded a tray with lasagne, garlic bread and chocolatey profiteroles, I went to join my new friends on one of the long rows of tables, along with other members of the crew. (I discovered that it takes a lot of people to make an episode of *Vera*.)

Just as I was about to sit down, I felt myself slip, and with no hands free to save myself I knew I was a goner.

But a cameraman, quick as a flash, jumped up and grabbed my arm to steady me, just in time.

'Whoa, you nearly went there,' said someone.

'Thanks for that.' I sat down next to my saviour and gave him an appreciative nod.

'It's so damn muddy here,' he said. 'You know, we filmed here a couple of years ago and the same thing happened then. It rained every bloody day.'

I nodded sympathetically as I tucked into the lasagne.

He carried on. 'I mean, it's in the middle of nowhere, it rains all the time, it's bloody freezing and there's not even a pub to go to. Who actually lives in a shithole like this? They must be soft in the head to farm out here!'

I stifled a giggle with a slice of garlic bread as my new friends looked from him to me in alarm.

'What?' he asked, seeing their faces and my own embarrassed smile.

'Actually, it's my shithole,' I answered, swallowing the lasagne. 'I'm the farmer here, and I quite like it.'

'Sorry.' It was the cameraman's turn to be embarrassed.

'It's OK,' I said with a laugh. 'You are right, anyway, I am a bit mad.'

There was a brief stunned pause before the rest of the table joined in the laughter.

When the post arrived later that day I discovered I had an interview for Broomhouse. I was delighted, but my elation turned quickly to guilt: what was I thinking of? I loved it here at Fallowlees. All the same, I was going to put my heart and soul into it. I'd be mad not to.

11

Fallowlees

I was excited and nervous on the day of the interview, but it turned out I had no need to be either. I could tell about one minute into proceedings that I wasn't going to get Broomhouse. There was lots of polite nodding and nice questions from the panel of three, but no getting down to the nitty-gritty of numbers. None of the in-depth quizzing I had been expecting and was prepared for. It was more meeting a new boyfriend's parents than *Dragons' Den*. Sitting at their posh table, glass of water in front of me, I could tell that they didn't see me as a potential tenant for the farm. It was very hard for me to keep my face neutral and not give in to my disappointment there and then. I remember sitting in the car afterwards, head resting on the steering wheel, dwelling on how very silly I must have appeared to think I stood a chance. I turned off my phone. I didn't want to speak to family and well-wishers who would soon be ringing with the 'How did it go?' question.

The tenancy for Broomhouse was awarded to a farming consultant who, it turned out, had similar ideas to mine. Later in the year, when the new tenant had settled in, one of the interviewing panel got back to me and asked if I would still consider holding dog and duck displays on the farm. I declined politely (gritting my teeth).

I should have known that I was aiming too far, too soon. But it still stung. I had really thought that Broomhouse could be the place for me, the place where I might even spend the rest of my life. If I'm being honest, I'd also hoped, deep down, that getting Broomhouse would make it easier for me to meet someone to share the journey with – that being the tenant there would turn my status as a farmer into a plus rather than a negative in others' eyes.

Those hopes were crushed. For a few days after the interview I fell into a kind of apathy. I became listless and lazy. I knew I was silly and ungrateful. I already had a brilliant life, and I felt bad that I wasn't appreciating it.

I had been so wrapped up in my plans for Broomhouse that at times I had almost forgotten how fortunate I was to have Fallowlees. As I looked at her now, I felt guilty to think how consumed I had been by my thoughts of leaving her. Without Fallowlees, I wouldn't be the person I was now. Without Fallowlees, who knows where I might have been? My life could have ended up taking a different course.

When I think of Fallowlees, it's of an oasis set in the barren landscape of the forest. The journey to it by car is a dull one: a rutted road bordered by acres of Sitka spruce. No real views to speak of, just towering trees on either side. Then, just when you think you have left all civilisation behind, the trees open to reveal her. I do think of Fallowlees as a 'she', in the way ships are always female, representing a mother and nurturing.

Despite the long drive through the forest to get to her, her situation is high and open. On a sunny day you can see the sun winking off the North Sea on the east coast. There is almost always a breeze. In the winter the wind can be so sharp it feels as if it's cutting you in half, but in the summer it keeps the midges away and brings the foreign, coconut scent of the gorse bushes.

The farmhouse has been here for hundreds of years, but there have been people on this land for thousands. The man-made cup marks (small depressions cut into rock surfaces and thought to be a form of prehistoric art) bear witness to Neolithic past guardians. A tumbledown bastle – a fortified farmhouse – lies next door. Its foundations are so deep in the earth, efforts made by past tenants to dig them up have ended in failure and they have resigned themselves to leaving the ruins be.

I was beckoned over in the pub one evening and told a story by the wise old boys round the bar. Apparently there had once been a concerted effort to remove the enormous cup-marked rock situated by the bastle. It took a full day, many workers, some heavy-duty machinery and a lot of cursing before they decided the rock must be set so deep it would never be moved by man. That night, they said, the entire crew fell ill with food poisoning. They put it down to a dodgy lunch ... or could it have been something more sinister?

I don't know for sure, but I would guess that much of the

stone used to build the farmhouse was stolen from the bastle. As it's still on the farm, I guess it's not really stolen, just repurposed. Things were built to last in those days, and most things do. All of the fields are hemmed in by well-made stone walls, hundreds of years old. It seems we aren't the only ones to appreciate them.

'Y'all must love those rock fences y'all got around here!' some visiting Texans said one day.

The walls of the house are outrageously thick, designed to keep out the cold in winter and make the place cool in the summer. The kitchen is the heart of the home in any farm-house, and that's where I spend most of my time. There is a huge fireplace with a massive stone lintel, exposed beams on the ceiling and red tiles on the floor. I pulled up some vinyl one day in the cupboard under the stairs to reveal gorgeous stone flags, which I assume floored the whole house at one stage. One of the tenants must have decided to concrete over them and replace them with more modern tiles. Perhaps they will never see the light of day again, but it's nice to know they are there.

I have made several changes to the house myself over the years. I put down carpets, sorted out the heating and had the generator totally overhauled. Those miserable trudges in dressing gown and wellies to fix a temperamental machine in an outbuilding on a freezing night are now just memories.

One day I had a farmer round who was buying a puppy from me. When he came to leave, he stopped on the doorstep, looked out over my fields and took a draw on his cigarette.

'Did ye hear of that young lass getting galloped to death on that fell over there?' He pointed to Greenleighton Moor, just beyond my own land.

By galloped to death I guessed he meant she had fallen from her horse but was held by her stirrup. I shook my head and shuddered at the thought. I get told lots of stories, but that was a new one on me.

'Aye, it's a wonder you don't have her round here on a night-time.' He winked. 'This place looks ripe for a ghost.'

If there are ghosts, I can only think they are friendly ones.

Sometimes I sit and think about the life these walls have seen, the good times and the bad times. People have been conceived, born and have died in this house for centuries, and many of them have left their mark in some way. Signatures on walls, scratchings etched in the stonework of the byres, even a bottle time capsule in one of the stone walls.

Fallowlees has so many secrets. I am only just discovering some of them. I guess I'll never know them all.

The area was more heavily populated in the past. Much of the land that is now forested would have been grazing land in times gone by, and there would have been more farms. The derelict farmhouses of Redpath and Chartners, barely a couple of miles from Fallowlees, were family homes only a few decades ago.

It makes me realise I am not so special, really – just the most recent occupant out of hundreds before me, no more signifi-cant than any other.

12

Archie

It was summer, and I had so much to look forward to. It was back to my favourite weekend occupation. I figured that tri-alling wasn't too strenuous for my back, the most physical thing I had to do being to close the gate of the pen once the sheep were inside. We had a wet spell, and some of the trials were cancelled due to waterlogged fields, but when they resumed in Belford at the end of July there was no stopping me. I had done little but train my dogs during those weeks of recuperation, and we were ready for the competition. I had high hopes for Roy and Alfie, who were both running well.

Roy and I came second in Belford. It was a great way to make a comeback.

I caught up with old friends and fellow triallists while I was there. There were lots of congratulations and enquiries after my health, as well as the leg-pulling I had expected.

'By, you've come back in fine fettle!' said my old friend Archie, his dog Dale by his side.

I gave Dale's rough coat a rub. It was wonderful to see them both again.

'Thanks so much for your help when I was just out of hospital, Archie. Mum and Dad would have been stuck without you and Dale.'

He shook his head in a way that indicated there was no need for thanks. 'You'd have done the same for me.'

'Of course!'

I could always rely on Archie to be honest with me about my performance, pointing out what I'd done wrong as well as congratulating me, so I was pleased with his praise.

'The time off's done you good,' he winked. 'I'll have to try a few weeks in bed meself.'

'Ha ha! Chance would be a fine thing! I've been on my feet training ever since they allowed me back to Fallowlees. It was the only thing I *could* do at first.'

'Well, lass, I always thought you were some woman, and I can see I wasn't wrong!'

Normally Archie would be telling me next he'd found the ideal man for me, as it was one of Archie's missions to see me married off.

'All his own teeth and hair, too,' he would tell me, as he gave the lowdown on the latest candidate.

I would argue that I didn't see the above as a selling point so much as a prerequisite.

'And the right side of sixty!' he would add, to my protests that I was still in my twenties.

But Archie kept off that subject today.

'It's made my day to see you back again, lass. Just keep off quad bikes for a while.'

Back on the farm, my other animals were also doing well. Penny was still besotted with her role as a mother and spent much of her time contentedly watching over her calves, getting frustrated whenever they went frolicking around the field in different directions. The juveniles were mushrooming on her plentiful supply of buttery Jersey milk.

Coquet was also growing, mostly in the leg department. It wasn't going to be long before he reached the dizzy heights of his mother's 16.2 hands. Coquet and Mr Tumnus still had the old rivalry going, though to be honest, it was more of a vendetta on Coquet's part. Mr Tumnus paid Coquet scant regard, preferring to roam widely across the farm, nibbling at things that shouldn't be nibbled, including newly planted trees, shrubs and the electric cable for my trailer lights.

I had shaken off my apathy. I knew I was lucky. I was doing the things I enjoyed, day in and day out. My life was a permanent holiday, training dogs and working with sheep in the countryside that was my office. I knew others would give their eye teeth to be in my shoes. If this was how the rest of my life was going to pan out, well, that would be just grand by me. Of course there would always be the odd day when the solitude would sap my resolve and enthusiasm, but they were few and far between.

I did what every farmer has to do: I dealt with the disappointment and moved on. It's a useful habit; in fact, to a farmer, it's more than that – it's an essential one.

*

The day the official rejection letter landed on the doormat, Arthur Davis rang out of the blue with commiserations – and another proposal for me.

Would I be interested in entering into a farming partnership with John and Rosalind Murray? I was flabbergasted.

Partnerships are common in farming, particularly within families, where different generations often work together, though other farmers might combine their finances and labour too. My first thought was to wonder what I possibly had to contribute. I couldn't cough up a load of cash, for a start.

It turned out that Arthur had had me in the back of his mind as a potential for this partnership after assessing Fallowlees for the environmental scheme. My meeting with John and Rosalind to help with the Broomhouse application had acted as an informal interview – a chance for them to see if they liked me and whether they wanted to work with me. And it seemed that they did.

Even after the call had ended, my mouth still hung open in surprise. What Arthur had told me sounded too good to be true.

The farm was called Healey Mill and was a twenty-five-minute drive away, near the village of Netherwitton. I would, effectively, be in charge of it. I would have two hundred and forty acres of ground at my disposal, rent-free, in return for looking after two hundred ewes for the partnership. I would need to stay at Fallowlees as Arthur and his wife Kirstine, one of John and Rosalind's daughters, lived in the farmhouse, but in reality that suited me. John and Rosalind were coming to Fallowlees the following afternoon, so I would find out more about it all then. If the deal was as good as Arthur had outlined, I would be able to give up my contract shepherding after all.

I hardly dared get excited for fear of more disappointment. I had passed my first test with the Murrays, but I knew, even without Arthur saying so, that their visit to me was a second test. Fallowlees needed to impress them, too, and I would hate to let them down. Fortunately, I had already put a lot of effort into tidying up the farm when I was applying for Broomhouse, knowing that a home visit is part of the interview process for serious contenders. All the same, I cast a critical eye over it and found other tasks that required my attention. Those who have gardens know that the work is never done, and it's the same on a farm – only more so. It was going to be a long twenty-four hours.

In the end, I needn't have worried. John and Rosalind were happy with all they saw at Fallowlees. They outlined the terms of the deal, and it was much as Arthur had said: I would pay no rent, and in exchange for looking after two hundred of their ewes, I would have the rest of the farm to stock with my own sheep. They would also provide and maintain both a quad and a tractor.

The partnership, it turned out, included several people with much expertise between them. John and Rosalind had four daughters, two of whom, along with their husbands, were involved in the business. There were also two other men – one of whom worked for the Wildlife Trust and another who had recently moved to another farm nearby and was the reason for the vacancy in the first place.

The crux of the matter was that they were looking for someone capable and reliable, and also someone they could get
on with and trust as there would be a great deal of crossover
between buildings and equipment.

I was over the moon. It was the first time I could take heart
in the saying, 'As one door closes, another opens.'

John and Rosalind left me with a map of the land and urged
me to take a look as soon as I could. It was all I could do to let
the dust settle on the forestry track after their departure before
setting out to see the new farm. My farm, dare I say it.

Netherwitton contained a mansion house, a small church,
some handsome stone cottages and little else. It is so
chocolate-box pretty it would make a perfect setting for an
episode of *Midsomer Murders*. Healey Mill lay on its outskirts.

My heart was jumping as I drove up the track and saw my
new farm laid out in front of me. I had my own steading, a
cattle shed and some sheep pens set firmly in concrete. But
the land was the real jewel in the crown. The terrain consisted
mostly of rolling hills, with some rougher land thrown in for
good measure. Some of the fields were edged by trees, others
were flat and almost arable. It was, in short, the perfect land
for schooling sheepdogs. In order to gain the experience to
compete at a high level, dogs need to practise their skills in a
variety of fields and landscapes. As I drove round on my des-
ignated quad, I just knew in my bones that I could really turn
my sheepdogs into something here. It was made for the task.

I thought too of my little flock back at Fallowlees – those
Texels who had survived the dog attack, and all the Blackies.
They would think all their Christmases had come at once

moving to such fertile, sheltered ground as this! My mind was racing with all the possibilities this new land offered. I would still keep some sheep at Fallowlees, I thought; I would use it to raise ewe lambs who would become replacements for the flock, as well as be used for training the younger dogs. Having two such different farms was an answer to my prayers.

I immediately gave notice on my contracts. I was terribly sad to say goodbye to all of them. I had worked for many of them for years. However, I think my former employers could see the joy bubbling over in my heart at the thought of being my own boss at last. They all wished me the best of luck in the next chapter of my life.

13

Caroline

My sister swept in on a breeze of glamour and scent. Caroline is a blonde bombshell, sophisticated and tastefully dressed, but hardy as they come. She can lamb a sheep as well as anyone. She's not a farmer (she has more sense), but is often called in to help out between me and my parents. She had been a godsend to me with my broken back.

Both Caroline and my other sister, Elizabeth, who is seven years younger than me, are my greatest friends. Growing up on the farm together we were always full of mischief. We also fought like cat and dog, and to this day I still bear the scars of some of the vicious fights we got ourselves into. Mum, who had her own ideas of how sisters should behave, would be heard lamenting in the background, 'Why can't you all be more like *Little Women*?' I did point out to her that the March sisters in Louisa May Alcott's book had their own conflicts too!

My mum also commonly says, 'Only family can be brutally honest with you.' I was about to get a taste of that.

'Are you living on cereal?' Caroline had only just stepped through the front door and into the kitchen, where she was confronted with the bowls in the sink, the telltale marks of dried-on muesli dotting the sides.

'And have you got all the dogs in the house?' She sniffed at the distinct aroma of work dogs.

It was true I had let things slip since I'd broken my back. Then with the application for Broomhouse taking up so much time, and my thoughts now being consumed by Healey Mill, I had stopped noticing and caring about the chaos indoors. Anything for an easy life. Outdoors had always been my priority. Normally all the work dogs would live in the kennels, and only Roy and Alfie would be allowed inside, but I had let the whole pack into the house in recent weeks. I found the hustle and bustle good company.

I had also started to enjoy a glass of wine every night while trawling social media. They were large glasses and they seemed to make the evenings go faster. I knew it wasn't a good thing, but it was the only social life I had.

'I know,' I replied, an answer that both confirmed her suspicions and admitted to my guilty feelings about them.

After giving me a talking-to about how I should start eating properly and relocating the dogs, Caroline – somewhat ironically – produced a tube of Pringles and a selection pack of dips. My sisters and I share an obsession with these snacks. It can really get out of hand at Christmas when we are all together, and the thought of those moreishly salty crisps dunked into tubs of hummus or soured cream and onion flavour dip makes our mouths water almost as much as Mum's lovingly prepared roast dinner.

'So, what's new?' Caroline asked, as we sat down and started munching.

'I'm in partnership,' I said, liking the sound of saying it aloud.

Caroline looked impressed, or she may have just been relishing her first delicious mouthful.

'Sounds very grown-up.'

I told her all about Healey Mill and how I was planning to move the sheep there in the next few months.

'I could do with someone to help when the time comes,' I hinted, testing the water. I knew I shouldn't push my luck – I had already leant on my family a lot lately – but it was worth a try.

Caroline dodged the question efficiently. 'You really should try dating again.'

'Yeah, right. That's going to be easy!'

'There's loads of options these days. Have you heard of Tinder?'

'Yeah, but isn't that like a hook-up site?'

'It's a new dating app. You should try it. Now you have mobile reception up here it'll be so much easier. In fact – what are we waiting for – you can do it now. It doesn't take a minute.'

Until recently, reception at Fallowlees had been so poor I had to rely on a temperamental satellite, which only worked on nice days and when the swallows weren't perched on top of it. But since the arrival of 3G, my life had been revolutionised. Well, it had made me feel less isolated, at least.

As we munched our way through the Pringles, I downloaded the app. It couldn't do any harm, I reasoned. I didn't have to do anything about it if I didn't want to. Caroline was right – it did look easy. All I had to do was create an account, put in a few personal details and decide on a photo as my main image.

'Not that one – use the one in your blue dress! That's a really cool picture. Now another four that sum you up.'

'OK, OK. I've done it.'

Caroline nodded her approval.

'Now I have to choose a geographical distance. What shall I say? Ten miles?'

'Hardly! There won't be anyone to match with out here. You'll have to set your circle large, like maybe as far as Newcastle.'

Job done, I put the remains of the dips in the fridge. 'C'mon, I'll show you the calves.'

The calves had grown really well on the super-butterfat milk Jerseys are renowned for. Penny and her new family were outside full time now, and her anxiety over their mischief-making had lessened. They really looked a great herd.

'They're beautiful. But I've never heard of a Jersey living on a hill farm,' said Caroline.

'I know, it's not ideal. I really need more cattle – some that suit the ground better.'

I was concerned that, come winter, the calves would need to be housed to maintain their condition. And with housing come all sorts of additional needs: silage and straw. And with silage and straw: a tractor.

I had always known a tractor would be on my purchase list. It was in my business plan when I first came to Fallowlees, but I hadn't really needed one that desperately till now. I had always managed with the quad and trailer and my own muscle power to get feed out when it was needed.

I had begun to trawl the agricultural papers for cheap tractors. I knew what I wanted: a four-by-four with a loader – it didn't need to be flash.

'But how will you afford it?' Caroline knew as well as I did that tractors weren't cheap.

'I think I'll have to sell one of the younger dogs.'

Caroline looked at me in alarm. 'But you love those dogs!'

'Yes, but I have Roy and Alfie. It's always been the plan to train to sell. To make my dogs a business.' This would be my first foray into the big world of dog selling. I was trying to justify it to myself as much as anyone. 'And I sold Fly, didn't I?'

'Yes, and it nearly killed you!'

Caroline was right. Fly had been my favourite dog and I had sold her out of sheer necessity when finances were tight. I had had several bills to pay at the same time, one of them, ironically, being the vet's bill for Fly's own life-saving operation.

'Anyway,' I added, 'it's just a thought.'

It was a gorgeous day and we decided to take the opportunity for a plod through the forest on the horses. Any of my previous daredevil tendencies had been well and truly curbed by the accident. We'd just take it easy.

So we set out, Caroline on Delphi and me on Piper. Piper was a big old gypsy cob, with fat brown patches. She was a kind, gentle sort and probably the type of horse I should have bought in the first place rather than the highly bred Delphi. She had been loaned to me by a friend who decided she needed a summer of happy hacking to recover from the loss of her foal. It's funny how quickly my little herd had grown – apparently that's a common side effect: once you have the first horse, they just multiply.

Coquet, of course, was leading the way. He understood himself to be the only man and the rightful leader of the herd, and took this role very seriously. Jogging alongside, with fast little steps to keep up with the long strides of the horses, came the unflagging, tenacious Mr Tumnus.

My Tumnus couldn't – wouldn't – be left behind. I had tried that in the past, tying him to a post, a bucket of food as a bribe. I wouldn't be repeating that again. The shrieks and screams could be heard for miles. They echoed in the trees and made him sound like a deranged monster. Which was partly true. He was a bit of a nightmare; he could and would travel everywhere on the farm eating whatever he fancied. I swear that goat had super-refined hearing – he could sense a bucket being moved forty yards away! If he wanted Penny's food he would poke her in the belly with his horns and she would move over. This was frustrating as Penny was rearing four calves and Mr Tumnus was only growing his fat belly. In the end I had to feed Penny in a specially constructed goat-proof pen.

I did have a notion at one point to cut off his horns, but when it came to it, I just couldn't bring myself to do it. He wouldn't be Mr Tumnus without them.

It serves you right, I thought, as I watched his barrel-like form jogging alongside us. You have to get fit. With his head swinging from side to side, he was wheezing like a forty-a-day smoker.

Delphi was still the love of his life. He followed her every-where. She acted cool as a cucumber, as with everything. Coquet, however, still hated him. If Mr Tumnus showed any sign of trying to move ahead of Coquet whenever we were out on a walk, there was hell to pay. Coquet wasn't beyond giving him a sly nip, or even letting loose his heels.

We were a funny-looking gang, picking our way across the dappled forest floor. Caroline and I talked nonsense, of days out, parties and men. We arrived on Greenleighton Moor, a huge expanse of fell ground opposite Fallowlees.

You know, I found out the other day that a girl our age got galloped to death here, I thought to mention, but decided against it.

A jay shot through the trees. Neither Delphi nor Piper batted an eyelid, but Coquet made a big song and dance about it, reeling back against his mum in mock horror. Caroline and I laughed. Some stallion he'll be! Not one to waste an oppor-tunity, Mr Tumnus quickly overtook him and led the way through the gate, whereby Coquet rallied, squealed and roared ahead, his masculine pride dented.

We had a quiet trot along the sheep trods on the fell – tracks worn into the ground by the regular use of sheep travel-ling the hill.

'Shall we try the double-ditch horror?' I asked Caroline, momentarily forgetting my new-found resolution.

The double-ditch horror was two large ditches, one straight after the other, so that you never knew what your horse would do. Would it jump both in one long leap, or would it do a series of bunny hops and bounce over each one separately?

It was a lovely day, so why not – though we were secretly thankful that we had safety stirrups.

We set off at a gentle loping canter, Mr Tumnus bleating as we gradually left him behind. Piper decided against jumping the ditches and came to a dead stop. I was slapped violently onto her neck before she manoeuvred her large backside over them in two ungainly bounces. Delphi, however, demonstrating the racehorse in her, decided to really extend herself, taking both ditches in her giant graceful stride. She and Caroline had landed safely when Coquet decided he wanted to swerve off to give the approaching Mr Tumnus a piece of his mind.

Seeing her offspring departing, Delphi made a sudden about-turn, dumping Caroline unceremoniously on the ground.

It was too much for me to bear. I broke down in stomach-aching giggles, slumped on Piper's saddle. Caroline, unhurt, stood up and saw what I saw.

'Christ help us if anyone sees that!' Coquet was chasing Mr Tumnus in circles, Delphi, trailing her bridle, was chasing Coquet, and Mr Tumnus was chasing her. A real merry-go-round menagerie.

We both fell about with helpless laughter.

Back at the kitchen table, we were still laughing as Caroline nursed her face with a bag of frozen peas I had dragged from the depths of the freezer, where they lay among unmarked carrier bags of dubious remains.

After she had caught up with Delphi, the horse had swung her head sharply, whacking Caroline on the side of the head. That marked the end of our ride.

Apart from Caroline, Mr Tumnus was the only one of the

party the worse for wear when we got home, lying flat out on the ground, panting like a marathon runner at the finishing line.

I made us both a cup of tea and we sat at the kitchen table and polished off the crisps.

I pulled out my phone. My first dip into Tinder had already produced results.

'Look, I've matched with this guy, a firefighter from Galashiels.'

Caroline took the phone from me.

'Mmmm, looks nice. But you know, being in the fire service is the most lied-about occupation on Tinder. And I bet he doesn't actually look like that. You have to take Tinder with a pinch of salt.'

'He's quite far from Fallowlees, too.'

'It's no distance really. I wonder if he knows anyone from Hawick? Galashiels isn't that far away from home, is it?'

'Yeah, I wonder. He does look nice, though.'

With his blue and white face paint and Scotland rugby top, I was reminded of Mel Gibson in the film *Braveheart*.

'What do you think I should do?'

'Ping a message!'

I had nothing to lose.

14

The Tractor

On a farm one season merges into another. Hints of the coming season sneak up on you slowly at first – the first green shoot or snowdrop, the glint of a handful of copper leaves on an otherwise green tree – then, before you know it, you find you have well and truly left the old one behind and are in the midst of the new one. With all that had happened to me this year, time seemed to be passing by even more quickly than usual. Summer was now slipping into autumn. Summer jobs had been done – sheep were clipped and weaned and were now putting on weight ready for the breeding season. I was on the cusp of taking over Healey Mill and was excited about the future.

Breaking my back so soon after the publication of my book in the spring had taken the edge off the excitement of being a published author, though I had managed to give a few interviews and make some TV appearances. There was a random trip to London to be on *The Alan Titchmarsh Show* with Roy and three of my Runner ducks, the ones I gave displays with. We all travelled down on the train – yes, the ducks included. As I got off at King's Cross, a lovely passenger approached me and told me how Roy must really love his little friend in the canvas carry cage (it was canvas so nobody could see the contents).

'He didn't take his eyes off his little friend throughout the whole journey,' he said, repeating that Roy must love him dearly.

'Yes, he does love his little friend so very dearly,' I agreed, making a hasty getaway before I could be questioned any further on the contents of the cage. I figured I would have great difficulty trying to explain the presence and purpose of Runner ducks and a sheepdog on a train!

It felt bizarre to be performing in a TV studio, with its fancy shelving and ornaments, but the three minutes flashed by. Roy was a star, lying there good as gold until his moment came. He herded the ducks from one cage into another in a jiffy. The audience were impressed. Alan Titchmarsh gave the book a quick plug at the end, though he managed to fluff the title and call it *One Girl and His Dogs* – a sort of mash-up of my book and the long-running TV programme *One Man and His Dog*. Oh well, they say there's no such thing as bad publicity.

The newspapers that wrote about the book loved those old clichés about me: 'Britain's loneliest shepherdess', or 'The shepherdess looking for love'. I was always grateful for the interest the press showed in me and my story – I figured spreading the word about my occupation could only be a good thing for farming in general, and if this was the best way to do it, then I could put up with the more annoying aspects. But some of the reporting did seem, well, a little irresponsible. I'd never asked the papers to act as a marriage bureau for me. I sometimes had unwanted visitors arrive at Fallowlees out of the blue. There was usually a good reason for their appearance, but I suspect the odd one had turned up hoping to solve my relationship dilemma!

The fact remained that – expensive or not – I needed a tractor before the winter months set in and the job of feeding my animals became more labour-intensive. After trawling the farming press every week I had finally found one I could afford – a yellow Renault Cergos, with bald slicks for tyres. It was a four-by-four with a loader, and as such it fitted my bill. It was sold by a big company that regularly took out a full-page advertisement in the *Farmers Guardian*. Better a large reputable company than to start trawling round machinery sales or farm steadings, I thought.

I decided to go and look at it on my own. I ought to have taken someone with me who knew more about tractors than I did, but it was quite a long drive to their site and I didn't want to inconvenience anyone. Truth was, I knew that at the price it was going for, it was the only chance I had of having a functional tractor, and that short of it sitting growing grass or spurting oil, I would be buying it.

The sales yard was very smart. A long row of shiny tractors was parked in a tidy herringbone formation. A Rottweiler chained to a barrel sounded a warning before wagging its stump of a tail and retreating to its kennel.

I entered the very male territory of the Portakabin office.

The tight space smelt of cigarette smoke, oil and men. The carpet was well trodden with grubby work boots; posters of nude women shared wall space with noticeboards displaying scribbled tractor jargon.

No one acknowledged me at first as I sidled in awkwardly. It was difficult to work out who I needed to speak to as I couldn't tell customer from employee, and didn't want to make a prat of myself by asking the wrong person.

Most of the men were talking to each other or looking at their phones. One, who was clearly a regular, was chatting amiably to a man on the other side of the counter as he handed over a stash of notes. Then someone nodded in my direction and all heads turned to look at me.

'I've, erm, come to see the tractor. I rang yesterday.' I felt awkward and silly.

''Course you did, darling,' said one of the men. 'I'll just grab the keys.'

I noticed him wink at the others as he plucked a set of keys from a hook on the wall.

At the furthest end of the herringbone row was the Renault, dwarfed by an enormous Massey Ferguson. In truth, I wasn't greatly impressed by any of them. They were just tractors, after all, a necessary evil in the mind of any shepherd.

The man passed me the keys and indicated with a sideways flick of his head that I should get inside. I hopped into the driver's seat and turned the keys to hear the click of a flat battery. I looked at the man queryingly.

'The battery's grand. We've just replaced it. It's just that she's been stood a while.'

Well, that can happen, I thought, as he whistled for one of the lads to fetch a jump-starter.

The hydraulics didn't seem to work well, being sluggish compared to what I was used to, and the tyres had virtually no tread left, but I guessed they could be replaced easily enough.

'The oil will just need a change,' said the man. 'I'll do that for you and service it before it goes.'

The side window was non-existent.

'I'll fix that before it leaves as well, and throw in delivery. We have a wagon going up your neck of the woods next week. If you get payment to us quickly, I'll send it up on that load.'

What to do? Decisions flicked through my head. It's about the best I'm going to get at that price, I thought. I hadn't seen a loader tractor anywhere near the same ballpark figure, and the loader worked grand. I was also swayed by the quick delivery – the calves and Penny were needing silage every day now, and I had the horses to think about as well. It was becoming a tiresome job handballing it to them each morning before work. It was just a little shepherd's tractor for dotting about putting bales in, and that was all I needed it for.

Back in the grimy cabin we shook hands and I agreed to send a banker's draft once I was home. They reiterated that the tractor would be with me within the week.

I felt elated on the drive home: a tractor would complete my little farm and make my life so much easier. I was basking in this new milestone I had reached, right up until the sun-shade on the windscreen fell off and I had to drive back to Northumberland squinting into the sun.

15

Coquet Grows Up

We had ponies when I was growing up, but they were more the feral kind, ridden at your own risk. Dad, quad and dog would have to be enlisted in order to gather them in. Once corralled in the shed and tack applied, we would ride them daredevil-style on the big silage field, leading them to the bottom before jumping on and letting them bolt to the top. It wasn't stylish, but it was great fun for my sisters and me. I think the ponies even enjoyed it – no sedentary happy hacking for them!

I really enjoyed having the horses at Fallowlees. I was lucky to have so much land for them, which stopped the fields looking 'horsified', as most farmers call it. Horses, unlike cattle, are selective grazers – they prefer the shorter, sweeter grass and will often graze it down to the bare ground, while leaving other plants to grow to maturity. For this reason, horses and farming don't always go hand in hand. They also pace a lot around fence lines, ruining the ground.

One dreary, plodgy day I shouted for them across the field.

I loved the way they all came running for a treat, so unlike the ponies of my youth. Coquet was getting pretty feisty – it wasn't just Robson Green who had been on the receiving end of the odd nip! He was starting to grow up and assert his authority. As the only male (Mr Tumnus had lost his crown jewels), he saw himself as the leader and liked everyone else to know that too.

Despite a couple of calls, the horses remained at the far end of the field. Piper began to move slowly in my direction but it wasn't the usual joyous thundering trot. I wondered why Delphi and Coquet weren't coming too. Aware of the fact that anything out of the ordinary is usually a bad sign in animals, I walked to the bottom of the field to see what was going on.

Delphi was standing by the wall holding up her front leg, the toe of her hoof barely touching the ground. She was trembling, too, despite her insulating rug. Horses and cows aren't very resilient to damage to limbs, so this was a bad sign.

I limped the whole sorry bunch up to the shed, where I managed to separate Delphi from the rest of her gang. I tried to give her a bute (phenylbutazone, a pain relief drug for animals), but even the treacle and apple I had mixed it with wouldn't tempt her. With a growing sense of dread, I rang the vet.

I hated to see my beautiful, delicate racehorse in such a sorry state, but there was little I could do except talk gently to her as we waited for the vet to arrive. The vet pulled the 'bad news face' when he saw Delphi. It's a kind of grimace that extends sympathy but admits at the same time a lack of hope.

I gave him Delphi's history: ex-racehorse, wind-sucker,

problems with her teeth, thirteen years old, docile as they come.

He examined her leg gently, but it still made Delphi flinch. He could tell that her lower leg was badly damaged, possibly broken. He would need to X-ray her in order to give a proper diagnosis. Perhaps she had been on the receiving end of a kick in the field, perhaps she had fallen; we would never know.

'It's up to you whether we go ahead with an X-ray,' he said, looking at me. 'But I'm afraid her prospects aren't good, and especially after what you've already told me.'

It had all happened so suddenly. Delphi had been fine when I last saw her. Now I was being asked if I wanted to choose a route that might only prolong her suffering, or end it all, here and now. She didn't even seem very old to me. But I knew a broken leg was the end of the road for any horse, and I loved her too much to be able to bear to see her suffer.

There was only one right decision. I took a deep breath.

'Can you do it now?'

It was more violent than I had expected. When dogs are put to sleep it all happens quietly, peacefully. The bang and thud gave us all a start. Though Coquet, Piper and Mr Tumnus were all outside, I heard Coquet squeal in fright.

But it was instant. And Delphi was free from her pain.

After it was all over and Delphi's body had been collected, I let the horses back in the shed. Poor Coquet nearly broke my heart as he looked everywhere for his mum. He couldn't understand how she had disappeared. Piper was no comfort. She was used to the comings and goings of horses, having spent much of her life in a busy yard, and was unconcerned by the absence. Mr Tumnus, though, was also bereft. He had idolised Delphi. She was the gentle, reliable one, the constant in all their lives.

In the shed later that night I found Mr Tumnus and Coquet standing side by side, their bodies touching. I like to think they drew comfort from each other, united by the pain of their loss. Coquet became an adult that night. The childish rivalry was never the same again. Coquet no longer chased or bit Mr Tumnus; the vendetta was forgotten. As for Mr Tumnus, he no longer spent as much time with the horses after Delphi was gone. It was as if she had been the glue that held them all together, and with her gone that bond had been weakened.

16

Newcastleton

The Blue Grey cow was a breed I had admired for some time. Known to be super-hardy, with great longevity due to the hybrid vigour of the cross, they aren't really a breed at all but a cross between a black Galloway mother and a Whitebred Shorthorn father.

Each breed brings something different to the table: the Galloway dam brings hardiness, a lack of horns and a strong mothering instinct, as well as the ability to live out all year round – thanks to a thick jacket – and survive on the worst of hill forage. The Whitebred blood evens out the wildness of the Galloway, bringing with it a peaceful and amiable nature and good milk yields. It also produces a longer, taller frame in its calves.

The Whitebred Shorthorn isn't the only white breed of cattle – there is the famous Charolais, while the British Blue and Beef Shorthorn can also be white. But weirdly, when crossed with a black, these more common breeds produce a diluting of the colour, so their calves are generally beige or cream or browny-black. The Blue Grey, however, has both the black hairs of its mother and the white hairs of its father combined in the same coat, giving it the unique blue-grey appearance.

They are an old-fashioned cross, and back when my dad first started out at the home farm they were all the rage, every upland farm in the north having some. In more recent years they have been largely replaced by bigger cattle, Limousin and Angus.

Never one to care about fashions in farming, I had always wanted some Blue Greys. Indeed, I was fascinated by them.

Now that I had made my first foray into the world of cattle with Penny and her calves, I was hungry for more. Penny had done a super job with the calves, who were starting to fend for themselves. But I knew the dairy blood in them might not suit the farm in the long term. They were certainly too soft to be turned out on the worst of the ground at Fallowlees, and to be honest, the worst ground was where I most needed to have cattle grazing in order to clear it to encourage birds for the higher-level environmental scheme.

So I had decided to indulge myself and the farm by making a trip to the only sale of Blue Greys to take place in the UK, in Newcastleton. I still had some of the location fee from *Vera* saved for this very purpose.

Newcastleton is in Scotland, just over the border, and hosts the Blue Greys sale over two days each year – one day for females and one day for males. The mart was built in the 1880s and has changed little since then. It still uses grass pens for the animals, meaning it can't fulfil the guidelines for washing out (most marts have concrete floors now), and it has an open-top roof. On arrival, you could swear you were going back in time, and for that reason it's one of my favourite marts.

It was raining when I got there – I've since learned that it always rains on Newcastleton sale day! The heifers were still arriving, scampering into the holding pens from the docks; wagons formed a queue all the way down to the village, waiting to unload their wares. The pens in Newcastleton are wooden, slimy and green with age and moisture, built high to keep the heifers where they need to be. For most it would be their first time off the farm, and for some, the first time they had been gathered up after spending the spring and summer on the hills nearby.

The mart was noisy, with cattle being moved all over. You had to keep your wits about you: if the easiest route was over the top of you, a heifer wouldn't think twice.

The heifers fell into two main age categories: the ones born this spring, eight to ten months old, and bulling heifers (unbred but of an age for breeding) at eighteen to twenty months. Most of the younger calves, only just weaned from their mothers, bellowed in anger and confusion. Steam rose off them as the damp air hit their warm hides. Each animal wore a number glued to its rump. Men in tweed caps stood next to their stock, leaning on sticks, answering questions and passing the time of day. Some smoked cigarettes. It was a scene that would have looked little different a hundred years ago.

The auctioneer passed through the pens outside ringing a large bell, announcing the start of the sale, and we all clambered into the ring, eager to get a good spot. The atmosphere was alive.

I drew the short straw here, not being very practised and not having been to this particular mart before. The best spot I could find was next to a giant pillar, which to some extent blocked me from the auctioneer. It would have to do.

Trade was on fire, right from the word go. Well, as it was the only sale of the year, no one wanted to miss out. Clearly I wasn't the only one keen to get my fill of Blue Greys. To my alarm, it wasn't long before we had been through the first one hundred lots. They were going for far more than I could afford, and I began to resign myself to going home empty-handed. But I stayed anyway, just because I love marts and, well, you just never knew what might happen.

As the day wore on a few of the younger calves came in, and although there was still a brisk trade for them, I did put in a couple of bids. The man I was standing next to was only buying the bullers, so we weren't in competition, and every time he saw a likely candidate for me he stepped to the side so that I could position myself where the auctioneer could see me. But the prices were still way out of my league.

The ring started to quieten as the day wore on. Satisfied customers went to pay and load up their wagons, ready to go home. I realised that with fewer customers, the price was dropping too. I had my eye on a pen of three calves, one of the last lots, and I wondered if, just maybe, I might be able to afford them.

The calves that trotted in were a lot smaller than I expected. They blared and looked confused as they entered the ring. A quick look at the board revealed them to be only four to five months old, old enough to be weaned but likely to take a backwards step in any new home, at least to start with.

The bidding started and the auctioneer quickly went down instead of up. This was a good sign.

'Two hundred, then?' he asked. 'Anyone at two hundred?'

I waved.

'Two hundred and fifty,' said someone else.

A look at me. I nodded three hundred.

The auctioneer looked across the ring to my competition. He frowned and shook his head. My heart was thumping. They were mine!

Then the farmer selling the calves shook his head angrily, mumbling. Nope, can't do them that cheap. The auctioneer took a last sweep around the ring, looking for another buyer, pleading with someone to up the bid. I despaired at losing the calves before I had even owned them. After a few heart-stopping seconds, the farmer, realising he wasn't going to get a higher bid, shrugged his shoulders and flapped his hand. The hammer fell and the calves were mine. They were ushered out of the ring.

I paid for them right away. I couldn't believe my luck. The fact that the farmer was unhappy selling them at that price made me even more sure I had got myself a bargain. Despite feeling a little bad for him, I could reconcile the thought with the fact that they were going to be well looked after, potentially for the next twenty years.

At three hundred pounds a head, the calves were fifty pounds per head cheaper than the baby calves I had bought for Penny. It was at this stage that I got myself a bit confused. For some reason I decided that because they were cheaper, and because they had seemed so small in the ring, they could be lifted into the back of my pickup. I backed my pickup to the docks and set off to find someone to lend a hand getting my calves to the loading bay and into the vehicle.

I found a lovely employee who was only too happy to help. Seeing the creatures now, close up in the pen, I was surprised at how big they suddenly seemed. I realised they had appeared small because I'd been comparing them to the heavier, older cattle that had preceded them. Yet I still didn't twig. Together we chased them to the dock.

When the mart man saw I didn't have a trailer hitched to the back of my pickup, he asked me how on earth I was going to transport them.

'Couldn't you just give me a hand to lift them in?' I asked him.

On hearing this he fell about laughing. I stood there feeling like an idiot – well, that wasn't new. The man beckoned to his mate, who came over, and on hearing my plan also fell about laughing. After the leg-pulling had subsided and my embarrassment reduced to a more manageable level, I grimly joined in. The calves were small, but still weighed over one hundred and fifty kilos each. It was a bonkers plan. I had to go all the way home and return with a trailer.

I sometimes see those mart men at the Carlisle auction, which is part of the same business, and to this day they still rib me about the time I tried to fit weaned heifers in the back of my pickup.

Back home I was thrilled with my purchases. The heifers were a super addition to the farm, and from that day on Fallowlees hasn't been without a Blue Grey cow.

17

Ewan

It was moving day! The fifth of November, Guy Fawkes Night, was chilly and mizzly – a typical autumnal Northumberland day. Some of the leaves remained on the trees, but they would all be gone in the next big storm. It is this time of year when the farming calendar really begins for me. Sheep mated on Bonfire Night start lambing on April Fools' Day, the traditional start for an upland farm. 'In with a bang, out like a fool,' the old farm saying goes!

I had had the land at Healey Mill for a month now, and taken over responsibility for John and Rosalind's sheep. The journey to work each day to check them was wonderfully easy compared to the long commutes of some of my contracts.

I had been wanting to get my own flock of one hundred ewes, born and bred at Fallowlees, to the better land at Healey Mill for ages. The grass at Fallowlees was running out and I had to go down daily and handball them sugar beets. But I needed the tractor to transport such a heavy load, and my latest purchase had not materialised. Yes, the tractor I had been assured would be with me within a week, over a month ago, was yet to make an appearance.

The cattle, too, were keeping me busy. Now that Penny's four calves were so much bigger, they were eating me out of house and home. And now I had my Blue Grey calves to add to the mix. They needed some tender loving care, being freshly weaned and therefore more vulnerable, but were starting to thrive. I was filling my quad trailer by hand each morning and handballing the feed to my growing herd, but they sure could pack it away quickly. It was taking me hours to do a job a tractor could do in minutes.

I wondered if I had been an idiot to let the tractor people have my money. I was too embarrassed to tell anyone what I had done, so instead I rang the company and grovelled week after week. It did little good. They patronised me with, 'Yes, darling, it will be with you in the next few days,' again and again. Now they had started to ignore my calls.

Then one day a wagon rocked up at the farm with that yellow goddess on board! They never did fix the window, and she still needed a jump to get her off the ramp, but I could overlook all that. She was finally here! Now I could get the ewes to Healey Mill.

That wasn't the only thing going on today. After a long text flirtation, I was finally going to meet the Scottish firefighter I had matched with on Tinder. Ewan Irvine from Galashiels had volunteered to give me a hand on one of his days off. So today, rather weirdly, was going to be our first date. I had it all sorted. I would transport the sheep to Healey Mill in the morning with the tractor. Ewan would meet me there, where he would hopefully be wowed by my impressive tractor-trailer combo as well as my amazing organisational skills. Then that afternoon he would help me with a job that was hard to do on my own – to colour (or raddle) the tups.

The tups are at their strongest at this time of year, and also their most aggressive. They can weigh in excess of one hundred kilos. In order to colour them they need to be sat on their rumps to give access to their chests, which are then daubed with oil-based raddle paint so that the tups leave a mark on the ewes when they mate with them. This helps me know when those ewes will lamb and when I need to bring them into the shed. It seemed a perfect job for a burly firefighter to assist me with. All the same, I wondered if he knew what he was letting himself in for when he offered his services.

Ewan had assured me that he would be happy to help; it would be an experience, if nothing else. In truth I would rather have met him on neutral ground, like a pub or restaurant, than on my newly acquired home turf, but with my demanding work and his shift pattern, we both realised that it might be the only way we'd manage a date this side of Christmas.

I jumped at his offer once I knew he was serious about it. It would be handy to have Ewan to hold the tups for me while I gave them their new colour scheme. Archie had helped me with the job the year before. I remembered our laughter as we began by trying to wrestle the tups to the ground and turn them over, neither of us being exactly built for the job, before working out a less strenuous solution. That's often the way in farming: finding a way to do a job based on the circumstances and who you have around at the time.

I was feeling deeply accomplished as I pulled away from Fallowlees in my new tractor, my fine sheep safely stowed in the trailer, all of them fit and ready to meet their man. I suppose, thinking about it, I was in the same boat! I had made a bit of an effort, with freshly washed and dried hair and plenty of mascara. I hoped I didn't seem too keen, though. It was hard to know how to play it when we'd already shared a fair amount of confidences and conversation. In some ways, I felt as if I already knew Ewan. I knew that he was divorced and had two young children who lived with their mother, and whom he saw regularly. I knew he was sporty – he played rugby and was keen on rock climbing and the winter pursuits of skiing and snowboarding. He seemed confident but also self-effacing, always a good sign, and I often found myself with a smile on my face when I was reading his texts. It all seemed to bode well. Yet who really knew how he might turn out to be in the flesh? It was only too easy to play fast and loose with the facts in a quickly bashed-off text message.

I wondered what he would make of it all. You never know how people will react when they first get a taste of the life I call mine. Healey Mill wasn't Fallowlees, but she was still a quiet backwater. I've known some to run a mile when confronted with a farm in the middle of nowhere: no shops, no local pub, the nearest takeaway fifty minutes away. Sometimes the only positive thing they can think of to say is that I won't have to go far for a Christmas tree!

I'd got to the end of the forest track and was on the road

just outside Harwood when a big red dashboard light started
to flash. Red lights are always bad news, I've discovered. This
one, even more upsettingly, was accompanied by an angry
STOP sign.

I pulled in. Sod it. I had no idea where to start or what to
do. I looked at the sign, willing it to disappear. No such luck.
I would have to swallow my pride. I hadn't done it for a while
but it was time to ring my dad and ask for his advice. Dad is
very mechanically minded, and given a hammer and a spanner
can fix just about anything.

'It sounds like the back-end oil transmission,' he said, when
I explained what had happened.

I bit my bottom lip. 'Is that bad?'

'Could just be a sensor. Check there's oil on the dipstick.'

'There ought to be. The guys I bought it from said they
would service it before they sent it.'

Even as I said it, I cringed at my gullibility.

'I'll check it anyway,' I said hurriedly, before Dad
could comment.

I pulled out the dipstick. 'Yeah, there's oil there.'

'Could be it's just not getting round the system. You could
keep driving, wait for it to cool down, then drive it again. See
how far you get.'

So that was what I decided to do. I would drive the tractor until the light came on, then stop for a bit, then carry on
until the light came on again until I got to Healey Mill, eight
miles away.

The problem was the light kept coming on faster and faster
each time. Time was ticking by, and I was still a few miles

away and falling further and further behind schedule. I was also starting to get concerned about the sheep, who had been confined for so long. I decided to pull into a farm and ask for help. I had got out of the tractor and was wandering round the empty farmyard when my phone suddenly pinged, having just come back into signal.

Where are you? I haven't missed you, have I?

Ewan! With everything going on I'd forgotten all about him! The poor guy had been waiting for me at Healey Mill for twenty minutes now. I texted him back, explaining that I'd had a bit of a hiccup, and pinged him directions to come and meet me.

Fifteen minutes later a nice silver Golf drew up to the farm and the firefighter from Galashiels got out of it. He was recognisable from his photo, even without the warpaint of his profile picture. In other circumstances it could have been a perfect moment, but with all that was going on I didn't know whether to laugh or cry. The tractor had decided she didn't want to give up her load of sheep just yet, and wouldn't drop the tow bar to unlink the trailer. Being new to the tractor, I had no idea how to do it. The farmer, who had looked a little bewildered at me showing up with a load of sheep in the first place, was becoming more bemused by the second.

'Is this a friend of yours?' he asked me, scratching his head, as a smiling Ewan made his way towards us.

I blushed at the awkwardness of the situation. 'Well, kind of, we've not met before.'

I grimaced, then attempted to put on a more welcoming face to Ewan.

'Sorry about . . . all this . . . ' I tailed off, unsure which one of the two men I was apologising to.

I couldn't even introduce them as I didn't know the farmer's name, despite landing in his farmyard with a tractor, a trailer full of ewes and now, well, a suitor of sorts.

Ewan, however, took it all in his stride. He donned a pair of overalls from the boot of his car (how organised) and gave the tractor tow a hefty bang with a hammer from his toolkit (also in the back of his car). This was my kind of man! The tractor released her grip on the load.

After finding out the farmer's name and making some hasty introductions and more apologies, I asked if I could leave the sheep with him until I came back with another tractor. He didn't really have much choice in the matter, truth be told. Then I asked Ewan if he could run me across to Healey Mill to borrow one of John and Rosalind's tractors. So much for the capable, organised farmer he had been supposed to meet! I had barely had a chance to exchange a civil word with the poor chap, but I was growing more and more aware of the amount of time the sheep had been standing and of the morning flashing by.

As I installed myself in the passenger seat, I realised what a mess I must look. My face felt flushed from the stress and exertion and I didn't dare check on my mascara. My hands were covered in grease and oil from the rear of the tractor, my nicely blow-dried hair was mangled and scraped back into a ponytail.

'I'm so sorry. And thank you! But honest, this is my life all over,' I sighed. 'Never a dull moment.'

He seemed unperturbed. 'Don't worry,' he said, grinning. 'It's pretty different for a first date.'

As we pulled out of the farmyard, I sneaked a glance at him. Ewan looked tough, no doubt about it. His hair was close-cropped, for convenience, I guessed, and showed two Harry Potter-esque zigzagging scars on his scalp. He was broad and well built, with standard-issue firefighter arms. In fact, he was exactly like his pictures which, judging from Tinder date horror stories told by my girlfriends, was nothing short of a miracle. His hands were strong-looking, clean, but not prissy and soft.

I took some deep breaths and allowed myself to relax a bit.

'Sorry,' I said again. 'Things don't always go smoothly, but I think everything went wrong that could have gone wrong today.'

'Stop apologising, it's cool,' he said.

'Sorry,' I replied, and realising what I'd said, we both started laughing. I knew then we were going to get on as well in person as we had in our text messages. It was a good job, as we had a long afternoon of work ahead of us.

Ewan dropped me at Healey Mill to pick up the Murrays' tractor, then met me back at the farm where I had left the sheep. He helped me to hitch the trailer up to this second tractor and take the sheep to Healey Mill.

'I don't know about you but I feel as if I've done a day's work already,' I said, after we had unloaded our cargo at my new farm.

The sun had come out since the mizzly start and it was a perfect autumn day. We sat on the ground and ate the sandwiches I'd packed.

'Sorry there's no cake to finish. I'm not much of a baker.'

'These are great.'

We drank tea from my flask and watched the new arrivals making themselves at home in their new pasture.

'I used to have a smallholding,' Ewan told me. 'So I know a little.'

'Oh, great! That will help.'

'But don't expect me to be an expert.'

'Oh, no one's an expert at raddling.'

I told him about Archie and me the previous year. 'In the end one of us had to trap a tup in the corner and the other one got down and applied the raddle. You should have seen us when we'd finished!'

A few minutes later, Ewan was throwing himself into tup wrestling with impressive enthusiasm.

'They're bigger than they look,' he exclaimed, as he tried – and failed – to get his first tup tipped over.

'Tell me about it!'

'And you sometimes do this job on your own?'

'Not if I've got a willing volunteer.'

But despite him being a novice, we got the job done. Ewan wasn't scared to laugh at himself either, thank goodness. When Horatio, the enormous Leicester, took him for a wee pony ride across the pens, swiftly depositing him in a corner, I had tears streaming down my cheeks and was holding my stomach with laughter.

'I'm sorry, I can't help it,' I groaned. 'I wish I'd got that on camera.'

At the end of the afternoon I realised that I hadn't laughed so much in ages. My stomach was hurting. As well as joining in my laughter – often at his own expense – Ewan asked lots of questions about my work. He seemed genuinely interested.

'I've really enjoyed myself,' he said as, job complete, he ran me back in his car to pick up my tractor where I had so rudely deposited it earlier. 'How would you rate my raddling skills?'

'Hmmm, ten out of ten for enthusiasm and style. Umm, sorry, but zero for technique.'

He laughed. We were both still in high spirits after our energetic afternoon. I liked Ewan. I felt that we had a lot in common. I wished the journey was a little longer, but we were at the farm in no time at all.

I found the farmer and thanked him for letting me leave my tractor with him.

'Well,' I said to Ewan, as I climbed back into it, ready for the crawl back to Fallowlees, 'goodbye, and thank you for your help.'

'I'll follow you until you're home,' said Ewan, ever the gentleman.

'Honestly, there's no need.'

'I insist.'

We said our goodbyes but agreed that Ewan would tail me in his car to the start of the Harwood Forest track in case the tractor let me down. That was far enough, I thought. I didn't want to show him Fallowlees just yet.

I had only gone a few miles when the red light came on again. I stopped, and Ewan waited patiently behind. The light went off, and I started again. By the time I reached the forest it had happened twice more. I had had enough. I got out of the tractor in fury and abandoned it at the side of the track.

I was too tired to be proud now.

'Any chance of a lift?' I asked, as Ewan pulled up alongside me.

'You say you just bought it?'

'Yes, more fool me.'

'You should get back in touch with them. Anyway, hop in.'

Now that there was no choice in the matter, I thought, Ewan might as well see sooner rather than later how far away from civilisation I lived. I liked him; I was pretty sure he liked me. But there was no point in things going any further if he was going to scarper as soon as he saw the isolation of my beloved farmhouse.

There was the track to negotiate first. If it bothered him, he didn't let on. Even when I cringed as the bottom of his car grated against a particularly high part of the road, he seemed unruffled.

I pointed out the farm when we got our first glimpse. He stopped for a few seconds. I was pleased to see his eyes light up the way mine always did when I saw Fallowlees.

'What a view!' he said. 'What a spot.'

A few minutes later we parked and I led the way into the farmhouse. Roy and Alfie gave him an enthusiastic welcome.

'They like you.'

'I grew up with collies,' said Ewan, getting down to meet them properly as I quickly rinsed a couple of mugs.

He sat down at the table and pulled out his phone.

'We have 3G,' I said proudly, as he tapped away to the sound of the kettle coming on to boil.

He was silent for a few seconds.

'The company you bought the tractor from – I've just goog-led them. They're not exactly reputable.'

I made him his tea and sat down. He showed me the phone. Trading Standards had become involved to investigate com-plaints against the firm, and there was an impending lawsuit.

My heart sank. Why hadn't I thought to do that earlier? I might have saved myself a lot of bother.

'I suppose it's too late to do anything about it now.' I was trying to play it cool. 'Probably more trouble than it's worth. I'll have to get it to a dealership and see what the damage is.'

I felt a bit of an idiot – a gullible girl who'd been taken for a ride (or not!) – but I was determined to put a brave face on it.

I changed the subject. 'So tell me a bit more about your work. It's not all rescuing cats from trees, is it?'

Ewan laughed. 'Where do I start? No two days are ever alike. It's like solving a new problem every time we go out, using the kit we have on the fire engine.'

I could see he was as enthusiastic about his job as I was about mine, and I listened in amazement to some of his stories.

When Ewan left an hour later, we did the awkward no-idea-how-to-end-the-first-date dance. Cringey, at best. Needless to say, I've moved the light shade in the porch now and no one has since hit their head on it.

18

Yellow Goddess

I continued to do well with my trialling into the autumn, scoring regular wins with Roy. My heart sang to see him being recognised by many as a 'good' dog, and what's more, I was being recognised as a capable handler for the first time. Maybe after everything I had been through I had become more focused. It had certainly been one of my dreams, while I was recuperating after my broken back, to get better with the dogs. To be known as a serious triallist. And I had had the luxury of spending more time with them when heavier jobs were out of the question. Now I was seeing the results of those efforts. With the Healey Mill partnership to add to my bow, I felt the sky was the limit. I was excited about the future.

By the end of the season I had even managed to accumulate a few trophies, which would be awarded at the annual dinner dance. The Northumberland League holds the dance each year to award prizes to the winning triallists and generally have a big old knees-up. It had long been one of the highlights of my calendar and I had been going since before I even started competing.

This year I asked Ewan if he would partner me to the dance. It was only a couple of weeks since we'd first met, and we did have a hiccup when, on our second meeting – a mutually agreed date to the Hexham machinery sale (we farmers are such a romantic lot) – he texted me to say he couldn't come after all because his car was broken. Aha, that old chestnut. I figured he simply wasn't interested. I thought back to the fun we had had that day with the tups. It had been a laugh, and we'd really got on, despite the disastrous start. Perhaps he thought I was an idiot with the tractor buying. I couldn't really blame him if he did. Or maybe he just wasn't keen enough to contemplate driving from Galashiels to Fallowlees every time he wanted to see me. Or, let's face it, he might have decided in the cool light of day that he didn't fancy me after all and that this was the kindest way to let the whole thing fizzle out.

In truth, I was crushed. I didn't reply, and deleted his number from my phone, drawing a line under the episode so I wouldn't think of him again. I set off to Hexham by myself.

Ewan appeared at the sale later that day in a hire car, much to my embarrassed delight.

'I thought you would think the car was a pretty shabby excuse,' he said.

'Oh, not at all,' I lied.

We came back to Fallowlees with a suitable array of

paraphernalia (garden fork, spade, spanner set, ratchet straps and a dog kennel) at bargain basement prices. He seemed as delighted as I was.

The dinner dance felt like an important next step. We knew each other well enough for me to feel comfortable introducing him to the people I spent so many of my weekends with. They'd want to know all about him and, when they discovered he wasn't a farmer, they'd be sussing out whether he'd last long in this strange new world. It would be interesting to see if he would stand up to their grilling.

The dance was held in Otterburn Hall, a popular wedding venue half an hour's drive away. I wore a backless little black dress paired with silver whistle-shaped earrings and a pair of sky-high heels that instantly made my feet ache for my worn-in wellies.

My best accessory was my firefighter, who appeared at my door dressed in a smart suit. Ewan looked very dapper and not a bit nervous.

As we set off it was snowing fat wet flakes. I hoped it wouldn't get heavier. We had a four-by-four taxi booked to take us home but these country roads are treacherous in bad weather whatever you're travelling in.

We left our coats in the cloakroom and headed to the bar. Although I had seen some of this crowd when I began trialling again, there were others I hadn't seen since before my accident. I knew I was in line for some ribbing over it – they wouldn't think twice about it, especially not when they knew I had made a full recovery. As a woman in a man's world, I was used to the teasing by now. It started straight away.

'I saw an advert the other day: quad bike for sale, one careful lady owner,' someone called out as I passed them.

'I did warn you,' I whispered to Ewan, before laughing and going back to introduce him.

I always do a double take when I see everyone at this event – it's the only time of year we meet each other out of our farming clothes. We are all transformed. Everyone – male and female – makes an effort for the dinner dance. Hair is always neatly combed, male faces have been given a proper shave, women who don't always bother have carefully applied lipstick and mascara. The smell of aftershave and perfume is strong enough to knock out a flock of sheep.

I steered Ewan to the bar where a group I knew were congregated. I was happy to see them all, and it was touching how genuinely pleased everyone was to have me back.

'Gave us a fright, you did!'

'Great to see you in one piece!'

'We wondered if you'd make it!'

'Couldn't believe it when Archie told us what you'd gone and done.'

'No dancing for you tonight, mind!'

'You wanna bet!'

After I had answered enquiries about my health, it was Ewan's turn to be the centre of attention.

'And who's this handsome fellow, then?' asked one of the old farmers, handing us both the drinks he'd bought us.

I introduced Ewan to the gathered crowd.

'Oh, aye, Ewan, we've heard all about you,' said one of them, giving me a wink.

Ewan looked chuffed. He shook hands and promised to try to remember names.

'You like your job, do you, son?' one of them asked. 'It must come in handy, mind, for Emma. She never could turn down a sick animal.'

Ewan, not quite sure what he meant but assuming it was a joke at his expense, managed a laugh.

I wasn't expecting them to go easy on him, but when some of the crowd started getting technical right away, launching into questions about worm burden in sheep and lactation of whelping bitches, well . . .

'Sorry!' I mouthed, as Ewan fielded their questions with his usual good humour.

Then Archie came up to the bar.

'Ah, Ewan! The firefighter! I've heard all about you from Emma,' he said, shaking his hand vigorously.

The group at the bar looked puzzled. 'Firefighter? Eeh, we all thought you were a vet,' said one of the party. They all looked at me.

I felt myself go a little pink. An ex-boyfriend, a vet, had also been called Ewan. This explained all the technical questions!

Luckily Ewan saw the funny side, and I endured yet more teasing, this time from him as well as from the others.

After a while I left him talking to Archie and went to catch up with a couple of friends I hadn't seen for ages.

'What did you make of my old mate?' I asked Ewan, when it was just the two of us again. I so wanted him and Archie to get along!

'He's lovely. Wants to know when I'm going to get a dog and start trialling!'

I took a sip of my wine. 'Well, do you fancy it? I could teach you the basics.'

I'd talked to Ewan about my love of trialling, and he'd seemed fascinated, but I realised that didn't necessarily mean he wanted to have a go himself.

'Only if you're interested,' I added hastily.

'Yeah! Why not?'

We sat at a table with some good friends of mine. They were a lively, boisterous lot, especially after a few drinks. I wondered what Ewan would think of them all, then told myself to stop worrying. He was a Scot, after all! He was soon chatting away as if he'd known them all his life.

After the meal – lamb, of course! – the presentations were made. Despite my limited appearances on the trial field this year, I had still managed a respectable placing in the league and won some silverware. There had never been a female winner of the Northumberland League, so I felt that my chance to claim this title for myself and make history might be getting closer. Maybe next year, if I managed to stay in one piece, the title could be mine. Archie and Dale were second, and I felt proud of my friend and rival.

Before the disco there was some country dancing, which everyone threw themselves into – some too vigorously. One woman, green to the dancing techniques of farmers, had her arm broken as she didn't hold on tightly enough during one of the ceilidh dances. Some of our companions won bottles in the raffle, and when the disco started we had lost any inhibitions we might have had about our dancing skills. By the time Abba's 'Dancing Queen' was on I had thrown off my heels and was barefoot.

I always request 'Come On Eileen' by Dexys Midnight Runners. It's a favourite of mine and a sure-fire hit in our crowd. Just about everyone was on the floor when those familiar beats started up.

Ewan and I were sorry to leave when the taxi turned up. What a great night it had been! Even in our slightly tipsy state though, I could see that the taxi wasn't the four-by-four I had asked for. It would have to do. Ewan helped to lift my trophy haul into the back. The snow hadn't abated – a thin, treacherous layer of it coated the road.

We were both laughing wildly, reliving events of the evening as we rode home. Ewan seemed to have enjoyed himself as much as I had. He had met some of the key people in my life and won them over. It occurred to me that he had covered some major milestones in just a couple of dates.

The driver took it slowly in the poor visibility, windscreen wipers working overtime.

'Up this road here,' I said to him as we reached Harwood.

The car began to bump its way up the forestry track. I heard a few nasty crunches as unforgiving Northumberland rock made contact with the metal underside of the car. I grimaced on behalf of the driver. It wasn't a good sound. When it had happened several times, the driver stopped the car and turned to face us.

'I'm sorry, guys, I just cannot take you any further. The car's not going to make it, and if I rip the sump out my boss will kill me.'

I could hardly blame him.

'That's OK,' I said.

He looked surprised at how cheerfully I had taken the news. But a master plan was developing in my brain as I was sobering up fast. We stumbled out of the taxi. In the car's headlights the scene before us looked like one from Narnia: swirling snowflakes, snow-dusted conifers. All that was missing was a lamp post.

Ewan looked bemused as I took his arm. 'C'mon, Ewan, our chariot awaits,' I giggled. My trophies clanged together in the cardboard box I was clutching.

The tractor still sat at the end of the road in solitary splendour. She had been there since the day I met Ewan. I was still furious at her for letting me down – well, probably more furious at myself, really, but it amounted to the same thing – and hadn't walked the four miles from Fallowlees to retrieve her.

'There she is. All ready and waiting.' I waved in the general direction of the tractor.

'You mean . . . '

'She'll be fine for four miles. It's lovely and cold, so she's hardly going to overheat, is she? Not when it's minus four! It's got to be better than walking. I'm not sure I could do it in these heels, anyway.'

I noticed the taxi making its getaway before we could change our minds and make a fuss about being abandoned in the snow, miles from our front door.

'Come on, Ewan, I'm freezing – and getting soaked!'

The journey that followed was reckless, dangerous and downright stupid, but we were completely stranded and it was the only option at the time. I shouldn't have been surprised to discover that the wipers didn't work. Ewan had to cling onto the side of the vehicle wiping the windscreen every few seconds so that I could see where I was going. At one point his hand slipped and he grabbed the first thing he could to regain his balance. He still bears the scar from the exhaust burn to this day!

We were both laughing, ecstatic at our own idiocy, as I parked the yellow goddess at the farmhouse. She had redeemed herself.

PART THREE

A New Start

19

Ewan: Firefighter

I was in my mid-thirties, living and working in the Scottish Borders as a firefighter, stationed in Galashiels, when I met Emma. I had been single for a year following my divorce, and I had two children. I knew that I wasn't exactly an amazing catch but I had been working hard to recover and find happiness in my life. At the time I was renting a semi-detached house with a garden just across the park from the fire station. It couldn't have been easier to get to work.

I have always had a passion for the outdoors and the natural world. Growing up in the countryside, south of Edinburgh, we always had Border or bearded collies, and my first weekend job was on the farm by my parents' house. Before starting in the fire service I worked as an outdoor pursuits instructor, teaching canoeing and kayaking and guiding rafts in the French Alps. In fact, if it hadn't been for a life-changing event which happened to me while I was working in France, I might never have chosen firefighting as a career.

It was 2007, I was in my late twenties and working a ski season in Meribel. One day, I set off with two friends, Timmy and Ryan, to explore the vast ski area. It was my second winter there, and by now I knew the hidden off-piste routes which held untracked powder days after fresh dumps of snow. We spent a tremendous day together, Timmy on skis, Ryan and me on snowboards, and I was looking forward to getting back to watch the Scotland game on the TV at half past four.

For our last slide we returned to a spot our boss had told us about that morning. We set off down a couloir – a steep, narrow gully – that we reached after a short walk in. The run then opened out into a large bowl. The visibility wasn't great, so we were descending carefully, as we knew there was a rock band at the bottom of the bowl before the last two hundred metres out to the marked piste. I was below the other two and called a halt when I saw the line of cliffs below us. I signalled to Ryan to join me and pointed out the snow-filled gap between the rocks that I planned to drop through. Ryan was going to watch me through and then pass that information to Timmy before dropping through himself. I was watching Ryan safely pass the rock band when I heard a shout and saw Timmy slide on his back head first over the cliff. He must have fallen twenty feet or so.

I couldn't really believe what I'd seen. I quickly unstrapped my board and climbed back up the hill. Timmy had landed just out of my sight and Ryan had reached him first. When I got to them, Timmy was lying on his side across the fall line of the slope. Ryan said that Timmy had been blue when he reached him and that he had cleared the snow from his mouth. There was blood around his head and he was unconscious and not responding to our voices or touch. I tried to phone for help but couldn't get a signal, so Ryan went to shout to the people skiing the slopes beneath us. With several people responding to his cries for assistance, he returned to help me as Timmy was starting to make uncoordinated attempts to move his arms and legs and was at risk of sliding down the slope.

We tried to scoop a shelf out of the snow to stabilise Timmy. Ryan held him still while I tried to see what his injuries were. Timmy had a bruise above his left eye and a cut on the crown of his head. Then I discovered a huge, circular, bulging open wound about the size of a fist at the back of his head. There weren't any other obvious injuries so I used Timmy's hood as a compress and tried to cup the back of his head to stop the bleeding, all the while trying to prevent him from moving.

It felt like the longest hour of my life waiting for the rescue team to arrive. I kept talking to Timmy but he made no response. The bleeding seemed to have stopped but his blood was all over me. I seriously thought he might perish. When the first rescuer reached us, I explained in French what had happened. The poor guy was ashen, as I'm sure I was. Seeing him struggling to get his medical gloves on, I used a large wound dressing and bandage to bind the ghastly head wound. More rescuers started to arrive with further equipment and a sled. It was unnerving, seeing them slide about in their ski boots as we tried to keep Timmy as stable as possible while they formed a mattress around him, drawing out the air with a pump to cocoon Timmy within it before loading him onto the sled. I gathered up Timmy's belongings, finding only one ski, his poles and his hat, which had a clean hole punched out of the wool.

Ryan had to leave for work, but I was with Timmy in the medical centre while the team there worked on him. I stayed until he was loaded into the ambulance for the run down to Grenoble and the specialists at the hospital there. They had wanted to fly him, but a blizzard had blown in. I returned to our staff quarters where all our friends and colleagues had gathered and tried to explain what had happened. It was awful trying to tell them just how serious it was. I remember someone said, 'He'll be all right, he always is.' I knew that if he had seen what I had he wouldn't be saying that. I was crying when I went for a shower and the water ran red as I washed off Timmy's blood.

I was working the following day, picking up guests from Geneva airport and driving them into the mountains for the start of their holiday. I was near tears all day as I hoped beyond hope that Timmy would live. After work I drove down to the hospital to meet Timmy's family, who had dropped everything to fly out from the UK. I was full of guilt and really distressed, trying to explain to his parents what had happened.

That event changed the direction of my life. When I finished that season I enrolled in a ski patrol course back in Scotland, working at the Nevis range near Fort William, after which I did an emergency medical technician's (EMT) course and went on to work as a rescue medic. That was when I started thinking about applying to the fire service.

I just knew that I wanted to use my new-found knowledge to help people in emergencies.

It was a long, slow road to recovery for Timmy, who, as well as his traumatic head injury, had four broken vertebrae in his neck and back, a shattered ankle and a snapped cruciate. He reckoned it was about five years before he was back to 90 per cent of his old self. He's been changed by the accident, of course, but he's written a book and made a life for himself as a life coach and mindfulness instructor.

After my divorce several years later, I knew I didn't want to remain single for ever. As time went on and I wasn't meeting anyone through work or out kayaking and climbing, I decided I needed to up my dating game. When a good friend told me about the dating app Tinder, I decided to give it a go.

With Tinder you can set parameters such as location, distance and age. The profile picture of anyone who matches your search pops up and you swipe left or right depending on whether you fancy them or not. It might seem savage to make an instant decision based on a profile picture, but I guess we know in a couple of seconds whether we are attracted to someone or not. The good stuff comes when we get to know that person.

I was looking for a woman who was smart, funny, attractive, independent, gregarious, fit, happy, loving, loyal and with a lust for life. Not looking for much, then! Is it even possible to glean all that from a photo? It seems you can . . .

Emma's profile picture was a stunning one. She was wearing a sapphire-blue ballgown and holding a shepherd's crook in one hand, with sheep in the background and hills in the distance. A click on her profile revealed more pictures of this beautiful woman with a gorgeous smile, and that she was a shepherdess. I swiped right and prayed for a match.

I remember the excitement of our flurry of messages. Everything I learned made her sound like the woman I had dared to dream of. Emma told me about her passion for farming and sheepdogs, and that she ran a remote off-grid farm in Northumberland. I was blown away that this intelligent, witty, beautiful woman was chatting to me. In our chats we talked about books, both having a love of reading, and Emma mentioned that she had written a book. Of course I bought a copy of *One Girl and Her Dogs* straight away. When I read it I laughed and cried at the stories of her life and started to fall in love with this woman I had yet to meet.

The first time I saw Emma, she was climbing down from her tractor, a vision in waterproofs, wellies and tousled auburn hair. She crossed the yard, shook my hand and told me about her predicament. I thought her even prettier in person and was glad that I could help unhitch the trailer. We had a good blether in the car running across to the other farm to borrow their tractor.

I'm not sure how much use I was in the pens putting raddle on the tups. Emma had some huge Texels that must have weighed a hundred kilos and then some. They had such a low centre of gravity, and I could barely reach from their chins to their tails in my attempt to fold them and tip them onto their haunches. I was amazed that Emma had the skill to manage these beasts! The best I could do was to pin the ones I couldn't tip in the corner while Emma applied the marker dye.

In one of the fields Emma explained that she had a Bluefaced Leicester ram which she would put over Scotch Blackfaced ewes to produce a Mule lamb. I was staggered at the skill of her dog Roy, who singled out this leggy tup, about the size of a small donkey, and backed him up to the corner of the hedge. I was still playing rugby at the time and when Emma asked me to catch him, I thought I would impress her with my skills. I caught him under the chin and flung a leg over his back, thinking I would walk him over to Emma. Much to my embarrassment, I was barely able to plant my feet and the tup took off across the field with me riding him!

When I first saw Fallowlees, the sight of the sandstone farmhouse, alone at the edge of the forest, took my breath away. I could see why Emma had fallen in love with the place a few years earlier. But as the car scraped its way up the rutted track – all four miles of it – I realised that it wasn't the most accessible place to get to. Emma told me that the track had been the nemesis of many a car's exhaust, and I could well believe it.

Emma decided to take me riding one day. I think it was at least twenty-five years since I'd last been on a horse. Helpfully, she had some great advice as we set off through the trees. The gist was to lean forward going uphill and backwards coming down. For the ditches I should try to keep hold of the mane. It was great fun as we cantered through the countryside and up across the valley from the farm. Emma had neglected to fill me in on the finer points of horsemanship, like how to steer or how to stop, and at one particularly boggy ditch I was rudely catapulted head first as Emma's trusty steed thought the better of it and sharply swerved to avoid the leap. I emerged completely plastered in mud, but none the worse, with Piper happily grazing, unfazed by the sudden departure of her happy hack!

As we started to spend more time together, Emma took me to some of the sheepdog trials that were such a big part of her life. They are very sociable occasions, full of banter and gentle ribbing. I watched proudly as Emma made it all look so doable, always seeming to make the prizes. I wondered if I would ever be brave enough to have a go myself. Perhaps the best part of the day was the trip to and from the trials in the car, during which we talked about anything and everything while also getting to see some of the gorgeous Northumberland country-side. Considering our different paths in life before meeting, I discovered that we shared the same views on lots of subjects. I realised I was falling in love with Emma.

I wondered if one day I might make the move from one side of the border to the other to be with her.

20

Hoggy

Ewan's shift pattern meant that he did two day shifts followed by two night shifts followed by four days off. He started coming to Fallowlees when he wasn't working. There were always jobs he could help me with, and he didn't seem to mind that our dates were in a farmyard or a muddy field rather than in swanky restaurants.

I knew I liked him a lot and he seemed to like me, too. But after Dan, could I really judge what a man was thinking about me any more?

'It's meant to be your day off,' I said guiltily, as I watched him mending one of my fences on a freezing December morning.

But Ewan was one of those men who liked to be doing something, and if it was in the open air, so much the better. I started to think I had found my ideal partner – though hadn't I thought the same thing about Dan?

He would return to Galashiels on his motorbike. It took an hour and a half. Quite a long commute, I thought to myself, every time I waved him off. I worried that he would get fed up with it before long.

I spent Christmas Day with my family as usual and returned to Hawick on New Year's Eve, which in Scotland is as big a deal as Christmas. Ewan was on duty, so Caroline, Elizabeth and I were planning to welcome in the new year in Edinburgh. We didn't get to do it that often these days, but when the Gray girls get together, a good night is guaranteed!

Earlier in the year, it turned out, there had been a secret romantic encounter between Caroline's sheepdog bitch, Nan, and my very own Casanova, Roy. Now Nan was no spring chicken and had never had a litter before. By the time we realised she was in the family way it was too late to do anything other than let the pregnancy run its course.

As luck would have it, that very evening, just as we were putting on our glad rags, Nan started to whelp. That quickly put an end to the night out.

There was great concern in the ranks because of Nan's advancing age, and sure enough, after making herself a nest of torn newspaper in front of the Rayburn, she lay down and gave us more to worry about. A pup was born, still and lifeless. Then another, and another. It was heartbreaking.

Poor Nan was forlorn, frantically licking her newborns, trying to love them back to life. Seeing an animal distressed is horrendous. Even worse when you see your sister so upset at the same time.

I knew everyone was annoyed with me for allowing Roy to have his wicked way with Nan, so I felt doubly guilty – I was making Nan and my family suffer as well as having already ruined what was supposed to have been a great night out.

Just as the chimes of Big Ben announced the new year, the last pup made an appearance. On the TV on the kitchen bench, Edinburgh was one big party. The rejoicing crowds danced on the streets of the great Scottish city, the castle illuminated by fireworks.

None of us felt particularly like celebrating.

Nan gave a final push, and the pup slid out onto the newspaper.

Caroline gave a squeal of alarm and surprise.

This pup was alive!

Nan was delighted, the dead pups forgotten. She now had something to love and cherish. The pup was beautiful, too, a traditionally marked black and white female.

'Wouldn't Eve be a nice name,' I mused, 'given that she was born on New Year's Eve?'

'We're in Scotland,' said Caroline. 'She was born on Hogmanay.'

'Well, you can't call her Hoggy!'

Hoggy it was, and she remained my sister's dog until she started taking off after sheep on the family farm. Then she came to Fallowlees to join my upcoming nursery trial team.

'It seems crazy you paying rent on your place in Galashiels when you're hardly ever there,' I dared to say to Ewan one day. 'And such a long commute.'

'Emma Gray, you are so romantic!' said Ewan. 'Are you suggesting I move in with you?'

'Well, having a handyman around would be great. And I've got a spare room.' I poked him in the ribs. 'What do you think?'

'I think it's a great idea!'

He gave notice on the place he was renting and seemed as excited as I was at the prospect of living at Fallowlees. My parents had met Ewan, and liked him very much, and I had met his family. He got on well with my sisters, too, always important.

Just as I was thinking how well it was all going, I opened the glovebox of Ewan's car one day and found a pair of knickers. They weren't the sexy, lacy type, but they were ladies' knickers and they most definitely weren't mine. A girl knows her own knickers.

My heart began racing and a hundred different stories started playing out in my mind. Stay calm, I told myself. There must be a logical reason. I decided to give Ewan the chance to explain himself and very calmly confronted him with the said pair of (clean) knickers.

Ewan shrugged. 'I've never seen them in my life.'

'Oh, and I suppose they magicked themselves into your car,' I replied sarcastically.

He just gave me one of those I-have-absolutely-no-idea-what-to-say-next looks. I was almost as mad about his under-reaction as I was about the knickers. Why wasn't he worried about them? That unnerved me. Surely he should have been either giving me a straightforward explanation or rolling about making excuses for how they got there. Instead he did neither.

When I went to Hawick to lend a hand the following day, I thought I would mention it to Mum and see if she had some advice to impart.

We sat in the living room with our cups of tea. Mum was there with Caroline and had her sympathetic face on as I launched into the story. I had just told them about pulling out the unfamiliar knickers when I noticed that my sister had stuffed her face into a cushion and was making strange snorting noises.

'What the . . . '

'I'm sorry,' she just about managed to say, laughing even more now. 'I'm really . . . sorry.'

'Well, I'm glad you find it funny . . . ' I began, before she managed to string something intelligible together.

'They're Mum's knickers,' I heard through her muffled laughter.

It was time for Mum to look affronted.

'Mine?' She frowned.

Caroline finally took the cushion away from her face and managed to speak.

'Remember when my washing machine was broken and I had to use Mum's for a while?' She wiped away her tears and sat up straighter to pull herself together. 'I ended up taking a pair of her knickers home with my own washing, so I stuffed them in my handbag to give them back. But then, remember how we both went to the races and borrowed Ewan's car? I didn't want to carry them round in my bag all day so I stuffed them in the glovebox. I ended up forgetting all about them.'

It was too much. All three of us were now falling about laughing. And I owed Ewan a massive apology!

When a big removal truck rocked up to Fallowlees one day in January, I could hardly believe my eyes.

'What's all this?'

'A lifetime's possessions. I've got a few years on you.'

Out of the truck came furniture, kitchen paraphernalia, sports equipment, books and records. Box after box after box.

'I'm not sure there's going to be room for all this. Are you building an extension at the same time?' Something caught my eye. 'Ooh, is that the sofa I like?'

I loved the big brown leather sofa from Ewan's house in Galashiels. It would look good in the living room. But as luck would have it, no matter which way it was turned, we couldn't get it inside.

'No problem,' said Ewan. 'Now, where's my toolkit?'

'What are you going to do?'

'Saw it in half.'

He looked at my astonished face. 'Well, have you got a better idea?'

Several hours later, exhausted after lugging all the boxes from the lorry and finding somewhere for them to go, we prepared to plonk ourselves down on our new settee – now looking whole again – and put our feet up.

'You're just in time to help me with lambing,' I said, as I went first to the fridge. 'Glass of wine, or a beer?'

'I knew there was a reason you were in such a hurry to get me here.'

I had been looking forward to this year's lambing. It was my first at Healey Mill, and the first time since I was seventeen that I wasn't trekking around the country lambing other people's sheep. I was finally my own master. And now, with Ewan by my side, I had even more reason to look forward to it.

It turned out to be the most enjoyable lambing I had ever done, helped in no small part by having someone to share the workload with.

Ewan wasn't a total novice to farming when we met. He knew something about keeping sheep and cows from his time having a smallholding with his ex. But I took a lot of pride and pleasure in trying to pass on some of the knowledge I had gained over the years. He threw himself into the work – and, as I'd already witnessed, at the sheep! Never embarrassed to ask a question or do something that might make him look silly, he was different from anyone I had ever met.

21

Strawberry

That spring of 2013 was exceptional, reflecting our high spirits. The sun shone and the ewes hardly saw a wet day. The lambs flourished like hothouse plants. The ewes we had transported the previous year couldn't believe their luck – born on the rough uplands of Fallowlees, the move to lower pastures provided them with lush feed they hadn't known before and they grew fat, round and contented. Even Lippy, the Texel who had suffered the facial injury in the dog-worrying incident, had rallied. For a while I had wondered if I might have to cull her, but the sweeter grasses of Healey Mill suited her disfigured mouth and she was thriving along with the rest of them.

What's more, Roy and Alfie were loving the work at Healey Mill as much as we were.

It felt so good to have finally found someone to share this wonderful life with. In the evening, when work was done, Ewan and I would reflect on the day's little dramas over a meal and a glass of wine.

I didn't feel as if I was forging ahead on my own any more, sometimes making decisions I wasn't sure about. I knew that if I had known Ewan earlier I wouldn't have made the same mistake with the tractor. I had sometimes rushed into things because I didn't want to bother anyone else with my questions. Dad would always provide a sympathetic ear, but he was a busy man with his own farm to run. Archie, too, was a fount of wisdom, but had already done far more than I could ever repay him for. Besides, I had my pride. The last thing I wanted was people thinking I couldn't do this job by myself – a young woman in a man's world. I had come up against sexism of this sort too many times in the past for it not to affect me.

But now I had someone I could sound ideas off, someone who had my back, and I felt so much more secure.

I thought back to the goals I had set myself when I was recovering from my broken back. It had been less than a year ago that I had written down that list of dreams, and today I had achieved far more of them than I could ever have dared to think possible. I had given up contracting; I was making progress on the trials field; I had met the love of my life; and I was adding to my pack of dogs.

The number of dogs at Fallowlees had been slowly creeping northwards for some time. I couldn't seem to pass up a well-bred pup. I had built an excellent team of experienced dogs as well as a good number of up-and-coming youngsters for the nursery trials later in the year. In my new pack I now had Jamie, a handsome, playful, black and white youngster I bought on the spur of the moment and had high hopes for, while also rising up through the ranks was Fred, a son of Roy and identical in all but name. Hoggy was showing early signs of being a good work dog, too. The varied terrain at Healey Mill was ideal for developing their education. But I was determined, too, to be businesslike about my pack. I couldn't usefully employ all of them for all of their lives: some of them would have to be sold.

It wasn't just the number of dogs that was growing. Penny was due to calve in the summer, thanks to artificial insemination. I was happy she would be able to keep her own calf for the first time. The calves had wintered well and I had weaned them from her. She seemed happy to be relieved of her brood, who were now far larger than her. They had grown long and tall – lanky teenagers. Chalky, the pure white one, was still my favourite. I hoped to repeat the experiment in the future, but with fewer calves next time.

The Blue Grey calves I had bought in Newcastleton were continuing to thrive, and were enjoying eating down the spring growth. As I saw the way the cattle had improved the land – how everything was working in harmony – it solidified my resolve to grow my herd when funds would allow.

Then there were the horses. Coquet was no longer a foal but now a rapidly growing gelding. He was losing his winter coat and looking every bit the racehorse his mother had been. He had become withdrawn since losing Delphi, and after Piper, the fat gypsy cob, went back to her owner, he was left with just Mr Tumnus for company.

Their relationship had certainly improved since the early

days. I think, because Coquet was lonely and Mr Tumnus reminded him of his mother, there was still a bond between them, albeit a weaker one. They were like brothers: they loved each other but didn't always like each other.

Coquet needed more than a goat for company, though, even one with the character of Mr Tumnus. Horses never live alone by choice, and need equine companions around them to live a truly contented life. I had been keeping an eye on the horses for sale pages on Facebook, hoping to find a little pony to run with him.

One day I saw an advert I could not pass by.

Appalooser [sic] horse mare
Make 16 hands plus
Two years old
Haltar [sic] broken
£300

With the advert was a picture of the sorriest little pony you had ever seen. She was skin and bone; her coat was mangy and balding in patches, and her mane and tail were lank and ungroomed. In the background I could see more horses, looking as emaciated as she was.

I rang my sister Caroline immediately.

'Fancy a horsey road trip tomorrow?'

'Damn right!'

Ewan was at work that day, so knew nothing of my plan. Caroline and I set off with the livestock trailer and headed down to Durham on our rescue mission.

We arrived at a tiny plot of bare ground. To be honest, it was exactly what I'd expected: motorway barriers were tied up in gaps of broken-down fencing, junk was piled in heaps, scrap cars were dotted all over. There was not a blade of grass to be seen, and yet wherever I looked I saw broken-down horses.

It must have been a bog in the winter or after a wet spell. I could see where the horses' constant pacing had worn deep tracks in the mud, which had now baked dry.

It was a very sorry sight.

'I'm not sure I like this, Emma,' said Caroline. 'Remember the time we went to test-drive that car ... '

I could hardly forget. Caroline had seen an advert for a cheap Fiesta that seemed worth checking out and asked if I would go with her. I felt a twinge of anxiety when the satnav directed us into the depths of a travellers' encampment. The people seemed friendly enough, and they agreed to let us take the Fiesta for a drive if we left my car with them. We promised not to be long. We stalled at the second junction, about a mile down the road, and the car wouldn't start again. We looked at each other. What to do? Should one of us walk back and get help? But we were in the middle of nowhere and didn't really want to split up. Should we abandon the car and both go back? What would the owners say? We tried the engine a few more times and after an age it finally fired and we took it straight back. When we got there we found that our car had been blocked in, and it took us some time to find someone to let us out so that we could make our way home.

'Christ, yeah, that was some day!'

But this mission felt important and so we opened the smashed-up gate and drove in anyway. Before we got out of the car, though, I checked my phone's reception and slipped it into my pocket. That previous incident had made me more cautious.

I saw the pony straight away, tied to a post in the field. Her head was hanging miserably.

I pointed her out to Caroline. 'Have you seen her?' I muttered. 'She's tiny. There's no way she's ever going to make sixteen hands.'

What I was actually thinking was that she'd be lucky to see out the summer. Next to her stood a slightly bigger blue and white colt, who was in a similar state. They were both lifting with lice. A stiff breeze could have knocked the pair of them over.

A lad appeared from nowhere, like magic, followed by several others.

I had already decided I was taking her, but I was no stranger to the art of negotiation.

According to the lad he had rescued both horses from a 'despicable' person a year previously, but could no longer keep them. He repeated the claim in the advert that the Appaloosa was going to make sixteen hands, as was her companion. This was a blatant fib. They were both about twelve hands tall and were most certainly ponies.

I said I would give him the asking price for the Appaloosa if he would throw in her friend. I could see that the blue pony was overly attached to her, and had no doubt they had been through a lot together. Having endured the trauma of reading

about Black Beauty's love for Ginger as a child, I had no inten-
tion of splitting them up. The sight of the cash and the fact that
I had the trailer there waiting was too much for the boy. He
shrugged and took the money. He handed over two passports
for Exmoor hill ponies. There was no way they were Exmoors
(little fat brown ponies with a distinctive beige muzzle) any
more than they were going to reach sixteen hands, but I said
nothing and tucked the passports away in the glovebox before
we got on with the job of moving them.

We dropped the tail ramp and the boy clipped a rope
onto the blue colt while Caroline took the other. The blue
colt walked dejectedly up the ramp, putting up no fight, but
the sight of the trailer caused panic in the little Appaloosa,
who shied and whinnied. I wondered what had happened
to her in the past. She must have had a bad experience at
some point, I thought, to be so frightened, even in her apa-
thetic state.

The commotion brought more people out of the wood-
work. Men, women and a bunch of scruffy children now
stood there too, eyeing us suspiciously. The Appaloosa was
wheeling, wild-eyed and terrified. Despite her size, she was
giving Caroline a run for her money, dragging her rapidly
backwards. And now the blue tied inside was starting to get
worked up, too.

An old lady moved out of the crowd and began smacking
the side of the trailer, yelling at the blue colt to calm down,
which wasn't helping.

The Appaloosa was backing further and further away, her
eyes rolling in her head, stumbling and shying despite Caroline

talking to her gently, trying to reassure her. She reached out to give her nose a stroke but the horse flinched and jerked her head out of the way.

Suddenly the weakened pony tripped, fell backwards and lay there, spent, the fight in her gone. That was when four burly men swaggered over to her and Caroline. They scooped the pony up, one at each leg, and dragged her into the trailer.

With them both safely installed, I set off before anything else could happen. It wasn't exactly the rescue I had dreamed of, but I told myself it was all going to get better from now on.

I breathed a sigh of relief as we reached the safety of the main road.

'Phew! I'm glad we're out of there,' I said to Caroline.

'I know. You just wonder, don't you, what's going on when there's no one there to see it. Those poor animals. It breaks my heart.'

We both looked at each other, then burst into slightly hysterical laughter at the absurdity of the situation.

'Oh, my God, that old lady!' I exclaimed, between bursts of laughter.

'Least we got the ponies, and it'll make a good story.'

We were both excited to get the ponies home. I don't think they knew what to do when they stepped out of the trailer into the wide expanse of Fallowlees and more grass than they could dream of. In fact, it was all too much for them at first. They stood there bewildered, as if they were waiting for permission to move or to start grazing.

When Ewan got home that evening he found the two sorry creatures in the dog paddock. Somehow, in the more bucolic surroundings, they looked even worse than they had at the travellers' camp.

'I leave you two alone for one day and what do you do? Buy some broken-down ponies,' he laughed. He gave the blue one a closer look. 'Is that one a donkey?'

I turned my head on one side. 'Actually, he might be!'

Before he could say anything else, I added, 'But look at them, Ewan. It was our duty to rescue them.'

Caroline and I had worked all afternoon to worm, delouse and groom them. They were so tired they just stood there, resigned.

We named the Appaloosa Strawberry and the blue Tramp.

The following day I let them out into the horse field with Coquet. He came trotting over as soon as he saw us coming. I could see his excitement. He was beyond delighted to have companions. He pranced and danced for them and gave them all his best moves. But the poor ponies just wanted to graze or lie down. They were shattered from their experience. Having real grass to eat was clearly a luxury for them and they didn't have the time or inclination yet to fool around and play. Coquet looked dejected.

'Never mind, Coquet, give them time,' I said.

A quick inspection by Mr Tumnus marked the ponies as not worthy of his love, and he sauntered back up the hill to eat some more of my garden.

The ponies stayed with us for two years. They never did make sixteen hands, but they did make the most wonderful riding ponies. Their transformation took a long time but was remarkable.

To this day, if Ewan knows that Caroline is coming for a visit when he's at work, he asks if we'll be needing the trailer!

22

Gypsy

I got back into trialling with a vengeance in 2013. I had a great season with the dogs. Both Roy and Alfie had hit their prime. I felt as if they and I knew what we were doing. We were in the prize list most weeks. It's funny how people say, 'It's easy when it's done.' I know what they mean now. Up until then I had had little success – just odd flash-in-the-pan moments – and then suddenly I became consistent. I knew I had been lucky to make a complete recovery after my accident and I was determined to reap the benefits of it.

Trialling was still a male-dominated competition. I remembered how at my very first trial, one of the experienced shepherds told me he had had a bet with some of the other old-timers that I would be the Northumberland champion one year.

'I can see your talent, lass,' he said. 'Go on and win me my bet!'

I laughed modestly, but secretly that had been my aim, right from the start.

I kept an eye on the scores. I knew I had a chance. At the end of the season when all the points from all the open trials over the summer were tallied up, Roy and I had come out on top of the Northumberland League. I had done it! I was the first woman in its almost forty-year history to have won. I was delighted for both of us.

Roy was my top dog, though some of my youngsters were showing great promise. That was important to me – to have a team of dogs at all stages of life and training. Roy might be number one now but one day, this powerhouse of a dog would be usurped by one of my juniors.

Ewan had been serious about learning how to handle a dog and started coming with me to trials when he wasn't working. I gave him a blue-eyed pup called Dennis. Ewan had a whale of a time teaching him basic commands.

'Watch him, Emma! Look at the eye he shows on the other dogs. He'll be ready to start on the sheep soon.'

I could see the fire, the impatience to start training, light up in Ewan. I knew from my own experience how sometimes the hardest thing to do is wait for a dog to grow up before beginning serious training. With a young, keen dog it's so tempting – but counterproductive – to rush ahead.

With that in mind, we decided to keep an eye out for a capable dog for Ewan to run. That would fuel his desire to learn and take the pressure off Dennis. We bought a competent little trial bitch called Gypsy from Aled Owen in Wales. Aled is a big name on the international sheepdog circuit, and two-time winner of the World Sheepdog Trials. He also sells top-quality dogs.

Ewan and Gypsy took to the field for the first time at a charity trial for beginners and novices. I had a feeling he would enjoy it. It was a friendly event, and an ideal opportunity for him to take his first competitive steps.

Ewan entered the novice class, a class for entrants who hadn't been placed in the top six at open level before. This class was where I cut my teeth when I first started out in the sport. The course was exactly the same as an open course.

Oddly, I found myself to be more anxious watching Ewan than I would have been running the course myself. I so wanted him to do well, and for him to enjoy my sport as much as I did. Added to that was the fact that his performance was a reflection on me, too. I was his teacher, but was I any good?

Calmly and confidently, Ewan set Gypsy away to gather the sheep. He told me later that he was so engrossed in trying not to get his commands muddled that he was hardly aware of anything else. But Gypsy knew the ropes and tucked the packet of sheep through the gates with no trouble, and with Ewan's assistance, successfully penned them.

We waited nervously for the results. When we discovered he had been placed third we were both ecstatic. And Ewan was well and truly hooked.

'I'm in for some ribbing at work next week,' he said, posting a picture of Gypsy and her rosette on Facebook.

I don't suppose many firefighters are sheep triallists in their spare time. His family and friends were surprised too when he confessed his new hobby – and even more to witness his delight at coming third!

Ewan was able to compete as a novice at all the

Northumberland open trials that summer, and in the winter competition for young dogs. That meant he ran the same course as me and was scored by the same judge. There was always a separate prize for the best novice, and as the year went on he was regularly coming away with that prize. On a good journey home we would be buzzing, discussing the intricacies of the course and the sheep, debating the judge's prize list. Or we might be commiserating with one another. We felt like a team now. And it was wonderful to turn up at a trial with the man I loved by my side.

It wasn't all plain sailing on the farm. My skills as a teacher were less polished there. I often struggled to verbalise what I was trying to communicate. So much of what I know is just instinctive. As a naturally sporty, outdoorsy person – 'Jack of all trades, master of none,' he would tell me – Ewan had probably thought that farming would suit his abilities and personality. He was about to find out it wasn't quite as straightforward as that. That things had a habit of not going according to plan.

'How did you know the sheep were going to do that?' he would say in exasperation. 'How couldn't I see that?'

'It's sheep sense. They have done me over so many times in the past, I have had to learn,' I laughed.

I could try to explain everything to Ewan, but it was no replacement for experience; Ewan would have to learn sheep sense from his own mistakes.

'It's not a science,' I told him, 'it's instinct.' I gave him a playful poke. 'Being strong and sporty isn't going to help with everything!'

Sheep sense is not taught – it's acquired, slowly but surely, through mundane, day-in, day-out tasks. It's learned from making mistakes – and sheep usually punish these mistakes soundly. As Ewan was finding out.

The Border collie has been bred for generations to have innate sheep sense. We humans, however, have to learn the hard way. It's not in our DNA the way it is in theirs.

Ewan hoped he would pick up sheep sense through being a good pupil. That wasn't a bad start, and I could only admire his enthusiasm. But I think he wanted a paint-by-numbers approach to some of the new skills he was tackling, and a list of rules to follow. I had to explain that as far as farming was concerned, it didn't work like that. Sheep and dogs have their own agendas, everything happens very quickly and there are so many variables that no one situation is like another.

Of course it helped that as a firefighter he had developed good problem-solving skills, and these were indeed transferable at times. But as he began to realise, there is no substitute for time spent working with sheep to develop a feel and respect for them.

There were times when I wished I were a better teacher. So much of what I do is unconscious that I'd never thought of breaking it down and explaining it in simple terms until now. It was a good exercise to try, though.

23

Making Hay

Our first summer together had flown by. When Ewan wasn't away firefighting he was at my side, helping me look after the two farms. I had never been happier. I had two partnerships now, a professional one and a personal one, and my life had improved immeasurably thanks to both. The Murrays had proved to be the best of people to work with. I was allowed a free rein to look after their sheep, and to stock and manage my side of Healey Mill as I saw fit. I loved getting up each day to work around my own schedule, instead of jumping to someone else's tune. Dreams of Broomhouse seemed like a long time ago.

The tractor saga had run and run – if that's the right term to use for something that spent so much of its time conking out! Machinery isn't really my bag – it's the animals that drive me. But there were times I did need that temperamental vehicle. When Dad sensed that I was at my wits' end, he accompanied me on a special trip to the dealers. After some careful negotiation on his part, they eventually sorted out a replacement. This tractor was the same model as the first, but newer. It also cost more. When it arrived it needed a bit of fixing too.

Seeing my predicament – one that he had faced himself in his early farming days – Dad generously gave me some money to help. I didn't ask for it, but I took it without too much protest. I was happy to say goodbye to the whole sorry affair. I had learned my lesson the hard way.

I knew I was deeply privileged. I heard a saying once, 'It's easy to fly high if you know you have a soft landing,' and I make no bones about the fact that my parents are there for me and were able to help me pick up the pieces of a very poor decision. I know not everyone has something to fall back on, and I admire those who take risks without that safety net.

As part of the higher-level environmental scheme I had signed up to at Fallowlees, I was to make hay in my front field annually. Previously I had got contractors in to do the work, and they had made large round bales. This year I decided that with Ewan's help and the addition of a working tractor of our own, I would make my own nice little square bales.

I figured these would be easy to store in one of the small sheds and handy to feed to the cows in the winter should it snow. Bales of this size fit on the back of the quad bike perfectly and don't require a big tractor to distribute them like the enormous round bales do.

Ewan and I went out one day and purchased a little square baler. It looked like a relic of the past, and was probably older than both of us put together. But I'm sure it was the envy of the neighbourhood in its heyday (pun intended)!

We duly hired a contractor to mow the field. He actually got a puncture on the forestry track on the way home and vowed never to come back. (Punctures and Fallowlees are an ongoing saga – the boys at Hexham Tyre & Battery reckon I should have a loyalty card.) However, the job was done, thank goodness.

Every day we lovingly turned the hay with our tractor and haybob – a two-in-one piece of equipment that aerates and rakes the hay – so it would dry evenly in the sun, happily watching the grass go from vivid green to dried-out yellow. Ewan and I felt quite accomplished. We studied the weather forecast closely and prayed every night that it would stay dry.

We made the decision to bale the hay one day when Ewan was off work. I had put a plea on Facebook: anyone who wanted to come and lend a hand would be most welcome, and there'd be beers and quiches when it was all over. I had a *Darling Buds of May* image of us all laughing and joking, swigging a cold beverage as we sat on the safely stowed-away bales under a reddening evening sky.

Unfortunately, by mid-morning we realised no one was going to turn up, and with rain forecast that afternoon we had to make a start on our own. I figured a couple of hours would bale the whole field.

It turns out you need a university degree to operate a baler as old as ours. And when you do fathom it out, you discover that the baler actually has a personality. Despite its age, ours was a huffy teenager. The first row was grand. Ewan chugged away, the new tractor powering the baler behind it, which did its job popping out even, nicely tied bales. I collected them with the quad and trailer, and safely stowed them. All fine so far.

Then the baler went into a sulk and started putting out bales with no string on them. Ewan got out his handbook, did a bit of tinkering and she was back, spitting out bound bales again – but instead of the standard two strings, ours had twenty-five! More tinkering, a pat and a cuddle and a promise of a treat when it was all over, and she was putting out bales with two strings once more – only now the bales were eleven feet long and I couldn't lift them! Oh, she had a sense of humour all right, but not one we were appreciating. A prayer and another tinker led to a few good bales, and then she spat out a load of miniature two-foot-long bales instead of the standard three-foot.

All day this carried on. It was a never-ending task. I went round the field dragging the well-made bales into the trailer and stowing them away, leaving an ever more frustrated Ewan to his coaxing and his prayers.

If anyone ever asks you to help them stow away square bales, just say no. It is the itchiest, heaviest, most soul-destroying job ever. Especially on your own. Late afternoon, with about half of the field baled, some black storm clouds appeared in the distance. Our urgency increased and our tempers shortened. It was around this time that friend and salesman Peter Forster rocked up to lend a hand. I'd never been so grateful to see anyone – I could have hugged him. The two of us worked quickly to get any acceptable bales safely put away.

If hay is rained on it goes mouldy when it is stored, and

understandably cows and sheep won't eat it. Plus, the presence of a single wet bale in a stack can ruin the whole lot. Making bad hay and stowing it is also a fire risk, as for some reason hay can spontaneously combust. This scenario in particular was one Ewan was keen to avoid, having seen too much of it in his work.

In the end we got about three quarters of the field baled and most of that inside before the heavens opened. It was disappointing to see the result of the previous week's work ruined, but there was nothing we could do to save the remainder of the hay, and at least we had enough crop to see us through.

Coquet, Strawberry and Tramp had found the whole process fascinating and as we finally sat down on the bales and chinked our beers, they came over to investigate. Or perhaps they just wanted to seek shelter from the rain.

'This one looks like a thoroughbred if it wasn't for the patches,' said Peter, with an enquiring look at me, as he stroked Coquet's nose. Ever the showman, Coquet kicked up his legs and performed a little frolic for his new admirer. The other two looked at Coquet disdainfully and resumed their eating, after lapping up some attention of their own. They had become far more sociable since I had bought them but would never be extroverts like their companion.

I told him the story of Coquet's mother, my beautiful Delphi, a real racehorse. Peter listened with interest.

'Are you going to break him in yourself?' He nodded towards Coquet.

I glanced at Ewan, who spluttered on his beer at the suggestion.

'Not blooming likely!' I laughed. 'I don't intend to have any more hospital visits.'

'Perhaps I can help,' he said. It turned out he was a part-time horse trainer himself, and he offered to take Coquet for some expert tuition at a yard in Hexham when the time came.

'I'll take you up on that! Cheers!'

We touched bottles again. The day had proved to be more successful than we thought.

The next morning when the rain stopped we collected the bales left on the field and set fire to them and the rows of hay we had been unable to bale. It was sad to see what had been perfect forage go up in smoke, literally, but that's farming life.

We sold the baler the following month. We couldn't cope with the thought of dealing with its teenage tantrums or sense of humour again. We also didn't want to put our own relationship under any more strain. There's nothing like a bit of temperamental machinery to put you at loggerheads with your partner, when really it's the machine you're both angry with. But that just seems to be the way it happens. I did feel a pang of guilt thinking of the next farmer to purchase it from the dealer's yard. We wrote down all the little tips we had learned that day in the back of the handbook, with a good luck message to him or her!

By late summer our lambs had prospered and reached market weight, and I had begun to sell them. I was proud of the stock I took to market that year. It had been hard to get animals to really thrive on the ground at Fallowlees, whereas the grassy goodness at the partnership farm did the job with little intervention from me. You only needed to look at the animals to see the results.

In the past I had hated going to market. I had a ridiculous fear of backing up the trailer after making a fool of myself one too many times. Backing up a livestock trailer is an art, and one I only seem able to master when no one is watching. Everything changes when I have a critical audience of farmers and mart staff. Not to mention a queue of other drivers impatient to drop off their own animals.

Like they say, practice makes perfect, and I had spent a long time backing in and out of the yard at Fallowlees until I could do it like a pro. I was finally confident enough not to have to turn up at 6 a.m. when no one was there to see me. It was a turning point for me, and now taking a trailer full of healthy animals to the mart is one of my greatest pleasures.

24

Flockstars

Flockstars was the brainchild of television company Liberty Bell Productions. They asked if I would be prepared to film a pilot and test run in the hope that the programme would be picked up by one of the commercial TV channels. I had been happy to oblige; it was extra money, and easy money at that. At least, that's what I thought when they described it.

The plan at that early stage was very different from the end result. The idea was to find the most unlikely candidate and turn her into a shepherdess under my tuition. With that in mind, they had interviewed and selected Abbey Marie, a model and beautician. I had just a few weeks to turn her into a farmer and dog handler. The showdown was to be a sheepdog trial in an arena at the end of the training, where she would compete against experienced shepherds. The pilot would then be shown to the commissioners in the hope they would give it the green light.

Abbey Marie had rocked up to Fallowlees as inappropriately

dressed as it was possible to be, which was, of course, part of the plan. Given her long nails, platinum hair extensions and deep bottled tan I didn't know whether to laugh or cry. A clubbing-style dress completed the outfit.

Her knowledge of dogs was limited to her little Chihuahua, and she confessed that she had never seen a sheep in real life before.

She had been asked to play up to the role of blonde bimbo for the pilot, and she did so admirably. The producers threw her in at the deep end, asking her – still dressed in her finery – to complete a series of tasks only an experienced shepherd would have been able to do, so that they could have a good old laugh at her expense as she failed miserably.

She was as game as they came. She ran here and there trying to catch a sheep, falling over in the mud and the muck, her beautiful tresses flying all over. The tasks she had to complete were written on placards, which she read to the camera before attempting them.

'Catch a . . . you-eee?' She pulled a face as she read it, drawing out the word. 'What's that?'

'A ewe is one of those animals behind you,' I replied. 'A female sheep.'

She clipped the muck off the lambs' tails, making suitably disgusted noises as she did so; she tussled with a ewe, yelping as she went. She had no authority over Mist, the half-white-faced sheepdog that was to be hers for the duration of the experiment. The little dog took full advantage and ran amok, sensing her new freedom in the same way an unruly class senses a rookie teacher.

And yet, I knew she had it in her to make the transformation. I could see she wasn't as silly as all that – that she was enthusiastically playing the role expected of her.

We spent four weeks together as I showed her how to do all the day-to-day jobs. I taught her how to handle Mist and get her to take commands to guide the sheep round the front field. I watched, pleased and proud, as Mist recognised her authority. She learned surprisingly quickly. I really enjoyed the time, and hoped she did too. Although we were poles apart – think Town Mouse and Country Mouse – we also had a lot in common. We were, after all, women of a similar age, looking for the same things in life: a stable job, enough money to get by, happiness in love . . .

She and Mist really took to one another, and a few weeks in they were looking like a proper team. If you'd seen them together you wouldn't have known that a few weeks earlier this woman had never set foot on a farm, never mind worked on one.

We were filmed throughout the experience, and we quickly got used to the camera. The best thing was just to forget it was there.

The day of the finale came.

I had been asked to provide two competitors. I quickly roped in Michael, my friend from the hill farm, and Jonjo, a local farmer with a keen interest in sheepdogs who had used Alfie as stud on one of his bitches in the past. I lured them to the arena with the promise of a cash handout for not a lot of work and, hopefully, a bit of a laugh along the way.

We arrived to find everything ready for our arena trial.

Trials are often held in a similar format to this in the US – a tighter setting than the fields of our own trials. Each of the three competitors was to take a packet of four sheep around the obstacle course using their dog. It was far less refined than a normal sheepdog trial, and quite simply the fastest team to complete the course and pen the sheep would be the winners.

Jonjo was up first with Red, son of Alfie, who set off to gather his charges with great gusto. However, used to the open hills and valleys of home, the close environment and bright lights gave Red a touch of stage fright. After a dazzling start he was quickly distracted and snuck off for a dirty protest next to the pen, much to the delight and hilarity of all watching. In fact, Abbey Marie and I broke down into that helpless sobbing laughter that cannot be stifled, even after the director had roundly told us off for being immature. It was a good few minutes before we could get a handle on ourselves, and we spent a while after that quietly shaking with badly held-in giggles.

Abbey Marie was up next with Mist. Dressed in a smart tweed gilet and carrying my stick, she looked every bit the expert. I couldn't help but feel proud of my little unit. She put Mist through her paces as well as any seasoned triallist, completing the course quickly and efficiently.

Michael was last to run. His dog, like Mist, wasn't fazed at all by the new experience. It was a good performance. They would be hard to beat.

It was all down to the judges and the time on the stopwatch. The judges deliberated for what felt like an age. But in the end Abbey Marie and Mist were crowned the winners, to the delight of everyone there, especially the producers.

I still tease Jonjo and Michael about their trouncing to this day!

Liberty Bell were going to condense the filming into a single pilot episode. They would take the pilot to the commissioners at ITV, hoping the powers that be would see the bare bones of a show in there somewhere.

After that I didn't hear anything for a while and thought it had perhaps been a non-starter.

Then one day, out of the blue, the producer rang to say the show had been commissioned, but with a new twist. They still wanted to turn inexperienced folk into shepherds, but they had decided to do it with celebrities. And because most of the celebs they had in mind lived in or around London, they wondered if I could come down to a city farm for a few weeks and train them to run dogs. Oh, and could I also provide the dogs?

The money was more than the farm would earn in a year; I bit their hand off. Ewan agreed he would manage the farm between his firefighting shifts and I would come home at weekends, when we would do the bulk of the work with the sheep. As part of my agreement with Liberty Bell, they arranged kennelling for several extra dogs so I could continue the education of Alfie, Roy, Fred, Hoggy and Jamie in my spare time.

I hadn't voluntarily left the farm in anyone else's hands before, and – apart from when I had broken my back – had never been away for more than a day or so. But, confident in

Ewan's ability to keep things ticking over, I packed my bags and drove to London.

I hadn't been to London a lot. The previous time had been when I was invited to the Women of the Year Lunch, after my book came out. Driving there was quite the experience. I got well and truly lost, and was unbelievably late for the welcome session the producers had set up. They rang me, all in a panic.

'I thought I was lost but it's OK, I'm on the ferry now,' I told them cheerily.

'The ferry?!' they exclaimed. They put me on speakerphone and I could hear sounds of cursing in the background. 'You should not be on a ferry! Where the hell are you? Get off the ferry now!'

'The satnav told me to get on the ferry,' I answered simply.

I was on the Woolwich Ferry, that links the North and South Circular Roads, but the producers were frightened I was on my way to France!

I stayed at a Premier Inn, just down the road from the farm where filming was to take place, with two other shepherds, and we travelled there together each day. Woodlands Farm is in Welling in Kent. It's a traditional working farm, run as a charity, that aims to teach people about farming and give city dwellers the chance of a countryside experience.

The other mentors were Ioan Doyle, a fun-loving shepherd and rock climber from Wales, and Ed Hawkins, a shepherd and sheepdog triallist from East Anglia. Both twenty-somethings, but quite different characters.

I had seen Ed briefly on the trialling scene at one of the Nationals. I knew he was an excellent handler with a reputation for liking a headstrong type of dog. Ioan was more happy-go-lucky, a comedian – no one was immune to his charms and plucky nature.

I had never met them properly before, but we hit it off right away – a shared love of dogs and sheep is always good for bonding, as well as being thrown together in such a remarkably bizarre setting. Ioan and I were very much the country bumpkins, in at the deep end, while Ed was far less naive.

I told them about my journey and we had a good laugh about the producers' breakdown over the ferry conversation. They had their own tales of random mishaps. Ioan told me his Land Rover Defender had hit the roof barrier in the Premier Inn's multi-storey car park, while Ed's van had been stopped by the police right outside for looking suspicious. Boy, what a trio we made!

We each had to provide three dogs, who were housed in fancy new kennels on-site. I had selected Hoggy, Ewan's bitch Gypsy and a bitch called Sky hired from a friend. Roy and Alfie were the more experienced dogs, of course, but I didn't really want a novice handler taking the shine off their well-polished skills. However, I hoped that I could attend some of the trials in the South with them while I was down there.

We were instructed to put our dogs into the kennel that had his or her name on it. A picture of the celebrity assigned to that dog was also pinned to the kennel door.

We walked along the line, looking at the faces, scratching our heads.

'Do you recognise anyone?' I asked Ed and Ioan, as I looked at the pictures of my own celebrity pupils. Their faces were familiar, but not familiar enough for me to be able to name them.

'Not likely!' they chimed.

That is not to say these people were not famous, it's just that most shepherds live sheltered lives and have little interest in celebrities.

Ioan had Tony Blackburn, the DJ, and Fazer from the hip-hop group N-Dubz.

Ed's protégés were Kelle Bryan from the pop group Eternal, Wendi Peters, known for her role as Cilla Battersby-Brown in *Coronation Street*, and Amanda Lamb, the TV presenter who is perhaps best known as the face from the Scottish Widows advert. Actor Laila Morse, who played Mo in *EastEnders*, was a reserve.

I had Brendan Cole, one of the professionals from *Strictly Come Dancing*, Lee Pearson, the Paralympic gold medallist dressage rider, and Lesley Joseph, the actor who played Dorien in *Birds of a Feather*.

We had been laughing at our cluelessness, but now I looked at their pictures and felt my mouth go dry. I was out of my comfort zone here. I had nothing in common with these people – people I was about to spend whole days side by side with. I was so terrified at the prospect of meeting my charges, I hardly slept the night before. I tossed and turned in the pristine Premier Inn bed. It was far too hot. I got up to open a window but it didn't move far. After being used to a cool, draughty farmhouse, the heat was unbearable.

The more I thought about it, the more bonkers the idea seemed – me, teaching total novices how to run dogs! And not just ordinary novices, but people who quite possibly had no real interest in becoming triallists and were taking part solely to provide entertainment (and earn money). I still didn't consider myself a teacher, but then I thought of Abbey Marie, and how she had come on in leaps and bounds in a few short weeks, and of how Ewan was now a confident handler. I had asked him for some feedback on my technique.

'You're useless at explaining but good at demonstrating,' was his reply.

So that was going to be my approach. It's almost impossible, anyway, to lay down the fundamentals of training a dog on paper; far better to just go ahead and show them how it's done.

It turned out I had worried unnecessarily. Celebrities are just normal people.

Lesley was like my mum. I felt comfortable with her from the second we were introduced. She was very dedicated and very driven. She was determined to do well. She needed reassurance that what she was doing was correct. She was also a great dog lover and fell hard for little Gypsy.

Brendan was born for the job. With his dancer's discipline, natural authority and the right instincts, I would have employed him on my farm any day.

As for Lee, I warmed to him straight away. We all did. He was the person everyone got on with the best. He was lively and chatty and had a great sense of humour. As he had travelled from his home in Staffordshire, he too had to stay in London, so he, Ioan, Ed and I would often have our evening meal together.

Every day was sunny, and I surprised myself – for one who

sometimes feels out of her depth in the centre of Newcastle! – by loving London's urban sprawl. We country dwellers think of it as noisy and busy and dirty, and I suppose it is all those things, but for me it was a noisy, busy, dirty novelty. Suddenly there were shops on my doorstep, restaurants downstairs, a train ride to all of the places I had only ever heard of. One night Lee took us three shepherds (sounds like the start of a Bible passage) to see the bright lights of the city in his Range Rover. I loved how London never seemed to stop; there was always something to do.

Lee had his medals in the back of the car and being a fiddler I found them and asked if I could have a proper look at them. He showed us a video of him winning one of his gold medals, his horse dancing on the spot in the arena. Wowed, I asked Lee if he taught the horse to dance like that when he was on its back. He told me he taught the horse everything on its back. Ioan's eyes were wide. 'How do you get it to roll on its back?' We all cracked up. Lee, of course, meant with *him* on its back.

I was shocked at how clueless some of our celebrities were. On the first day I was asked by one of the contestants (who shall remain nameless) what breed of dog Hoggy was crossed with.

'She's not crossed with anything. She's pedigree all the way back, for generations.'

'Oh, I thought you said she was a bitch.'

'She is a bitch.'

'I thought all bitches were cross-breeds.'

It took all my self-control not to fall about on the floor.

'No, a bitch is just the term for a female dog.'

Every day is a school day!

Of course, the crew loved it when someone slipped up, or did or said something funny. They had one such priceless moment when it was decided that Lesley should be given some farm work to do. The manager suggested that she help check the bees. Lesley is tiny and the only suit that would fit her was a child-size one, which meant the headpiece was too small. She wasn't entirely happy about it, especially as her nose was touching the fine mesh at the front, but the director, keen to get some footage, assured her it would be fine.

Well, you guessed it – an angry bee landed right on the end of her nose and delivered a painful sting.

Lesley was pretty put out, but not the director, who watched the clip over and over muttering about it being 'pure TV gold'.

Gabby Logan was the host. She is as stunning in real life as she is on television, and has time for everyone. One evening, not long before the final, we had all congregated in the celebrities' hotel, where she bought a round of drinks. Ewan had come to join me, and he and I sat there, star-struck. Ewan, who had had a few by that point, gazed at his glass in wonder, declaring to me or the glass, I'm not sure, 'Gabby Logan just bought me a drink.' Perhaps a boyhood fantasy fulfilled!

There were four head-to-head rounds in the show, after which the four winners and the two best losers had the chance to compete in the semi-finals. All three of mine got through to the semis, and Brendan and Lee both made the final along with Amanda Lamb. The final took place in a huge arena in front of an audience. I felt sick with nerves. I wasn't just nervous about seeing my protégés in their ultimate test, and one in front of a lot of people – my reputation was also at stake here. None of the contestants had been able to complete the course in rehearsal, which I felt was going to reflect badly on us, the trainers. If that happened, the last episode was going to be an awful anticlimax, and the whole show might seem a pointless exercise.

Thank goodness Brendan Cole came through with his strong desire to win and saved the day in the nick of time, complete with a cartwheel in the closing seconds! He and Hoggy were crowned winners. I was incredibly pleased that Brendan was under my tuition, and that Hoggy was a dog I had trained from a pup. I planned to run her, Jamie and Fred in the upcoming nursery season.

I know the sheepdog community wasn't exactly over the moon about *Flockstars*, and indeed, a complaint was raised at the International Sheep Dog Society's AGM. But I would do it all again happily if I got the chance. It might have been entertainment, but it also allowed the viewing public to see the skill involved in training sheepdogs. It was educational as well as fun, and I'm all for that.

At the end of filming I asked if I could buy the kennels. The company said no, they were holding out for another series. Further down the line, when it became clear that the programme had not been the success they had hoped it would be, and a second series was ruled out, I asked again. This time they said yes, and my kennels were upgraded overnight!

25

Training

The one constant throughout my life has been my dogs, and the Border collie sheepdog in particular.

I have been lucky to have had a succession of talented and devoted companions who have each given me so much. It began with Bess, a gift from Grandpa Len when I was thirteen years old, all the way through to the dogs I own today. To own a sheepdog is to know unbounded loyalty.

I am often asked what I look for in a dog, so I thought it would be helpful to put it all down here.

I don't think you can pick a champion from the nest – that would be a valuable skill indeed – but you can pick a pup that pleases you from bloodlines that you admire. That's the cake mix. Then it's just up to you to bake it properly.

First, I look for a dog who likes me – a dog who wants to try for me. If a dog wants to please you, you can overcome most challenges. A will to please can even help to make up for a lack of talent to some extent.

If the dog's attitude to you, and to work, is right, the rest is easy.

Talent is the next ingredient, and an elusive one at that. I wish I could define it, but that's impossible. Talent is in the dog to start with, but it is up to the handler to bring it out. Even the most talented dogs can be ruined by poor training and handling.

Then comes heart: I love a dog with a big heart, one who will give everything to his cause. This type of dog will dig deeper when the chips are down, and try harder to get the job done. It's not something you can put into a dog – it has to be there – but allowing a dog to complete progressively more difficult tasks as a youngster will give it a never-say-die attitude as it grows older, allowing you, the handler, to reap the rewards. Equally, a young dog with a big heart can be ruined by expecting it to do near-impossible tasks, where it is doomed to fail, at too young an age. Too many failures early on will cause it to lose heart and throw in the towel early.

And finally, power – though this is a hard thing to measure. I used to think those dogs charging about and gripping sheep were powerful dogs, but time has taught me to re-evaluate. Now I believe that the really powerful dogs are the quiet ones – the ones that just get on with the task without any dramatics, who calmly approach the sheep with a presence that could part the sea. This is probably the rarest element of them all.

All dogs have these attributes in varying quantities, and as a trainer I believe it is my job to try to bring them out as much as I can, so that the dog can be the best version of itself. If a dog is well trained and well mannered, it is useful and will be respected.

Some people don't understand how I can train dogs to sell, and I can sympathise with this view. At the beginning I had a really hard time coming to terms with selling them myself. I remember my dad talking to me after I had sold my first dog. She was a nearly pure white Border collie I had been given by a farmer who told me she was no good as a worker. I proved otherwise, and set about bringing out her full potential.

Dad told me that now I had sold her, she would go to a good working home, which was a far better outcome for her than selling her untrained. And now, he said, I had room to train another dog and do it all over again. Not everyone can train dogs, he told me.

I still cried myself to sleep thinking about my dog, but I knew he was right. I had finally found a talent I could use not only to make extra income for myself, but also to help dogs achieve what they had been bred to do. I had identified a gap in the market: farmers could run dogs but they did not always have the time to train them properly. I could increase a dog's value and provide a useful service by selling a farmer a ready-trained collie.

I know there are people who, even after reading this, will still think me cold-hearted – and to some extent I have had to harden myself in order to do what I do. But I have made peace with the process now.

Training a large number of dogs each year allows me to filter through them and find the gems. Truly great dogs don't come along all that often. By trying out different bloodlines

I get to see what works for me. Bloodlines are important in all pedigrees, but never more so than in a working dog. It is the dog's lineage – like tracing its family tree and seeing the attributes of the ones who went before it. But of course it's not an exact science – you still never know how that dog will turn out. Occasionally one comes along that I just cannot part with. These are the Roys and the Jamies (of whom more later) of this world.

It's not all work, though. I allow my dogs a happy, carefree puppyhood, with lots of free running and rough and tumble with other dogs. I try to leave exposure to sheep as late as possible. Having sheepdogs on a sheep farm is a bit like having vampires running a blood bank, so the later they are switched on, the easier it is for me to keep tabs on them. Once they have their first exposure to sheep, I try to limit it to once a week until they are eight or nine months old, when I feel they are ready to understand the training. Just because a pup is keen to chase does not mean it has the mental development to be trained. For a dog, training is like playing football while being taught mental arithmetic – it is both fun and exhausting.

Most of my early training takes place in a fifty-metre-circumference fenced pen. I find this round pen is the best place for me to maintain control and protect the sheep from any overly exuberant pup antics.

I use 'light' sheep, who are well used to dogs. Light is the term for flighty sheep, who are very sensitive to movement, while 'heavy' is the way we describe sheep who react more slowly. I like to use little black Hebridean sheep for these first encounters. They react swiftly, which means that the dogs can see the results of their efforts straight away. Using slow, heavy sheep in these early encounters is boring for the pups and can dull their instincts – or it can make them rough and snappy in an attempt to liven up their charges, which is just as bad.

Once we have had a few sessions and I am confident that the pup is obedient to basic commands, I move out to the big field. The pup at this stage will be wearing an extra-wide collar attached to a light line about eight to ten metres long. This is my most important tool: it means that when things get a bit too exciting I am able to step in and restrain the pup. It also means I am able to catch a pup at the end of a session. Over the years I've noticed I need longer and longer lines – either the pups are getting faster or I'm getting slower!

I condition the dog so that every time they move round the sheep in an anticlockwise circle, they hear the command 'Away', and every time they run in a clockwise direction, they hear the command 'Come bye'. These are the traditional commands passed down the generations. (I have a friend whose business is brilliantly called Come-Bye and who sells – what else – sheepdog semen for breeding purposes!)

From then on it's just a case of regular tuition, teaching the dog to respect its sheep as well as the fundamentals of left and right. I aim to start taking the dogs to work with me when they are between fourteen and sixteen months old, and it's really the work that makes the dog.

Some tips for first-timers: don't crush your dog's instinct. I have people proudly tell me they have chastised their dog for chasing the chickens and they have stopped doing it now. All they have done is tell the pup not to listen to its instincts.

If the pup wants to chase chickens, put the chickens somewhere else.

I also see a lot of people making the mistake of rigorously drilling their dog – waving a big stick and continuously barking orders – so that the process is both unpleasant and boring. Your dog is your friend, so be kind, be fun. If the dog enjoys itself right from the beginning you will have a solid foundation to work on.

I always make sure a dog is praised for its efforts and that it is allowed to succeed at every stage before moving gradually on to the next one. If a dog has built up enough confidence it will be able to complete the most difficult task because it will believe it can't fail.

I aim to have a dog fully trained by around its second birthday. It happens earlier for some, and later for others. At this stage I decide whether I want to compete with the dog, use it solely for work or sell it.

Needless to say, my kennels are full of dogs of all ages and at all levels of training.

26

Jamie

Flockstars aired in the summer of 2015, and though I got teased about it, it was a brilliant experience for me. It was also great for the dogs. I came home with three dogs who had seen and done it all: Fred, Jamie and Hoggy. There was nothing that fazed them. I had gone to *Flockstars* with Roy and Alfie as my most experienced dogs, but as the filming drew to a close and we made our way home and back to reality, I realised that my two older dogs had aged. It was time to take the burden off them. I looked to my youngsters, and what I saw made me happy.

I had never had such a consistent or experienced team going into the nursery season. I had high hopes for the autumn trials.

The nursery season is a series of trials held in the autumn and winter months for dogs under three years old. The course is shorter, but the fundamentals are the same as they are for any trial and the sheep can be just as awkward. It's a good opportunity for young dogs to gain experience away from home turf.

Northumberland typically holds ten to twelve of these trials throughout the winter weekends. Although decades ago, when nurseries were first invented, they were supposed to be a sort of training ground for young dogs, they have become fiercely competitive.

The trial begins with the handler standing at the post with the dog by his or her side. On a command the dog sets off on what is called the 'outrun', making a wide loop around the sheep, who might be a few hundred yards away. The manner in which the dog approaches the sheep is called the 'lift', and is possibly the most critical part of the process as the dog must avoid panicking his charges. The dog then brings the sheep towards the handler in a controlled manner (the 'fetch'), taking them through a set of gates en route, before driving them away from the handler (the 'drive'), negotiating two more sets of gates. The run ends with the 'shed' – separating one or two of the sheep from the others – and finally the 'pen'. The shepherd is allowed to leave the post during the latter part of the operation to manage the dog more closely.

A maximum score is assigned to each element of the test and points are deducted for any faults.

The dog with the most points at the end of the season is crowned Northumberland Nursery Champion, and there is also a championship trial where the winners of each of the dozen trials can compete for the championship trial title.

The top three dogs from each county go forward to compete at the All England Nursery Final.

After *Flockstars* I hit the nurseries running, and despite it being a strong season, Jamie, Fred and Hoggy were a force to be reckoned with and made the prize list at almost every trial. At the end of the season Jamie and Fred both qualified as two of the three dogs to go forward to the All England Nursery Final in March 2016. It was the first time I had ever run at it, so it was a big deal for me.

The final was held down in Staffordshire and Ewan and I decided to make a proper trip of it and stay down there the night before. Well, why not? We didn't get away that often.

The day of the final dawned crisp and frosty. Forty of the best dogs in the country would compete on the huge course, and it really was huge, far bigger than any my dogs had seen in competition. But I was reassured by the fact that they had gathered bigger fields during the course of their day-to-day work.

The standard was high, and I had a bad case of pre-trial jitters. It was good to have Ewan beside me, reassuring me and helping me to keep my nerves in check. The competition was also the chance for a reunion with Ed from *Flockstars*, who had qualified with his dog. And Sky, the dog I had hired from a friend, Ben Smith, was competing too.

Fred was up first. Now Fred was a great dog, but the overnight stay in the car had wound him up. He was like his father in that respect. Roy was the best dog I ever had on home turf, but he would get worked up and excitable if he was in a new place for too long.

This mood carried over onto the field. Fred performed well and enthusiastically, perhaps too enthusiastically. In his volatile state, timing the turn for the gates was difficult and when we missed a gate I knew we were out of the running for a win. But we still had a decent score on the board.

Jamie was still to run. Deep down I felt he could be my trump card. He wasn't fazed at all by the new setting. I had noticed when we were in London how he just took everything in his stride, how nothing seemed to ruffle him. Whether he had a crowd of three or three hundred, it made no difference to him – he performed as if he were at home every time. We waited patiently for our slot. I slugged on a bottle of Lucozade and forced down a banana. I had used this combo to settle my nerves and pass my driving test when I was eighteen, and figured it was worth trying again.

As I stood at the post with him, I felt confident. At that moment, with the spectators and other competitors behind you, out of vision, it's just you and your dog – and the sheep, of course. You block out everything else, if you can. I had a good feeling about our chances. We've got this, Jamie, I thought.

He ran out like a gem. A beautiful curve, disappearing underneath the trees for a second or two before reappearing, not too close to the sheep, not too wide. It was a perfect lift: he approached them smoothly and the little troop came trotting steadily towards me in a straight line. They came into the ring, passed behind me, then set off for the first gate, between the trees. At my whistle Jamie turned the sheep as soon as they had passed through the gate, and drove them in a straight line, keeping his distance, to the other side of the field and the next gate. He was making it look easy. It was as if the sheep had decided of their own accord that this was where they wanted to go. Again, Jamie turned them tightly and they came trotting into the shedding ring, where our job was to separate two sheep from the other three before reuniting them and heading them towards the pen.

Everything had gone well so far. I felt a nervy excitement. Throughout the whole process I had been counting in my head what the judges might be deducting. I knew there wasn't much. He'd easily been the best dog so far.

The shed came easy, the pen was a piece of cake. My heart was racing and I felt elated as I shut the gate, with all five sheep safely inside.

Until now I had blocked out all thoughts of our audience, but now I could almost sense the ripple go through the crowd. The competitors who hadn't yet run knew it wasn't going to be easy. We had laid down a score that had to be beaten. I couldn't resist a fist pump round the back of the cars when I thought only Ewan and I were around – it turned out later a photographer had captured the moment!

All Ewan and I could do now was sit and watch the final twenty or so competitors try to better our performance. It was an anxious time. It's hard to be sporting when you are sitting at the top of the tree watching your friends try to knock you off.

The judges stopped releasing any scores when it came to the last round, which added to the tension. I knew I had a good score, but some of the dogs who came after us had done well too, so I really had no idea what the final result would be. I could feel the butterflies in my stomach twirling around with the Lucozade and banana. The time came for announcing the results. Ewan squeezed my hand.

The judge announced them from the bottom up, just like *The X Factor*. In sixth place … in fifth place … in fourth place …

still no mention of me. I was either in the top three or I was nowhere. They announced third place – still not us.

I looked anxiously at Ewan. He appeared to be calm but I guessed he felt as nervous as I did. Second place. Still not me. This was it. Had we done it?

'And the winner is Emma Gray and Jamie.'

Oh, I could have cried! We had done it! Champions!

Ewan gave me a big hug and I subtly wiped my tears on his jumper before shaking the hands of the people congratulating me.

It was the biggest thing I'd ever won. It took that trial for me to realise that Jamie really was something special. He had that little bit extra that turns a good dog into a great dog. The sheep loved it when he worked them; he made friends with them and asked them nicely to go where he wanted. He wasn't a bully, and as a result the sheep just accepted him and did his bidding. It all looked promising for future competition in the open trials. Perhaps Jamie would even be an English National Champion one day. I dared to hope, anyway.

That long drive back to Fallowlees seemed to pass in no time. I spent a lot of time thinking about where Jamie could go next, the future seemed so bright.

As we got closer to home, we drove along the Military Road. This is the local name given to a stretch of road in Northumberland that runs parallel to Hadrian's Wall; in fact, part of it is constructed on the wall's foundations. Cars were randomly parked all along the side of the road, which seemed strange for this time of night in the middle of nowhere.

'I wonder what they're all there for,' I said to Ewan.

I peered out of the window as we passed.

'Oh my God, Ewan! Look! Pull in!'

The inky-black, star-studded sky was a constantly moving pattern of green, blue and purple. The Northern Lights were putting on their other-worldly display above this World Heritage Site. It was almost too perfect an end to the day. The man I loved was by my side; my dog was the National Nursery Champion. For the second time that day I gave in to tears.

27

Blue

I have owned a lot of dogs in my time. My work and trial dogs of the past grow old, and eventually pass on, and younger dogs come along to take their place. It's sad to see loyal friends entering their twilight years, but I take satisfaction in the knowledge that I have given them a good life, and I have the memories of the happy years we have spent together.

Roy and Alfie had been beside me for many years now. As well as being champion trial dogs, they had been true companions, the closest to what non-farming folk would call a 'pet'.

Alfie, the younger of the pair, had been partially lame since tripping at a trial I competed at when I was in the South filming *Flockstars*. I was in new territory, and I suppose I went to the trial hoping to show off in front of all of those strangers, but after I set Alfie off, he never brought the sheep. This was not Alfie. He just stood there at the top of the field, frozen to the spot. I whistled and whistled and finally he staggered his charges down the field towards me. It wasn't until he got close that I realised his shoulder wasn't working properly. Goodness knows what had happened, but I guessed he had had some kind of stumble. No matter how much physiotherapy he got or quack treatments I tried, the shoulder never worked again and nor did he.

Roy, who had been showing signs of arthritis in his front toes for some time, just retired himself: one day he decided he had had enough, and that was that. My little black dog joined Alfie as a kitchen dog from that moment on, and both now lived in front of the Rayburn.

It was time to give the junior dogs a turn.

Since the Nursery Final in March, Jamie had gone up in the ranks and was now my number one work dog. He had proved to be a cracking lambing dog, enjoying his work, while his early runs in the opens had seen good results.

I sold Fred to a friend in Spain, just after lambing. He was an excellent dog, but I knew I wasn't the right partner for him. As for Hoggy, the dog who had partnered Brendan Cole and won *Flockstars*, I gave her to Archie. Here was my opportunity to repay my friend for some of his kindnesses to me. Dear Archie had lost his old dog Dale a few months earlier. The whole of the Northumberland League missed him at the trials. Some people tried to encourage Archie to take on another pup, but he always refused. I could see why – a pup would take a long time to train. Archie had had a heart attack in the past while training a young dog, and I didn't want to put any more strain on him. Giving Hoggy to Archie seemed the perfect solution – she was capable and friendly, and it meant that Archie could get back onto the trials field.

Along with Jamie, my other main work and trial dog was a daughter of Alfie, a little red bitch I named Blue.

The International Sheep Dog Society pick the top one hundred and fifty dogs to go through to compete at each of the four Nationals – those of England, Ireland, Scotland and Wales – that are held annually, and I was hoping that both Blue and Jamie would qualify.

The selection is made on a points system: six points for first place at a qualifying trial, down to one point for sixth place. You put forward your three best places, all the entries are collected and the top one hundred and fifty are selected to run.

I had competed Blue in the opens the year before. She had sixteen National points, and therefore her place was a pretty safe bet. Jamie, on the other hand, had only been competing at open level since May, which was also the month of the cut-off date for entries to the National, so I realised it was a big ask to gain the points we needed in time. Despite the tight window, we managed seven points.

The list for the National came out in June and Blue was on it. Jamie had not made the cut – but he had made it as one of the five reserve dogs. So should a dog drop out, he could take its place.

It was to be Blue's first National. I had mixed feelings about running her. Blue was a bitch, and a hormonal one at that. I am often asked why I mostly compete with male dogs, and my answer is always the same: 'There's only room for one hormonal bitch in this partnership!'

Blue could run like a true princess when she was on form, but the rest of the time she ran like a wicked lady of the night.

It depended on the moon and the stage of her season. As a woman, I totally get it – I've been there too – but it didn't make for an easy life as her handler.

The National was held over three days at Castle Howard in North Yorkshire at the beginning of August 2016. The weather forecast was good and Ewan and I had taken the weekend off to go and enjoy ourselves.

Only the week before, Blue had made a fool of me at a big hill course in Lancashire. She set off on her outrun, ran half-way, then decided she had gone far enough and lay down in a ditch. I was dizzy with whistling by the time I finally motivated her to get up again and fetch the sheep. Blue had talent, that was undeniable, but not all dogs are cut out for trialling, and Blue was perhaps better suited as a worker.

So I wasn't exactly feeling confident as I waited for our run, late on the first afternoon. Why, oh why did we not get just one more point, I asked Jamie for the umpteenth time. He had something Blue didn't – consistency. He was a trial dog through and through.

The large field, situated in the middle of the Howardian Hills, an Area of Outstanding Natural Beauty, looked chal-lenging, with dips and rises. The sheep were big, strong Mule ewes, and becoming more obstinate as the day wore on, with good lines hard to achieve. They made it clear that they didn't like erratic dogs. That didn't bode well for Blue and me.

Then I learned that two dogs had been scratched from the list of competitors. Should one more drop out, Jamie was guaranteed a run.

I looked at Ewan. 'If I were to scratch Blue today, Jamie would get a run.'

I think I had made the decision even before I voiced it. It made total sense. Jamie was running so well, whereas Blue might run like an angel or waste her run, and with it a shot at making the National team.

I scratched Blue and Jamie claimed her place as a reserve dog.

Later that day I stepped out to the post with adrenaline zipping through my veins. It was Jamie's first National. He was one of the youngest dogs on the field, and perhaps because I knew we had nothing to prove, I just went out and enjoyed myself. Jamie seemed to enjoy it as well. He sailed round that field like a veteran and took total command of those tough Mules.

That evening, after rewarding Blue and Jamie with a leisurely riverside walk and settling them for the night with an extra-special dinner, Ewan and I walked into the hotel where a lot of the competitors were staying. As we approached the bar a ripple of appreciation broke out. Then a spontaneous round of applause.

I could feel myself blush bright red with a mixture of pride and embarrassment. As the clapping continued, the course director, Boggy, came over and bought us both a drink.

'Well deserved,' he said, slapping my back and chinking glasses.

Jamie had laid down the top score of the competition. We were that day's winners.

We had taken a risk on the final element. Coming into the

shedding ring to split the single off to complete the course, I had asked Jamie to slice in on the very last sheep, a dangerous move. It takes skill for a dog to hold a sheep when she can see her mates making a getaway; it's not uncommon for a sheep to bully her way over a weaker dog in order to rejoin the rest of her group. But Jamie was in like lightning. The risk paid off and we were awarded a perfect score.

It was a dream come true for me. What a year it had been! I was so proud and so grateful.

As the sun began to set on the final day, Jamie and I had to run off against the winners of the other two days for the title of overall champion.

We were the first to compete, and I was pleased with the run. The competitor after us needed a second attempt at the shed. That potentially put them out of the running. It was all down to the final competitor. In the end, Jed and his dog Zac were in excellent form, and beat us by a narrow margin.

Jamie and I were crowned Reserve National Champions. From Nursery Champion to almost-England Champion in five months! And with it, a guaranteed place in the team for the World Sheepdog Trials next summer. I could hardly believe how far we had come. I was realising what for me had always seemed so unachievable. A childhood hope, germinated back in those early days with my first pup, Bess. If I never did anything else in the sheepdog world, I would always have this.

Later that week a friend from Northumberland came to visit with his dog, a bitch named Stella. Jamie and Stella had a romantic liaison, brief but fruitful. Nine weeks later Stella delivered a healthy litter of six puppies. As owner of the stud, I got to choose my favourite to take home as a fee for Jamie's services.

Since Jamie was named after a character in *Game of Thrones*, it seemed only appropriate to carry on the naming tradition with this pup. So we called the dark, slick-haired pup Joff. Right from the outset he was full of mischief, but adored people so wholeheartedly it was hard to be cross with his antics. His favourite trick was to jump up and wrap his front legs around you in a bear hug, sighing with contented love. His second-favourite trick was to scale the top wire in the garden and gather up the sheep when no one was looking! He had talent and grit for sure.

But could he repeat what his dad had done? Only time would tell.

28

Snow

I had timed 2017's lambing at Healey Mill for April Fools' Day once more, the traditional start date for a northern lambing. This is to coincide with good grass growth for the ewes and milder weather to help the baby lambs with their thin coats. Mother Nature, however, threw us a curveball that year.

The demands on a pregnant ewe are at their greatest towards the end of her pregnancy, when the bulk of lamb growth happens. It is also when she fills her udder with life-giving first milk, ready for her hungry offspring. For these reasons, the end of March, a few weeks before lambing, is the worst possible time for it to snow.

But snow it did. The sky was forever grey as the whole country lay trapped under a sodden cloak. Cars sat stuck in drives while their owners stayed at home, huddled in front of their TVs; supermarket shelves were stripped bare and replenishing delivery wagons floundered. The UK ground to a halt as no one wanted to risk a polar expedition for anything less than absolute essentials.

It is at times like this that a farmer's lot is at its most demanding. The daily trip to Healey Mill became more like an expedition to the North Pole as Ewan and I packed shovels, blankets, food and drink – emergency provisions should we fail to make it home. The trip was strewn with hazards. The forestry ditches at either side of the road filled with drifted snow and became impossible to distinguish from the track – until the pickup nosedived into them. These nosedives were always accompanied by a great deal of swearing as we each blamed the other for the mishap. Even with a four-by-four, chunky tyres and chains, we might get stuck half a dozen times on each journey. The local council's snowploughs, understandably, had more valuable routes to plough than the comparatively little-used byways of this part of rural Northumberland. Thank goodness we had the tractor to get us through the worst parts. We spent a lot of time just driving our little orange peril backwards and forwards on the track to keep it open.

If we had had no need to go anywhere else we would have happily holed up in Fallowlees and seen it out. What better excuse to batten down the hatches, put the kettle on, curl up in a chair and read or binge-watch DVDs until it was safe to venture out.

But that wasn't an option. We had to get to the pregnant ewes at Healey Mill, so we blazed our trail every morning. Some of the drifts were higher than the bonnet of the pickup and we had no option but to smash or dig our way through them. Sometimes the best way to get through the drifts was to hit them hard, reverse and hit them again, and repeat the whole process. The snow shovels became our most valuable assets. The pickup bumper took some serious abuse, and I cursed the fact that I hadn't invested in bull bars.

Perhaps this was the truest test of our relationship so far. I can't pretend it didn't grow strained under the pressure of hours spent digging snow from under spinning wheels, our faces frozen and our fingers numb and aching. We didn't always agree on tactics, but we knew when to hold our tongues. It was only too tempting for one of us to say to the other 'I told you so' at times, but we started to learn when that might cause irreparable damage to our relationship.

The sheep were totally reliant on what we brought them to eat; there wasn't a chance they could dig through the snow to the grass beneath. They were eating the silage as fast as we could bring it, and often the younger, smaller ewes were being pushed out before they could have their fill. They were all burning up hundreds of calories just to stay warm – and alive. I felt as if I was watching them diminish in front of my eyes. Farming teaches you to be completely responsible and reminds you that you are utterly helpless.

Sheep will often stand next to a wall for shelter in a snowstorm, little knowing that the snow – when it's really bad – will drift over the wall and envelop them. Before they know it, it is too deep for them to move and they are stuck.

Ewan and I found a number of young sheep completely trapped in this way. It took a good deal of effort, patience and brute strength to heave them out of their cocoons, hungry but none the worse for the experience.

I decided to use this opportunity to see if the dogs had the sheep-finding ability their forebears were blessed with. As a child I had read many stories about the faithful sheepdog who would sniff out snowbound sheep and save the day. Was this a myth, I wondered, or could a Border collie instinctively locate its charges? I wondered if Jamie, my pride and joy, would be any good, and was quite excited to try him out. But if sheep-finding was a trait of his collie ancestors, then the genes must have skipped his generation as he was useless! He did enjoy joining in the digging, though, once we had found the sheep, so he was quite helpful in his own way. I live in the hope that if it happens again (God forbid), he will know what to do next time.

When the snow finally left us at the end of the month, the sheep were shadows of their former selves. I like my girls to be in the best condition possible heading into lambing, but this year they looked gaunt and had lost some of their sparkle. The snow had really taken its toll. They had little time to rally before they would be giving birth.

Ewan and I had a helping hand with the lambing that year. Dennis was a German office worker with a passion for Border collies who had contacted me to ask if he could stay and lend us a hand. In exchange for his assistance, we would help him to train his dogs and teach him something about the craft of shepherding as he hoped to get his own sheep one day.

You can't be too sensitive if you come to stay at Fallowlees, and a sense of humour helps, too. It's an open house with a kitchen that welcomes everyone, both two-legged and four. If you are sitting at our table it won't be long before a wet nose is pushed into your hand, or worse, you end up with a dog on your lap. Our guests need to be deep sleepers, or at least be able to get back to sleep quickly after being woken. This is because something as small as a mouse running in front of the kennels during the night can set a dog off barking, and one dog will start the rest off, and they can really make some racket.

Poor Dennis, did he get a baptism of fire! He arrived on a chilly day in March, and if he was looking for a hot shower after his long drive, he was disappointed. We hadn't had heating or hot water in the house for a week – the delivery tankers for the oil we rely on had a backlog of orders, thanks to the weather, and we were low on the list of priorities. Fallowlees doesn't hold the heat well or for very long, and had quickly turned damp and frigid. Dennis's shower, alas, was freezing cold. He never said a word as I apologised and vowed to make it up to him with a hearty home-cooked meal.

I had decided on slow-cooked Northumberland lamb with all the trimmings. About halfway through the meal Dennis mentioned that UK lamb tasted very different from German lamb. This seemed odd to me, but on reflection I did think it tasted, well, not like lamb at all. It turned out to be a leg of venison! I don't bother labelling the meat in our freezer as it's mainly our own. I just stick it into plastic bags and pull them out when I need them, without a thought. So Dennis didn't exactly have the best start, but at least he liked venison.

The three of us battled on with the lambing. Thanks to the weather, the ewes were thin and produced less milk than normal. However, by keeping a careful eye on everything, we were limping along OK. It was a blessing to have both Dennis and Ewan on hand. Over the years Ewan had become something of an expert himself in lambing, and I felt happy leaving him to make his own decisions.

We were about halfway through the operation, with two hundred ewes already lambed, when Mother Nature decided she wasn't done with us yet: the forecast spoke ominously of twenty-four hours of driving rain to be followed by piercingly cold clear skies and temperatures as low as minus eight. You'll need an umbrella and your warm socks, the presenter advised. Hmmm, for city dwellers that might have done the trick. The forecast was a recipe for disaster for us. Baby lambs' thin coats are easily penetrated by driving rain, ruining the ability of the fleece to protect them from the elements. And if this is followed by freezing conditions, they can quickly perish.

There was only one thing we could do to give them the best chance of survival, and that was to get all of the ewes and lambs less than a week old under cover as quickly as we could.

It's not as easy as it might sound – even a lamb a few days old can outrun a human. I buzzed around on the quad bike, trying to gather them into the trailers with the help of the dogs, while Ewan and Dennis dashed around on foot, helping me to catch them. Many of the ewes weren't keen to follow, even when their offspring were carried into the trailer, and had to be caught with man- and dogpower – not much fun for either party, but necessary. We were worked off our feet – sometimes literally. Poor Ewan and Dennis spent the odd occasion flat on their faces in the freezing slush. All the while the rain pelted down. Icy, face-numbing rain. The quad threw up a mix of mud and slush everywhere it went, splattering us and our fluffy charges. It was miserable work, all the more stressful for being pitted against the clock. The dogs did a great job. They seemed to understand the urgency of the situation and they all worked double time as we collected up those creatures who needed protection most.

Some of the slightly older lambs proved impossible to catch, and rather than make a big deal of it and stress them out, we instead herded them into the shelter of the adjacent woodland. We would have to work out how to get them out later; the immediate danger was so great that it called for desperate measures.

Every available inside space on the farm was filled to the gunwales with ewes and lambs. There were sheep in the stables, sheep in the woodshed, sheep in the coal bunker, sheep in the kennels and sheep in the trailer (top and bottom decks).

At the end of the day the rain stopped and the howling wind drove away the storm clouds to make way for one of the coldest nights of the year. The only thing for it was to head back to Fallowlees and wait till dawn to survey the damage.

It was dark when we drove home. The road was already frosted and the sky so starry you would think some of the stars were touching. A strange kind of camaraderie emerges in crises like these, where you've worked together as a team and know you've given it your best shot. It had been a wonderful show of what can be done under pressure. I was worried, but knew there was nothing more I could do.

The three of us were exhausted that night – as were the dogs – and despite my fears I slept solidly.

The drive across to Healey Mill the next morning was an anxious one. None of us knew what awaited us. My jaw was set. Dennis and Ewan knew better than to speak. I wasn't in the mood for any small talk. It was still dark when we arrived, the security lights snapping on as we drove into the yard. Stepping out into the shock of the freezing dawn air I had no idea what I was going to find. The lambs were still so young, so vulnerable. I headed first to the shed, flicking on the lights, almost too scared to look.

The sheep were all huddled tightly together. Their coats had been wet when we stored them and the night air had frosted their fleeces with a thick, crunchy rind. Even so, the lambs were clustered round their icy mothers, seeking comfort and shelter. Sure, they were cold and looked pretty miserable, but to my surprise not a single lamb in the shed had perished overnight.

I breathed a huge sigh of relief, though I wasn't finished yet.

I went next to the stables. All was quiet in the yard. Even the birds hadn't woken up yet. I opened the door of the first one with trepidation and peered inside. A ewe blinked at me in surprise. There too I found huddled family groups, bewildered at this early-morning interruption, but all living and breathing. The coal bunker, the woodshed and the trailer all yielded the same result.

There had been some new arrivals in the night, born outside, but even they were none the worse for wear. I decided that newborn lambs must surely be the hardiest little things on the planet.

It took us a good number of days to reinstate the sheep to where they belonged. We had a dodgy couple of hours when the ewe housed in the coal bunker refused to accept her black lamb, she was so sure she had given birth to a white one.

29

Shortface

Since my first foray into cattle with Penny and the Blue Greys, things had gone from strength to strength.

Penny's adoptive calves had all thrived, and when they were a year and a half old, I took three of them to the mart to be sold as breeding heifers. As much as I loved them, I knew it made sense to put the money they raised to buy native breeds more suited to the hilly landscape at Fallowlees. I couldn't, however, part with Chalky, the brilliant white one. She had become a firm favourite, who loved nothing more than having her back scratched.

The Blue Grey heifers grew up and we sold them at Newcastleton, where I had bought them as youngsters, as breeding cows for a large hill farm in Scotland.

The money from all my cattle sales was recycled into purchasing younger calves to rear, with some to spare.

Having the Blue Greys had perked up my interest in both the parent breeds, that is, the Whitebred Shorthorn and the

Galloway. I wanted to start breeding my own. Jonjo Pattinson, who had so gamely cooperated in the *Flockstars* pilot with Abbey Marie, happened to be a breeder of the cattle I wanted. Jonjo and his parents farm Hotbank Farm near Bardon Mill on Hadrian's Wall. The fifteen-hundred-acre windswept farm is famous for the sycamore tree that grows in the gap in the hill-side there, inventively named Sycamore Gap. It's the image in many a local painting, postcard and photograph.

Hotbank Farm has a long, unbroken line of white breeds going back generations. When foot-and-mouth struck in 2001, almost the entirety of their stock was slaughtered, including most of the herd of pedigree Whitebred Shorthorns. However, a twin set of heifer calves were being wintered away from the farm on some better grass at the time of the cull. They were named Lucy and Lucinda, and they were the only ones spared. Together the pair allowed Jonjo to rekindle the blood he almost lost. Since then all his cows are named Lucy or Lucinda, depending on which cow they relate to.

The first two Whitebred Shorthorn heifers we bought from Jonjo were descendants of Lucinda. One had a long face and the other a shorter face. They instantly became Longface and Shortface. It seems I am not so inventive with names either! But their official names were Lucinda 18th and Lucinda 20th.

I knew Jonjo had been very generous in letting us have such good blood as the foundation for our stock. When I offered my thanks, he brushed them off. 'Just name your first bull Jonjo,' he said.

I couldn't justify the purchase of a bull when Longface, Shortface and Penny were mated for the first time, and used artificial insemination. Longface never held to the service, and the following year I sent her to a neighbour who kindly let her run with his herd and be mated by his bull. Shortface and Penny, however, turned out in calf.

When Shortface was due to deliver, I didn't want to let on to Ewan that my knowledge of calving wasn't that extensive. I had never calved a cow on my own before; I had always been the runner: 'Run and get the gel!', 'Run and get the calving jack!', 'Run and get the vet!'

When he asked me, I bluffed it and told him it was pretty much like lambing a ewe but on a grander scale.

I also told him about the calving experience that stood out in my mind from my youth.

I was around fourteen years old, and one of the two-year-old heifers Dad had bought to fatten started to calve late one wet night. This heifer wasn't supposed to be in calf at all and hadn't had the treatment or care she would have had if we had known she was expecting. Despite my dad managing to get the calf presented correctly and most of the way out, it got stuck at the hips.

No manner of heaving would get the dangling calf out, and the heifer was getting very tired. The vet was duly called. He had no better luck. He heaved and heaved, but all to no end. By this point the calf was very much the worse for wear. The vet and Dad were busy discussing the benefits and logistics of killing the calf and taking him out in bits, when a young woman, a student who had accompanied the vet, asked if she could have a go. The vet gave a dismissive hand movement that said, 'Do whatever you want.' You could tell he didn't think much of her chances.

The veterinary student quietly slid her hand along the calf's pelvis and felt for a minute or so. At this point the vet was sorting out some wire and Dad was looking for a saw. I stood there, feeling pretty helpless. It wasn't a pleasant situation to be witnessing. I watched the student closely. I could see the look of quiet concentration on her face. Suddenly, with a little flick of her arm, the calf slipped out of the heifer and landed with a slap on the concrete floor.

We all stood there in amazement. Dad and the vet promptly dropped their chopping-up gear and set to work reviving the calf, drying him with bundles of straw, as the vet dripped kick-start drops onto his tongue.

When after fifteen minutes he hadn't rallied, we thought we ought to warm him up in the house. It was three in the morning by then, still raining outside, and we were exhausted and chilled to the bone ourselves.

Dad pulled out the bottom drawer of a large sideboard we used for storing stuff in the shed and scooped the calf into it. We carried him into the house and put him in front of the Aga while Mum poured coffee for everyone.

I had decided to make a massive tray of fudge that afternoon, and those thick chunks of cream and sugar revived us all along with the piping-hot coffee. Dad was telling the vet he didn't owe him anything because his student had done the work – he would pay her instead, he joked – but the vet failed to see the humour.

The calf was still flat as a pancake. Mum tube-fed him some powdered colostrum, after which there wasn't much more anyone could do. Besides, we all agreed that saving the heifer was the priority. The calf wasn't going to get up to much overnight, and we all stole off to bed.

We all lay in a bit longer than usual the next morning, even Dad, tired from the late-night shenanigans, and were still in bed when there came a knock at the door.

Panic ensued as Mum and Dad tumbled down the stairs. They had forgotten they had a meeting that morning. In the kitchen the calf was alive but still looking very listless and making no effort to move from his drawer.

Before opening the door to the visitor, Mum and Dad scooped up the drawer and carried it and its sorry-looking load into the office next door. They plonked the drawer on top of the spare bed that had been relegated to a corner of the office.

Disaster averted, they welcomed their guest, who happened to be none other than a farm inspector. I had surfaced by now, too, and Mum gave me a poke and indicated that I should offer him some fudge while she cleared the mugs from the night before. All was fine and dandy until the inspector wanted to see the paperwork and decided to follow Dad through to the office.

I still don't know how Dad explained the live calf on the bed, but I would have liked to have heard!

The calf went back to his mother that day and she was happy to see him again, despite the ordeal he had put her through. The heifer got a stay of execution and entered the farm's breeding herd, where she remained until she was an old lady.

In the end Ewan and I didn't have any dramatic calving stories of our own to hand down. Despite our inexperience, our first calving was painless. The calves simply arrived in the night with no need for intervention and were standing there with Shortface, happy as Larry, the next morning.

As our herd grew, so grew the need for better facilities. Good pens are required in order to move cattle easily, safely and efficiently. As I was to realise, they are better for your relationship, too. We couldn't afford a large outlay on expensive pens at the very beginning, so we made do with whatever we could pick up cheaply. As a result, no day working with the cows was ever dull.

Poor Ewan was often shouted at. 'Be more instinctive!' I would order him, which, thinking about it, is a terrible thing to say. It's like telling someone to be more artistic.

At the beginning that lack of instinctive awareness around cattle made things difficult. He hadn't grown up with animals, and sometimes stood in the way. When I'm working, I'm the first to admit I'm not the most, er, sensitive, shall we say, and can be rather sharp.

But as always, he was game and never took things too personally. And I think that over time I became more patient and started to become a better teacher, that I learned how to break down my reasoning and communicate it to Ewan.

With more cattle, it finally made sense to purchase a bull of our own. I would be delighted to say goodbye to the artificial insemination man. So off we went bull shopping to a friend of Jonjo's. A pedigree Whitebred bull duly arrived at Fallowlees, much to the appreciation of our girls. We of course named him Jonjo.

Jonjo wasn't the spectacular beefcake I was used to seeing. Whitebreds are in a different category of size and presence when compared to other breeds. This lad was built to breed a hardy hill female, and as such wasn't the muscular bodybuilder of the more common Charolais and Limousin bulls. Jonjo was also young and had a bit of growing to do, but he knew the job. He charged out of the trailer with his top lip curled and his wedding equipment dangling outrageously.

We were fond of Jonjo. He turned out to be a kind-natured lad who carried out the job we had bought him for efficiently, and didn't make a fuss at all when handled.

It wasn't only cattle we had got from our farmer friend Jonjo. Our cat, Salem, also came from Hotbank Farm. Salem is such a good hunter I don't ever need to feed him. He's our resident pest controller, yet despite his independence he's the most tolerant cat you can imagine – quite unlike the cats I grew up with – and will let puppies swarm all over him in their play, registering the intrusion with barely a flick of a superior eye.

30

World Trial

In July 2017 I found myself on the wrong side of the road, headed to the World Sheepdog Trials in Holland with my friend Lisa. Jamie's 2016 National performance had automatically qualified us for this prestigious event, which is held every three years. Here the three hundred best dogs from across thirty nations compete against each other over four days to find a world champion.

I had hoped Ewan could accompany me, but there had been no alternative other than to leave him holding the fort. It was too much to ask of anyone else, and I knew that he was the most capable person for the job. It was hard to leave him, especially as I knew how much he wanted to attend the event as well as support me. And despite knowing the farm was in such good hands, I was anxious – I always am when I'm away from home. Travelling doesn't suit me – I find it stressful at the best of times. I'm not ashamed any more to admit that I'm a bit of a homebody.

Why on earth am I going, I thought for the umpteenth time. I was finding it hard justifying the expense and time away. Plus, I didn't expect to do well. I had run on continental sheep once before and they proved to be very heavy, dull and unexciting. Not the best challenge for Jamie, a dog whose talent lay in his ability to sweet-talk even the wildest of ovines.

The first roundabout on foreign turf just about blew my brain as cars came at us from the wrong direction. Thank goodness I wasn't driving. It didn't faze Lisa, who zipped through the traffic easily and confidently. I marvelled at how quickly her mind snapped into driving on the right-hand side of the road.

Lisa is German but has a Scottish islands accent. I can't actually pinpoint the moment we met, but we have been in regular contact for years, swapping dog-training tips, talking sheep and general gossip. Lisa and her boyfriend have a large farm on the Isle of Bute. She wasn't competing, but, good friend that she was, had volunteered to be my chauffeur for the trip. She knew as well as I did that this was a big deal for me and that I could do with some friendly support.

Our drive took us on various detours around random parts of Holland, but we got to our destination, Hoogwoud, at last. On arrival we were grouped into individual nations to walk with our country's flag through the streets of the town, our dogs in tow. The whole town had come out to wave and cheer us on, at least that was how it seemed. The dogs were the stars, of course, but I got a feeling of what it must be like to be a top athlete, about to compete at the Olympic Games! As I stood under the English flag, with Jamie by my side, I had never felt prouder. In front of and behind me were some of the best handlers in the world. Jamie and I had earned our place beside them, at the highest level. This was beyond even my wildest childhood dreams.

Jamie was still a young dog, one of the youngest in the competition, so I knew the chance of a performance good enough to go through to the semi-finals was unlikely. But the opportunity for us both to gain experience at this level was invaluable.

The event began with two days of qualifying trials. Jamie and I weren't running until day two, so on the first day we had time to watch the competition. There were three fields, with forty competitors running in each. We wandered around, taking it all in.

The biggest problem I could see beyond the sluggish, unimpressionable sheep was the absolute flatness of the fields. British dogs are used to hills and valleys. Here in Holland the long – you might call it boring – flatness made the sheep difficult to see and the gates hard to judge.

We spent the whole day watching. Studying the field I would run in the following day, I saw with growing alarm that there wasn't a weed or molehill to be seen. At home we can generally use the odd thistle or rough patch of grass to help us make sure the sheep are in line for the gates. Here there was nothing but a vast expanse of uniform green grass. Time and time again I watched as the British dogs fell foul of the flatness, purely because of a lack of distance perception. The Dutch handlers, used to such conditions, were faring much better.

The sheep themselves were not the type to be easily charmed. A dog would need all of its power to push them round as they were used to capable dogs and would quickly suss out any who didn't have enough courage.

Lisa and I made the most of our time and finally got to see in the flesh a selection of dogs we had long admired from afar. We were also there with our business heads on, looking to see which pedigrees were breeding well and seeking out potential stud dogs.

Sometimes farmers give trial dogs a bad rap. They often tell me that their work dog is better than any trial dog, who only has to gather four sheep. I disagree. I think that putting a dog under pressure on a trial field is the truest test: a trial dog has to run on foreign ground, on sheep he has never met before, and to complete a course only on commands given by his master. It's the difference between driving on a road you have driven every day and racing on a rally track you've never seen.

Some of those same people are often surprised when they come to the farm and see Jamie working ewes and lambs in the pens, or nipping the nose of a cow who doesn't agree with the direction of travel. Good trial dogs make the best work dogs. And in Holland we were surrounded by the crème de la crème.

The following morning I was hit with the standard bout of nerves. This was the most demanding audience in the world, and no matter how often I told myself I had no expectations, the nerves just grew and grew. I had a banana and took a gulp of Lucozade, my now go-to snack before any big event.

We watched each run critically for mistakes I could avoid. I decided the best option was simply to let Jamie power on and use his own sheep sense as much as possible. In the UK sheep often need handling with kid gloves in order to be nudged in the right direction, but these Dutch sheep needed a tougher approach. They didn't need to be guided, they needed taking!

I was very worried about the third set of gates. They were proving exceptionally hard to judge. So many people had come unstuck trying to hit them and I didn't have a lot of hope for my own distance perception, a definite failing on my part.

It was a hot day. Time dragged on until, suddenly, we were in the competitors' box. Jamie, unperturbed by the whole event, sat quietly watching the proceedings. Here goes nothing, I thought.

Lisa mouthed a 'good luck' from the sidelines as I made my way to the post.

Jamie set off on the outrun as focused as ever. As he arrived at the top of the field my nerves suddenly disappeared. I knew we were off to a good start. I gave Jamie a 'power on' whistle, normally reserved for working tough sheep at home. He didn't need to be asked twice. He brought those sheep down the field on the end of his nose, through the first fetch gates, striding with purpose. It was magic. They turned sharply at my feet and made a perfect line for the second set of gates, bang through the middle, without a waver. The crowd quietened as the sheep were taken by their confident little black and white master straight to the notorious third set. A groan went up as the sheep skimmed the very edge of the hurdle. One ewe even stopped for a sniff on the way past. Inwardly I cursed. That would cost me points. I needed to be foot-perfect now if we were to make up for it.

I quickly collected myself from my disappointment. All was not lost. We entered the shedding ring that had been mowed into the perfect lawn. Two of the sheep wore collars, and it was Jamie's job to shed two of the three who didn't. As if by telepathy, Jamie shot into the tiniest of gaps and separated them. Next up was the pen. I didn't even need to work. Jamie had cast his spell on these sheep all right, and they didn't put up a fight. I took a deep breath as we moved to the last test, the single. A ewe wearing a collar had to be shed. I was hardly back in the ring when I saw my chance. Jamie saw it too and split her off, to the applause of the crowd.

Knowing his work was done, Jamie jumped into the large container of water that was sitting in the competitors' box. He took a good slurp, his tongue hanging out of his mouth. He was unused to the warmer climate.

My elation quickly disappeared as I came off the field to be greeted by a tearful Lisa.

'Are you OK?' I asked, concerned that something bad had happened.

'It was just so wonderful!' she said, wiping her eyes as she gave me a hug.

Relief and joy nearly set me off as well.

Points were released quickly after each run, and one look told me we had gone to the top of the leader board. Despite the slip-up at the third set of gates, the rest of the performance had been good enough to make up for it.

I had my leg pulled about the error and had to put up with several 'You should have gone to Specsavers' comments. But it was wonderful to have people congratulating me. There was also a lot of interest in Jamie's bloodlines, and enquiries about stud services.

We watched closely as the remaining competitors took to the stand. The sun was going down as the final competitor retired.

The results were announced, and Jamie and I were third in the competition. We were going through to the semi-finals. Jamie was one of the top forty dogs in the world!

My elation was short-lived. That evening I could see that Jamie wasn't himself. During the night he was sick and had violent diarrhoea. I felt my heart sink. The next morning he had improved, but with another challenging course ahead, on a new, far bigger field, I didn't feel very optimistic about our chances. I wondered what had happened to my usually healthy dog. Perhaps it was the upheaval of a long trip, I thought, or even just the heat, something we rarely worry about in Northumberland.

I took him to the trial vet who, it turned out, had been seeing similar cases all morning.

'You didn't let him drink out of the trough in the competitors' box, did you?' she asked.

'I thought that was what it was there for.'

She pointed out that the water had been sat in and drunk by almost every dog on the field. If one of them had a bug, it was the quickest way to transmit it.

I gave Jamie some hydration therapy and cursed my own stupidity before walking the course we would have to run that afternoon.

The field was bigger than the previous day's and seemed to stretch for miles into the distance. The lack of fences made it seem even bigger. Instead of the traditional fences we have in the UK, flat fields in the Netherlands are divided by enormous ditches, twelve feet across. This gives the impression of a vast, unbroken expanse that can trick the dogs.

The day felt even hotter than the previous one. I fanned myself with my catalogue.

'It's never like this in Northumberland,' I said to Lisa.

'Nor in Bute.'

The vast field was causing problems, as I'd thought it might. A lot of the British dogs were running too wide, assuming they needed to gather all the ground they could see, and even one of the Dutch dogs landed slap bang in the middle of one of the deep ditches. He was finding it difficult to get out, so his handler ran up the field, shedding clothes as he did so, to dive in and rescue him, much to the amusement of the crowd.

'I wouldn't put it past Jamie to do something similar,' I told Lisa.

'You'll be fine. I just hope you've got matching underwear on, though, just in case,' she said with a wink.

Away from all the excitement, Jamie and I took some time out before our run. He really was one of the most balanced dogs I had ever owned. He didn't seem to be fazed by anything. Although Roy had been an outstanding work dog, he could get very hot and excited away from home, and I felt he never showed himself off as well as he could. I also never quite felt that he had my back at a trial. With Jamie, however, it was almost like taking a machine out of the box each time – all new and shiny and in perfect working order – following the instructions and, hey presto, everything going according to plan. It was as if he was saying, 'OK, Mum, tell me what you want me to do and I'll do it.'

He also never fed on my nerves the same way my other dogs did, and always gave his all to any situation.

We were on.

As I walked to the post I saw to my horror that a large group of dairy cows had been let out after their afternoon milking. They currently stood next to the ditch line on the left-hand side, the side of my chosen outrun.

My mind began some frantic calculations. Should I change my plan and run right? The field seemed to lend itself to a left-hand outrun, but the cows were far more visible to a dog than the tiny specks on the horizon that were the sheep. And because of the way the ditches were set, the cows looked to be in the same field. But there was just so much opportunity for things to go wrong on the right-hand outrun, so much ground for the dog to get lost in. I had hardly seen a British dog do well on that side.

We were at the post. Jamie looked fixedly up the field to where the sheep were. Left, I thought to myself. It's got to be left. Don't change your mind now.

'Come bye,' I whispered, and he was off, bang on the right trajectory. He ate up the ground with a positive pace. He was looking good.

Then I saw him lift his head, and my heart sank. He had spotted the cows. He swerved deeply into the field, heading swiftly for the ditch near to where they were standing. I shoved my whistle in my mouth and blew a hard 'Stop'. Jamie skidded to a halt on the bank of the ditch, just as he was collecting himself for a mammoth jump.

I whistled at him to continue up the field, and he did, for a while, but once he was level with the cows he made another attempt to cross the ditch, so sure was he that I needed him to bring them to me. I cursed inwardly, knowing we had already shed a good number of points. I eventually guided him to the sheep, but I had gone to pieces in my head. I knew we were out of the running, and the run that followed fell far short of Jamie's usual standard. I could sense his own frustration, too, how he was unsettled by the commands I was giving him on what he thought was a well-thought-out outrun. His movements were sluggish, and I found I had stopped trying too. It wasn't our day.

There was lots of commiseration as I came off the field, but I couldn't feel too downhearted. It was just one of those things.

'Next time, Jamie,' I told him, looking at his sleek black head. 'Next time.'

We watched for the rest of the day to see who would make it to the final fifteen. Some dogs were well and truly showing off their mettle, while others were coming unstuck. After a while I realised Lisa wasn't watching but had her head buried in the catalogue, her phone in her hand, adding up scores on its calculator.

'You know, I wouldn't feel too sad,' she said, nudging me. 'I've checked this three times.' She showed me her adding-up. 'Unless my maths is wrong, I think England have got the team gold.'

If Lisa was correct, there it was in black and white – the total scores of each of the five team members from each nation from the qualifying trials put England on top. Jamie had actually posted the top score of the England competitors.

I rang Ewan, who was delighted but also gutted he had missed it.

'I watched Lisa's live stream,' he said. 'Jamie looked awesome! I'm so proud!'

Lisa had been spot on: England had won the team gold. And Jamie and I had played a big part in our victory. Celebrations were in order that night. Everyone at the trial (apart from the sixteen who had qualified to run in the final) let their hair down. We all sat on the grass outside the beer tents in the evening sun until long after it had dipped below the horizon. We drank the native beer, ate bratwurst and talked pedigrees and training. It turned out that Dutch beer is very strong and before long we were all very merry. All the different nations mixed happily together, and I came away with loads of new friends.

'To the dogs!' we toasted, and raised our glasses.

The next day found Lisa and me groggily waking at dawn in a tent with the mother of all hangovers. That sweet Dutch beer had a hell of an afterkick.

We nursed our sore heads with coffee in the trial marquee and fed our cooked breakfast to Jamie, who was back to his chipper self and delighting in all the praise he was receiving. I felt my cheeks flush as a memory came back from the night before, around beer number five, when I had declared him the best dog in the world.

'Did I really say that?' I groaned to Lisa. I might think these things myself but I am usually very modest when I'm with other people.

Nothing could dampen our spirits as we watched the final.

Once again, the course was huge, the dog expected to run eight hundred yards for the first packet of sheep and a further eight hundred yards for the second. It was a spectacular feat for a dog, even a champion.

Sixteen worthy competitors took to the post to compete. We watched each run on tenterhooks. Some dogs made small errors, some couldn't even find the sheep, and yet one more dog took a bath. But when Jaran Knive and Gin from Norway finished their run, we all knew they couldn't be beaten.

Disappointingly, we couldn't stay for the ceremony as our boat was sailing that night, so I didn't have the pleasure of being presented with the gold medal. However, we had our own presentation of the medals at the National later that year. I was very proud to be part of the England team. It had taken me thirty-one years to get to this point, and I felt that I had finally arrived. If I did nothing else, no one could take this away from me. I had it for ever.

I owed it all to an unassuming little black and white dog.

31

Nessie

My birthday is in January, not exactly the best month of the year to celebrate. It fell on a Friday in 2018, and Ewan and I went away for the weekend to stay with Lisa and Ian on the Isle of Bute. My long-suffering sister Elizabeth held the Fallowlees fort.

It was a few months since the eventful World Trials, and I was looking forward to reliving that time with Lisa. She had bred me a cracking little bitch, and we were going to collect her and have a good old chinwag at the same time. Yes, another dog for the pack. And it never gets any less exciting. Every dog is different, and you're always hoping that the latest addition will have that little bit extra – that he or she might turn out to be another Roy or Jamie.

Bute lies off the west coast of Scotland, in the Firth of Clyde. Ian and his father run a sheep and cattle farm on the west of the island. Bute is a wonderful place to unwind, a paradise for walkers, anglers and anyone who appreciates the great outdoors.

Lisa and Ian rent out the adjoining part of their nineteenth-century farmhouse as self-catering holiday accommodation.

It's hard to believe as you watch Lisa with her dogs that she used to be a book-keeper in her home town of Frankfurt. She's a classic example of the person who quits the city for a new rural life. She met Ian when she moved to Bute after a year learning the ropes on a farm in the Borders. Like mine, her pack of dogs has grown rapidly over the years.

'She does understand English, doesn't she?' I asked Lisa jokingly, as I admired Nessie, my pretty new pup.

Lisa laughed. Her main dog, Harvey, who was born in Germany, was famous for understanding commands in both German and English.

A few minutes' walk from the farm is the secluded Scalpsie Bay, with views to the Isle of Arran. Lisa, Ewan and I walked the dogs along this beach, watching the seals lazing on the rocks. Lisa said if you were lucky you could sometimes see porpoises and basking sharks in the water.

Today Lisa pointed to a spot on the edge of the beach where she said she was going to put a glamping pod.

'It's actually going to be a shepherd's hut, small, but with all mod cons.'

'Oooh, what a brilliant idea! I bet you'll get loads of visitors.'

'I hope so. Glamping is really popular these days.' She added, 'You don't fancy doing something like that at Fallowlees?'

'With the midges? People would need danger money!'

'Well, with your cooking you certainly couldn't do bed and breakfast,' she joked.

'Oi, less of that, you cheeky cow!' I laughed. Lisa is famously blunt, but we are good enough friends to be able to say what we want to each other.

The evening before we were due to return home, at the end of what had been a wild and windy January day, Ewan asked if I would like to go for a walk down to the bay. He might have had a special twinkle in his eye, but I didn't notice.

I pulled a face.

'You're joking, Ewan. Have you seen outside? Can't we just stay in and have a glass of wine?'

I spend enough time out and about in the worst of the weather, thanks to my work, so felt no need to subject myself to a Scottish island gale on a well-earned day off. Especially when the alternative was a cosy farmhouse and a drink with friends.

Ewan just shrugged, and said something about it being our last night.

I caught his eye as we sipped our gin and tonics half an hour later. I thought he knew me better than to drag me off for some exercise, however well intentioned. But never mind; he looked to be in a good mood as he laughed with our hosts.

One of the nice things about leaving Fallowlees – whether for a few hours, a day, or longer – is the welcome I receive on coming home. The dogs are always delighted to see me. The sight of their wiggling, enthusiastic bodies, anxious for their share of my attention, makes everything seem worthwhile.

I could always be sure of a welcome from Coquet too.

Coquet was now a fully grown horse, and he was

magnificent. He was every bit the racehorse, and as full of himself as ever. I had taken our friend Peter up on the offer he had made us all those years ago when he helped us with our haymaking, and loaded Coquet off for a couple of months' training at a yard in Hexham when he was old enough. Peter had done a great job with him, and he paid me the compliment of telling me that Coquet had been one of his top five nicest horses to break in.

Tramp and Strawberry had left me some time ago. They had flourished in the years since their arrival as scraggy ponies, making an incredible transformation into rather good-looking specimens. As they were really only suitable for children to ride, I felt that they could have more useful lives elsewhere and, with a heavy heart, set about finding them new homes. Strawberry's striking looks immediately attracted the attentions of a friend, who snapped her up for her daughter. As she lives nearby in Rothbury, I often see Strawberry grazing in her field when I drive through the village.

Tramp had turned into something quite special. He was a proper athlete, like a racehorse in miniature. He was taken on by another friend who had also had a Border collie from me, and from there he was broken in and turned into a remarkable show-jumping pony. Last time I enquired he had been sold for a large amount of money to an excellent show-jumping yard. I was so pleased that someone was helping him realise his potential.

So Coquet was the only horse at Fallowlees now. He had been to my sister's in Kelso to get an education in traffic, before coming back to Fallowlees for the winter.

Mr Tumnus – he who had never left Delphi alone – didn't give a hoot about horses any more. He must have been quite an age by now, but he was still as sprightly as ever, and still making a nuisance of himself eating things he shouldn't.

PART FOUR

Changes

32

The Ring

I was so lucky to have a man like Ewan by my side. He always threw himself into whatever work needed doing. I think he loved farming as much as I did. I wondered if it acted as an antidote to his work as a firefighter. I encouraged him to talk about some of the difficult days he had, rather than bottle up his feelings, and he said that it helped him to do that. I knew his job could be tough; I knew he saw things a lot of people should never have to. I sometimes pull his leg about firefighters sitting around watching TV and drinking tea, but in reality I know that few people could do what he and his colleagues do. Every call-out could mean risking their own lives. Ewan never wanted to talk about the worst things that happened, and on the days when he arrived back at the farm exhausted and ill-tempered, not like his usual self, I knew not to pry too much. Though I couldn't help asking, 'Saved any lives today?' as I was always massively curious to know.

A few days after our return from Bute, he had got in from

work and gone to get changed and came back into the kitchen where I was preparing tea. I was chopping an avocado when I wondered what he was doing on the floor beside me.

I saw he had got down on one knee.

'Emma, will you marry me?' he asked.

I didn't hesitate. 'Yes!' I cried out, throwing my arms around him – after I had put down the knife, of course.

That was when I learned I had scuppered his plans for a more romantic proposal of marriage on the beach at sunset while we were in Bute.

'Remember our last night there, and how you refused to come for a walk with me? I'd tried to get you to myself all weekend, but with you and Lisa glued to each other's sides for most of the time, I didn't get a chance. In fact, I've been carrying the ring around for almost a month, waiting for an opportunity.'

He presented me with a French antique emerald and diamond white gold ring. My heart soared when I saw it. I couldn't have chosen a better one myself. It was beautiful.

'So, just think, you could have told people we got engaged on a Scottish island rather than at your kitchen table.'

I laughingly apologised. But somehow it seemed more appropriate that it had happened here. Fallowlees had been the stage for so many great things for us both that it just felt right. I wondered if any other proposals had taken place under its ancient roof, or if a young suitor had stood nervously in the same spot as Ewan to ask permission of the farmer to marry his daughter. I suspected we were merely the latest in a long line.

I couldn't wait to tell my family. In fact, I think I was straight on the phone to my parents, followed by my sisters.

My parents were delighted, as I'd expected them to be.

'About time too,' said Dad. 'I hope the wedding isn't going to cost me a fortune.'

'Let us know how we can help,' said Mum. 'What lovely news!'

33

Uncle Toffa

Ewan and I planned to get married in August 2018. We couldn't bring ourselves to spend an outlandish amount of money on a wedding; money was hard-won and we had so many more pressing things to buy. Dad was very generous and gave us a contribution for the party we wanted to hold. We hummed and hawed and finally came up with the idea of concreting the floor of the cattle shed so we could host the reception there. That way we could reap the benefits of the work for years to come.

We worked all summer getting ready for the party. It became quite a stressful affair, and I wondered if we had bitten off more than we could chew. We wanted Fallowlees to look her best. Many of our friends had never actually been on the farm and we didn't want them to be disappointed.

We fenced and we walled, we cleared and we cleaned and we scrubbed, we weeded and we sprayed. We organised the concrete and laid it ourselves. That was before all the other things you need to consider for hosting a wedding reception: tables and chairs to hire, food and drink to order, toilets, car parking. I spent a lot of time writing lists and crossing things off them, only to start another list with yet more jobs on it.

I chose the very first dress I tried on, white lace and off the shoulder. It was from a bridal warehouse and had a reasonable price tag, which was just as well given the punishment it would get on the day.

We decided to put in a proper drainage system for the shed. Until that point it had flooded every year. We figured that while we had the machinery and labour to do the concreting, we might as well take advantage and get some new ditches dug. We got my uncle Toffa in to help us with his digger.

Toffa (short for Christopher) is my dad's brother and has been there for me throughout my life. During my college days I would work weekends on his farm with my dog Bill to earn my beer money, and he often came to lend a hand at Fallowlees.

Toffa is well known throughout the farming community. He's the hardest worker you could meet, but he is also notorious for having nine lives.

One day when Dad and Toffa were young boys, their father, my late Grandpa Len, bought a nail gun from a travelling salesman. The salesman proudly proclaimed that it had enough power to shoot a nail into a steel girder. My dad, being of curious mind, decided to put this to the test one day. He loaded the biggest cartridge he could find into the nail gun and placed its nose against a steel girder in the cattle shed. A split second after he pulled the trigger, he heard a loud shout from Toffa, who had just walked into the shed. The gun had not only blown the nail into the girder, it had punched the nail all the way through, and it had flown across the shed, grazing Toffa's ear in its flight. Just a few millimetres and that could have been the end of him!

When Toffa was a young man he spent his summers as a shearer, travelling to farms all over the country, shearing hundreds of sheep in a day. One blisteringly hot day he was hard at work outside. All of the shearers had stripped off in the heat. Toffa stopped briefly for a drink and took a swig from a bottle lying on a wall next to the shearing trailer. Though it looked like lemonade and was in a lemonade bottle, he quickly realised it wasn't lemonade and spat it out, caught his next sheep and continued his work.

His sister, my auntie Elspeth, who was rolling wool for them, sniffed the contents of the bottle and realised Toffa had just drunk cattle pour-on. This is a noxious and deadly poison poured onto the backs of cattle to kill external parasites.

Alarmed, she tried to get Toffa to stop shearing so that she could take him to hospital. He brushed her concerns off, telling her he was fine. When he started to sway on the trailer, she called an ambulance.

Toffa's heart stopped three times on the way to hospital. He was brought back to life each time by the skills of the ambulance crew. It was a miracle he survived – and a lesson in labelling medicines.

Years later, on a wet winter's day, he was working alone, feeding the cattle in the sheds on his farm near Hexham. He was towing a forage box with a tractor. A forage box has a conveyor belt that dispenses silage in an even amount in front of the cattle barriers as the tractor drives along. The forage box became blocked and Toffa jumped off in his cumbersome wet-weather gear to switch the power over.

The power take-off on the rear of the tractor (known as the PTO) is the means by which power is transmitted from the running engine to another machine. It was spinning at one thousand rotations a minute when it caught hold of some of Toffa's loose clothing.

He was very nearly skinned alive as the PTO chewed off every piece of clothing he was wearing and a fair amount of his skin, and flipped him over, before sheer strength and determination helped him to wrench himself free. Another lucky escape.

Toffa had lived to tell the tale after one too many near misses and, generous with his time as ever, came along to lend us a hand a couple of weeks before the wedding. We left him with his excavator, doing some exploratory digging, while we got on with the hundred and one other tasks that still needed doing. He was looking for a field drain in the front field so that he could direct the guttered rainwater from the shed roof into it.

A few hours later he stumbled into the kitchen, white as a sheet – he had dug through the armoured electric cable from the windmill to our batteries.

'No guard tape,' he muttered, lighting a fag. 'Nearly blew me sky-high.'

Another life gone!

34

Mushrooms

In the weeks leading up to the wedding, we had a bumper crop of field mushrooms on the farm. Fresh mushrooms are just the best. They have pink ribs underneath instead of the brown ones on the mushrooms you find in supermarkets, and they are made even more delicious by being organic, home-grown and free. I have always loved mushrooms, and it was wonderful to have this bountiful crop on our doorstep, a true gift from nature. For a fortnight they formed the main part of our diet. We ate them on toast, we fried them, we made omelettes and risottos. They were unreal.

I was still trying to do a thousand different things to get ready. This was probably why most people chose to hold their wedding parties in hotels, I mused. So much of the planning was taken care of for you. I wasn't sure if it was the stress or too many mushrooms that started to give me a gippy tummy. I guessed it was both. I couldn't do anything about the wedding, but decided I had better cut down on my mushroom consumption. It seemed to help.

Just a few days before the wedding, I trailered a batch of store lambs to the auction at Hexham Mart. When I got out of the pickup I felt sick. It was a few days now since I'd overindulged in mushrooms, and though I'm a notoriously bad passenger, I rarely get carsick as a driver. I sat back down for a while, the window wound down, breathing in some fresh air. I hoped I wasn't coming down with something, with the big day so close.

The lambs were drawn a late ballot, so I had time to walk across the road to Tesco's. Something else was niggling me, too.

I bought a pregnancy test in the supermarket and took it back to the mart. I was all alone in the ladies' toilets when the second blue line appeared, confirming my suspicions. Apparently taking two contraceptive pills when you miss a day is not effective birth control.

The result knocked me sideways.

I remember standing next to my lambs, about to run them up for sale, and a farmer friend chatting about his children.

After hearing a long story revolving around childish misbehaviour, he sighed contentedly. 'Couldn't be without them, though.'

Hmmm, I thought to myself. He hadn't exactly sold parenthood to me.

'Kids not on your agenda?' he asked.

I swallowed. I'd been asked this question many times, and was so used to the reply I always gave that the words just trotted off my tongue, same as usual.

'Nope, not for me. I'll just keep popping those little pills!' Then I added, 'I'm really not a maternal kind of person.'

I said it with a smile, but inwardly I shrank. Kids hadn't been part of my plan. Ewan had come pre-packaged with two lovely children. I certainly didn't feel any pressure from him or anyone to have a baby. My view of the future was, well, just more of the present: me and Ewan and a whole load of dogs and sheep. I'd never thought beyond that.

I was a bit anxious about telling Ewan. I knew he loved kids and adored his own. We had great fun with them when they came to visit the farm. They particularly loved being pulled by the dogs on their sledges in the winter snow. (Ewan's mum was a fan of our dog rig, too!) But we hadn't been planning to start a family of our own.

Ewan found me in tears in the kitchen when he got home from work later. He put his arms around me. I could see he was worried as I'm not usually a crier. I managed to tell him the news.

'But that's wonderful! What are you upset for?'

'I don't know. It's a shock, I suppose.'

'A lovely shock!'

'It'll be just my luck if it's due at lambing time.' I managed to laugh as I wiped away my tears.

Nothing was going to dampen Ewan's mood.

'I'll take my holiday when it's due and I'm sure both our mums will be more than happy to help out. When can we tell them? They're going to be thrilled! Is it too soon?'

Ewan was buzzing as we prepared our meal, and it helped to lift my mood too. We'd manage. Of course we would. But it was a big piece of news for me to absorb. Our future had just changed radically.

But first of all, we had a wedding to celebrate. Most of the jobs had been crossed off the list. The concrete flooring was finished, and Uncle Toffa had dug our ditches – and lived to tell the tale. We were all set.

35

The Dress

The day of the wedding was also Ewan's fortieth birthday – and the last fine day of the summer.

We were married in the registry office in Kelso, which is located in the town hall. Ewan, being better travelled than me, commented that the pretty building with a clock tower and flags flying, centred within the town's cobbled square, is just like a *mairie*, lifted straight from a French town.

I walked into the registry office, all nerves and excitement, on my dad's arm. I could see mine and Ewan's entire families there, waiting expectantly. Ewan was no doubt expecting to be blown away by the sight of me. I might have known I would cock it up. Somehow I managed to snag my beautiful dress on the door as I went in. It brought me up short and tore a great hole in the lace down the side. Well, start as you mean to go on, I thought, as Dad unhooked me from the door to much laughter from the room. I might have ruined the supposed grand entrance, but the rest of the ceremony went without a hitch – well, apart from Uncle Toffa and Granny Gray missing it completely! They arrived a wee bit late and the registrar had locked the door.

We had a small reception back at my parents' house for close family. Mum had gone to a lot of trouble to make sure the garden and house were looking their best, and it was hard not to overindulge in the delicious spread she had laid out for us.

Still in our wedding finery – Ewan in his kilt, me in my dress – we headed back to Fallowlees to get the party started. We stopped at the abandoned farmstead of Redpath on the way up the track. There on the boarded-up front door we drew a big red love heart and an arrow with sheep-marker spray to point the way for our guests.

Time flew as we raced to make final preparations before our guests arrived. The photos were taken in the front field with the dogs and sheep, and the bottom of my dress got covered in all the usual muck you find in a field full of sheep.

We had the shed blinged out with chandeliers, and our families had helped us decorate it with wild flowers and heather. We had borrowed chairs and tables from the local village hall in Elsdon. The Bird and Bush, our local pub, had been roped in to run a one-pound bar and we had a disco, a bucking bronco and a hog roast. We borrowed a couple of huge firepits from our shearer and built a giant bonfire in the field behind the house with the old wood from all our tidying. With strings of lights to guide the way from the car park paddock and all along the house, as darkness fell, Fallowlees had never looked more enchanting.

The bucking bronco was a big draw at the start of the evening.

'Come on, Emma,' said my sister Elizabeth. 'You're not getting out of this.'

'But I've got my dress on!' I protested.

She wouldn't hear of it. It was no wonder – after the beating that dress had been receiving all day – that I was back in jeans and a shirt by 10 p.m., the dress relegated for ever.

Elizabeth wanted to get Ewan on the bronco, too, but he said that as he was in his kilt, it was best he gave no one a fright.

'Why is no one dancing?' I asked Ewan as the disco got going.

'Haven't you been to a wedding before? You two are supposed to kick it off!' said Caroline. 'What have you chosen for your first dance?'

'Umm, I haven't even thought about it. What about you, Ewan?'

Neither of us is a gifted dancer, and we just wanted something to carry on the relaxed vibe. We opted for 'Sweet Home Alabama', and were soon surrounded by our guests on the dance floor.

It was wonderful to have all our nearest and dearest together in the place that had been my mainstay over the past years. I had grown up here. I had arrived as a naive twenty-three-year-old and I was now thirty-two. Not that I felt any different on the inside.

I watched everyone enjoying themselves in the beautiful late-summer evening. The grey and violet clouds slowly gave way to a sky of purply-black. People were happily drunk, aided no doubt by the one-pound bar. Even the bar staff joined in the party.

I saw Ewan giving someone a big hug. He called me over and introduced me to Timmy, the friend whose life he'd saved in the Alps, and his partner, Whitney.

'It's wonderful to meet you both. And what a long way you've come,' I said, knowing that Timmy lived in south London.

'I wouldn't have missed it for the world,' he replied.

Timmy told us about his business, The Mindful Baker, and it was wonderful to know he had made such a satisfying life for himself, one that drew on his terrible experience and used it in a positive way with his love of baking.

I spotted Archie talking farming with my dad, and Lisa swapping dog stories with some of the other triallists. Well, that's what happens when your job is also your passion. We are fortunate people. I managed to drag Archie away and coax him onto the dance floor.

'There's still life in you yet, Archie!' I exclaimed, as we strutted our stuff to Sister Sledge's 'He's The Greatest Dancer'.

'Hmmm, try telling that to my old bones in the morning.'

Lots of our friends were camping around the farm, so didn't have to stay sober or leave the party early. Many of them were still throwing logs onto the firepits at three in the morning.

I took some of my friends to their accommodation. Chartners, another of the abandoned farmhouses in the forest, had recently been repurposed as a bunkhouse, often used by Scout groups, and we had booked it for the weekend.

'You can't drive, Emma, you're mortal!' one friend told me, looking aghast as I hopped into the driver's seat.

'It's OK,' I told them. 'I'm feeling quite sober.'

Little did they know I had been drinking orange juice all night! Ewan and I had only told our families about the baby, figuring that as I was just a few weeks pregnant, it was too early to spread the news more widely.

I made my way to bed, with Jamie by my side, at 3 a.m., exhausted but content. Ewan stumbled in beside me three hours later.

We both agreed it had been a perfect wedding.

36

Brenna

'Well, Emma Gray, you're a married woman at last!'

Archie and I were at a trial. After swearing he'd never trial again when he lost Dale, it was great to see him back. He and Hoggy made a good team.

'Surprising, isn't it? I thought I was going to be single for ever at one point.'

'Well, I seem to remember you were pretty fussy when it came to men.'

'Quite right, too. I might have been pushing my husband round in a wheelchair by now if I'd gone for one of your choices, Archie.'

We both had a chuckle as we looked back on those days. Not so long ago, really, but in other ways, they felt like half a lifetime ago.

'Yeah, you've got a good one in Ewan. Mind, I can see some marital discord when he starts beating you.' He nodded towards my new husband, who was about to take to the post with Dennis.

'Healthy competition, Archie.'

After the World Trials, I felt I had discovered how to train dogs well. As I had hoped when I first set eyes on it, Healey Mill had proved to be the perfect training ground. It had the right mix of terrain in order to get the dogs used to varied landscapes. By the autumn of 2018, a year after the World Trials, I had three promising young dogs: Nessie, the dog I collected from Lisa on Bute; Brenna, a talented tricolour who was the daughter of Aled Owen's Cap, an International Supreme Champion; and Joff, the offspring from Jamie's mating with my friend's bitch after the English Nursery Final.

To be honest, Joff was the one I really had high hopes for – he wasn't a sweet-talker, like Jamie, but he was tougher-natured and had power to burn. At the end of the season Joff was winning the Northumberland Nursery League, closely followed by Brenna. Nessie was not far behind.

The final trial in the Northumberland winter nursery series was held on the military ranges of Rochester, a steep rush-covered field, and not one for the faint-hearted.

I had a blinding run with Nessie. She was foot-perfect, the sheep loved her and she was in total control. It was one of those runs that make the crowd fall silent. The sheep walked into the pen as if they were pet lambs, not straight-off-the-hill mountain sheep. I released them and was just lining them up to take the shed when the judge appeared beside me.

'Sorry, Emma, but you are disqualified,' he said.

I dropped my stick in shock. 'Why?'

'You didn't close the gate properly when you penned.'

'Oh!' I was stunned. 'Can I just re-pen them and try again?'

'No, sorry,' he said, and walked to his car.

There was nothing to do but walk my sheep off the course. Everyone watching was wondering what on earth had happened. I was close to tears, mostly born of frustration. It seemed that although I had swung the gate round, it hadn't touched the clashing post, which meant disqualification.

I still had Joff and Brenna to run. I was careful not to make the same mistake again. Brenna went on to win the trial.

The championship trial was held directly after, open only to those dogs who had won one of the nursery trials. This was a bigger challenge, and included a shed and a single. The single is the most difficult task to accomplish with a dog, who has to separate a single sheep from the others without any assistance from the handler. Sheep are flock animals, and it is their natural instinct to want to stay together, so to persuade one of them to break away from the security of her companions is a big ask for a dog, especially a young one.

Nessie was first up, and another foot-perfect run left no doubt in anyone's mind that she had won the championship. On penning, I pushed the gate hard against the clashing post and held it there, adding the flourish of a little showman's bow, to the cheers and laughter of the crowd.

Afterwards people asked me if I was sore about the disqualification for the pen. Of course I felt hard done by at the time, I can't lie, but in reality it was a valuable lesson, and better to happen there on a nursery field than at a national or international competition. No, in the end, the truth was I was grateful for it.

The result that day meant I qualified for the English Nursery Final the following February, with both Brenna and Joff.

I was, however, in a quandary. I had a lot of dogs now and, realistically, I knew I couldn't keep them all. It had been my plan, back when I was recuperating from my broken back, that I would earn part of my living from the sale of top-quality sheep-dogs, not that I would keep every dog I spent time training for myself. I knew I needed to be hard-nosed about this. I also had a stack of bills to pay – not that that was anything new.

I had to sell one of the three. But which one? All three were talented. Joff, being the son of Jamie, my star, was now the apple of my eye. I felt particularly close to him because of that link with Jamie, who was still my number one dog. Nessie, meanwhile, was proving to be a natural – she had a talent I wanted to develop further.

I realised it had to be Brenna, and following her success I had had a great deal of interest in her from abroad. I had no idea how to value her, and so I entered her in the Skipton auction.

Skipton is a world-renowned auction for working sheep-dogs. It hosts three sales a year, and there, the best – and occasionally the worst – sheepdogs are sold. I had never sold a dog at auction before and the thought terrified me. The Friday of the auction also happened to be the weekend of the 2019 Nursery Final that I was supposed to be attending with both Brenna and Joff. Could I do both?

I entered Brenna in the auction with the proviso of still being able to run her at the final. It would perhaps dent her value, but my place at the final had been hard-won and I didn't want to give it up.

Ewan and I travelled to Skipton with the dogs. I was feeling pretty uncomfortable. The first scan had revealed that the baby was due in early April – yep, lambing time. It could hardly be worse timing for a shepherdess. Large and round with persistent indigestion, I now had blistering nerves to contend with too.

I had seen dogs I thought quite good flop badly at sales like this, but I had seen others soar, so I knew I could take nothing for granted. I had never been out on the sales field before and was anxious about meeting such a critical audience.

I drew great comfort from having Ewan with me. He reminded me that if we weren't happy with the price, we could always take Brenna home again. It was a consoling thought, but we both knew that with a baby on the way and the farm racking up the usual bills, we needed the money.

Our lot number came round in the early afternoon and I took to the field for what I guessed would be the last time as Brenna's owner. It's customary to put a dog being sold as a working dog through his or her paces at a sale like this. Brenna didn't let me down – she ran as she always ran, with great flair and power, the sheep obeying her will. While Brenna was running, the auction was taking place behind us. I was concentrating so much on her performance, I didn't hear how things were panning out. Or perhaps I had tuned everything out deliberately.

Job accomplished, I whistled Brenna to me and we walked down the slope towards the auctioneer. It became clear that the bidding was winding down.

'Fourteen thousand – are we done?' the auctioneer was saying. 'Last chance, fourteen thousand!'

Fourteen thousand? Had I heard right?

'Selling now! Fourteen thousand!' he shouted to the collected crowd.

He glanced at me, checking it was OK to sell. My gobsmacked face must have told him it was, and the hammer fell. The crowd burst into spontaneous applause as we walked out of the field to massive congratulations. At fourteen thousand guineas, Brenna had just broken the centre's record price for a bitch. (Sheepdogs are traditionally sold in guineas, a pound and a shilling, so one pound and five pence in today's money.)

Ewan was there waiting, pride in his eyes. We had hit the big time! I felt the baby do a flip inside me. Everyone was buzzing. I could almost feel electricity in the air.

Brenna had been sold to an American, Pamela Helton, who I knew from our communications on Facebook. She was a university professor who did trialling as a hobby. Brenna was going to live with her in Maryland, and eat grilled chicken, as well as be her primary work and trial dog. I was delighted for both of them. It was a brilliant scenario.

But we had little time to reflect, because on the Sunday both Brenna and Joff were competing for Northumberland in the All England Nursery Final in Westmorland.

I knew there was a lot of pressure on me. The last time I had run at a nursery final had been three years earlier in 2016, with Jamie, Joff's father, and he had won the competition. And after Skipton people were expecting great things of me and my dogs. I had a lot to live up to. Equally, I knew that there would be a contingent of people who would revel in my misfortune should a fourteen-thousand-guinea dog make a fool of us both.

The final was being live-streamed to the world on social media. The thought of it had been making me feel sick for days. I hadn't slept properly for the last week for worrying about the weekend, and it was starting to show. And my heartburn was even worse. The only thing I was really consuming was Gaviscon, swigged straight from the bottle. Hardly nutritional.

The final was one of the biggest held, its location and the dawn of a fine day meaning that cars were wall to wall and parking spaces at a premium.

The field itself was lovely, not massive, but tricky in its own way. The sheep were Mules, my favourite.

The stakes were high when I stepped out late morning to take to the post with Brenna. She ran like fourteen thousand guineas should, flexible and responsive, a Ferrari. A wide turn at the last set of gates and tricky sheep in the shedding ring took us out of the running for one of the top slots, but it had been a smartly completed run, one that ensured her reputation.

It was well into the afternoon before Joff and I had our turn. The time wore on terribly slowly for a heavily pregnant woman awaiting her fate. Performances varied enormously; some were outstanding, and in other cases, it was just too much for the dog. Often young dogs can feel the sense of occasion and the pressure makes them behave erratically. All I could hope was that Joff had inherited his father's ability to pull a performance out of the bag, despite the pressure I knew I was inadvertently applying.

I waited beside the judge's box with Ewan, fluttering with jangly nerves. Joff was just, unconcernedly, cocking his leg on the steps when I felt a terrible gripping in my stomach.

I clutched Ewan.

'What's the matter? Are you OK?' he asked, looking at me with concern.

I put my other hand on my stomach. 'Fine.' I paused. 'It was just a twinge.'

'Christ, don't have the bloody baby here!' said Ewan, panic in his eyes, while the course director, standing beside us, visibly blanched.

Whether it was nerves or the baby moving, I don't know. It wasn't the best time for it to happen, that was certain, and now our names were being called. Nothing for it but to concentrate on why we were here and walk to the post.

At a word, Joff snapped into work mode. What followed was a real cracker of a run; he showed everyone what I had known all along – that he was a class act and had a bright future. The sheep clearly had ideas of their own as the little party came trundling towards me and the first set of gates, but every time they veered off course Joff brought them back into line. He knew how to get them where he wanted while always keeping a respectful distance. He was a natural, like his dad. He brought them behind me, then through further sets of gates, smoothly and efficiently. Some of the sheep made it clear they would rather sit around munching on the grass, but Joff moved them on swiftly. Stay focused, I said to myself, as the five sturdy creatures trotted into the shedding ring. When he had separated two from the other three, easy as pie, I was happy that it couldn't have gone much better. Soon after that all five sheep were safely penned.

I trotted off the field to Ewan with a big smile on my face.

'That was great!' he said.

Because we had run so close to the end of the day, we didn't have many more competitors to watch before the trial concluded. After that, we could only wait, as we had done three years before with Jamie, for the judge's decision. As we all gathered round the judge's box, I was hopeful, yet also trying not to hope too much. Ewan was by my side and the next generation tucked up in my stomach. I wondered briefly if our child would be doing the same thing in twenty-odd years' time.

Then the results were announced. First prize and English Nursery Champion, Emma Gray and Joff. Ewan hugged me; we had done it!

It was one of the most remarkable weekends of my life. And I could be honest now and admit that Joff was the favourite of my young dogs. He had his faults, for sure, but I felt that his will to please would help us overcome anything.

The money from Brenna was unexpected but very welcome. It burnt a hole in my pocket and I quickly invested part of it in some Suffolk cross gimmers and one-crop ewes. These heavy-boned lowland ewes were due to lamb around the same time as our main flock, which was also the same day our baby was due. Perfect, I thought, and snapped them up. They were delivered a week later.

Ewan had taken time off work to do the lambing. I hoped I wouldn't be out of action for very long. Having seen so many animals in labour, I felt that it wasn't a big deal, and planned to be at his side as soon as I could make it after my own delivery. It was all part of nature, wasn't it? How hard could it be?

The Suffolks were a problem almost immediately. A few weeks after arrival, some started to abort, and the foetuses didn't have white faces as expected, and promised by the seller, but were horned and black-faced. Clearly the farmer had an errant Blackie tup somewhere.

But this changed things for us, too. Some types of abortion in sheep can lead to complications or miscarriage for a pregnant woman. It just wasn't worth the risk.

I handed the sheep over to Ewan. I was going to have to sit this one out.

37

Roy

Not long after the Nursery Final, I realised that Roy was nearing the end of his life. Alfie had passed away a couple of years earlier, and at the age of twelve, Roy was an old man for a Border collie. He had been retired to the kitchen for a few years now, and did little more than have an occasional potter outside. In the middle of the night he would suddenly start woofing at nothing. He also started climbing on the kitchen table and cocking his leg in the house, something he had never done in his youth. I think he had developed some form of dementia. I let him get away with murder – he was, after all, the one who had been with me through it all – the only dog I still had who had been by my side when I took on Fallowlees. It was hard to watch that brainy dog deteriorate.

A previously slow-growing tumour on his spine picked up pace in the early part of 2019, and by March I realised Roy's time had come. His quality of life had gone downhill steadily, and I wasn't going to wait until he was in pain. Sheepdogs are the most stoic of creatures, and I knew the dullness in his eyes meant it was time to let him go.

The vet put him down quietly in his basket in front of the radiator in the kitchen. It was very peaceful. Feeling a friend who has been one of the constants in your life go limp and heavy in your arms is an agonising experience. We had been all over the country together, from Devon in the south of England to Thurso in the north of Scotland; he had partnered me during long hours of lambing and shared the fun and excitement of a trial field. He won me the Northumberland League and my first team cap. He could also be hard to hold, and sometimes made me look a fool as he ran as strongly as a train, with a similar stopping distance.

I had so many memories of our time together, but my favourite one remains one evening at Gilsland Agricultural Show in Cumbria.

I had carried on to Gilsland after attending Alston Sheepdog Trials. I was full of beans and enthusiasm as Roy had come second in the trial that day. I had to go into the beer tent to try to drag my boyfriend Dan from the bar to go home. One thing of course led to another (show bars have that tendency), and before I knew it, I was also sinking a drink or two. Everyone was quite well oiled, and I found myself taking part in the age-old debate about trial dogs versus work dogs with a drunken farmer. He argued that a fancy trial dog couldn't do his farm work – he needed a rough-and-ready type of dog; I argued any trial dog worth its salt was a good work dog first and foremost.

It turned out that this farmer owned the land just across the road from the show field.

'Let's see your dog gather that, then,' he challenged, waving at the wide, steep slope that was filled with ewes and lambs grazing happily.

Tipsy as I was, I was determined to prove my point and collected Roy from the car. The drink that had fuelled my bravado in the bar made my legs wobble out in the open air. I hopped the fence with Roy, crossed the road and bent the wires to let him in.

A hiss, and he was off.

Meanwhile a crowd had gathered. Roy made his way neatly round the field, before, to my horror, disappearing through the fence on the skyline and out of sight into the field beyond. I took a step backwards in surprise – this wasn't like Roy – and fell into the ditch behind me, much to everyone's merriment. The alcohol had well and truly gone to my head. Bugger, I thought, as I stood up, dripping, provoking more hilarity from my audience. I prepared to blow my recall whistle, aware that not only had Roy shown me up, but I had also shown myself up, when four ewes and lambs came pinging through the fence, the very one Roy had shot through, hotly pursued by one diligent little black dog. Roy continued to gather the escapees and unite them with the rest of the flock, which he then brought in their entirety neatly to my feet.

After I'd called him off, the farmer grinned as he patted a panting Roy.

'Well I never! You've proved me wrong.' He shook his head. 'I guess trial dogs can be good work dogs. I never thought he would know those ewes were back there!'

That farmer brought his bitch to be mated to Roy later that same year.

When I remember Roy, I like to think of that evening and his proud, panting face.

Losing Roy in the final weeks of my pregnancy, and with lambing just round the corner, made Fallowlees a stressed and emotional place to be at that time.

38

Len

I was induced on the evening of 9 April 2019, as there was some concern over the size of my baby. We were in the thick of lambing, and the Suffolks were in full swing. It was all Ewan could do to get away and drop me off at the hospital, with reassurance from the doctors that it would be at least twenty-four hours before anything started happening. Comforted by this knowledge, he went home so that he could feed the sheep in the morning and check that things were OK before coming back to join me. We both agreed that there was no point in him hanging around waiting when there were lots of jobs to be done.

That night my contractions began coming very close together, and by early morning the midwife told me the baby was close to being born. She was diabetic and needed a break to go and get something to eat, she told me, but she reckoned she would wait as the baby would be here in less than ten minutes.

Eek! Ewan hadn't come back yet. He's going to miss the birth, I thought. A thick wave of disappointment swept over me. As if that wasn't bad enough, I felt dreadful – as well as the contractions gripping me like a vice, I was being violently sick on a regular basis. I hadn't even been able to ring Ewan to warn him that things were moving faster than expected.

Just then a midwife walked in.

'I found this gentleman outside.'

Ewan breezed into the stifling room, smelling of lambing and fresh country air, just in the nick of time.

Almost in the same breath, all hell broke loose. My midwife looked at the monitors and decided the baby was in distress. We were all whisked off to theatre.

Three failed attempts at a forceps delivery meant that our baby was delivered by caesarean section. This was the last thing I had been expecting, or hoping for, but our baby boy was delivered alive and wailing, albeit a bit battered.

We named him Leonard Ray Irvine after Grandpa Len, my paternal grandpa, who gave me my first dog, and Mum's dad, Raymond Connell, who was happy to see his name put to good use. Granny Gray cried when Dad told her that Grandpa's name had been handed on to his great-grandson.

Ewan, who hours earlier had been lambing one of those pesky Suffolks, was now proudly holding our son. While they stitched me back together, I was sick on his feet.

I changed after Len was born, even though I had promised myself I wouldn't. I was a faded, more tired-looking version of the usual Emma Gray. I've always made an effort with my

appearance – I was even a bit of a make-up junkie in the past –
but I didn't have the enthusiasm or energy for anything but
the bare minimum now. It was hard enough just to get out of
bed and throw on some clothes.

But I was changed in a deeper way, too. I didn't know
myself. And I didn't know what had happened to the life I had
had before.

People often assume that because of my job I must be
maternal, a natural mother. I have helped skinny lambs slither
into the world and coaxed life into them. I have birthed cows
and pigs. I have caressed tiny pups, a few minutes old. But
until I had Len I had never held a human baby in my arms.
Not once. Perhaps I held my sisters when they were babies,
but I had no memory of ever holding a baby as an adult. In
fact, I was the sort of person who would avoid doing so. It just
wasn't my area.

And yet I'd assumed that when it did happen it would all
come to me naturally. I had seen how sheep, dogs and cows
took to motherhood so quickly, without a manual. I thought
that would happen to me too. How wrong I was.

I wasn't able to hold Len for the first few hours of his life. I
was exhausted and numb from the chest down after the epi-
dural. I have often wondered, if I had held Len straight after
his birth, would I have felt a closer connection to him sooner?
A sheep in the same situation, not able to mother her lamb for
several hours, would have rejected him outright.

As it was, I didn't get that lightning bolt of overwhelming
love I had heard so many mothers talk about. I just felt empty.

And then we were home. And I was on my own, or, on my

own plus my new appendage. Ewan was at Healey, taking care of the lambing, all day and every day. It was, after all, our busiest time of year. Had it not been for Ewan the flock would have had to be sold, which would have meant an enormous loss of earnings, not to mention the loss of generations of sheep raised from scratch.

I might have laughed if I had been in the mood to do so, thinking about how carefully I planned lambing time for my ewes and yet had made such a mess of my own.

I longed to be out there with Ewan, doing the job I did best. Instead I was confined to the house, a nappy-changing milk machine.

Caroline and my mum came down to stay for a few days. They helped Ewan with lambing and looked after the dogs for me. Ewan's mum arrived, too, and was super-helpful. I think if one of them had suggested taking Len home with them and looking after him for a few weeks or months until I felt stronger, I would have readily agreed!

I fell hard into the baby blues. I was stiff, sore, tired and unhappy.

I had never felt so utterly responsible for anything before. I was required all the time. I had assumed that a newborn would sleep for twenty hours out of twenty-four. Which was partly true. Only they wake up every hour demanding a feed, and often when you are only just getting off to sleep yourself.

You lucky thing, I thought to myself, as I watched Ewan leave the house for a shift in the lambing fields with his dogs. You lucky, lucky thing! I wanted to be out there with him, working, not stuck indoors with a baby.

Then at two weeks old Len got colic. He cried night and day. Ewan was already drained from lambing and I was permanently exhausted. It was one of the lowest times.

I realised that I didn't have time to give all my dogs the attention and exercise they needed, so, reluctantly, I sold off some of the youngsters.

This wasn't how I imagined motherhood would be.

I make no bones about the fact that I had been horribly naive about the whole thing. How could I have been so arrogant to assume I would pop the baby out and go right back to work, baby in tow? I'd pictured going about the farm, getting on with my jobs, Len in a sling; or strapping him into his car seat and popping him in a corner of the shed while I got stuck in to lambing, occasionally breaking off to admire my new production or give him a feed before he settled back into a blissful milky slumber. I guess anyone who has kids will be reading this thinking what a total idiot I was. And I agree.

It took all my resolve not to break down when the health visitor came round asking her set questions about how I was getting on, how baby was feeding, how my scar was healing. Ticking away at her boxes.

I told her I was fine. I told her that I was enjoying my new role. Somehow I held back the emotion that was lurking. Perhaps if she had seen through me or asked one more question, these feelings might have been triggered. But I was terrified that Len would be taken away if she found out how miserable I was, so I kept up the pretence and told her what I thought she wanted to hear.

I wondered if I had ruined for ever what had been a pretty amazing life.

As my scar healed and I gained a bit more energy, I was able to go outside, with Len in the sling. I still couldn't drive or visit my sheep, but I realised I could start to train my dogs again.

But my overriding feeling was one of guilt. After a session with the dogs I felt guilty for having Len in the sling for so long. If I spent a day in the house with him, I felt guilty for neglecting the dogs. And I felt guilt all the time for leaning so much on Ewan, who was still a full-time firefighter but who now had the bulk of the farm work to do on his own.

Len's colic carried on for the first four months of his life, and throughout that time he cried incessantly. Health visitors told me it was normal. Up to that point, the only colic I knew was the agonising pain a horse suffers before it is shot. I mentioned this to the health visitor, who was not impressed at what she regarded was a flippant remark.

I was given various tips about cutting out dairy products and coffee, but whenever I asked whether I should bottle-feed Len, the mantra was 'Breast is best'.

One day Ewan came home and put his arm round me. It was one of those trigger moments. I started to sob, and once I started I found that I couldn't stop. I cried all that evening, really ugly crying, all snotty and red-faced.

It was, however, the turning point. Ewan listened to me as I blubbed out my guilt and misery. Together we set out a plan of action. Ewan fed Len a bottle that evening, and every evening after. Len was immediately happier. If I had been a ewe I would have had my ear notched and been sent away on a wagon as a failure.

The colic improved with time, until one day I realised it had all but gone.

I also realised that I loved Len more than anything. It had snuck up on me, not the lightning I was expecting, but there all the same.

My crying, clingy baby became a cheerful outgoing one, who smiled readily at everyone. It was a relief to see that the colic, although bad, had left no ill effects – at least not on him!

I really think that having a baby is an incredible feat. I take my hat off to mothers around the world: they are amazing!

Spring turned into the summer, and we were firing on all cylinders once more.

39

Ewan: A Dad Again

Our wedding day flashed by in a giddy blur. I'm smiling now as I think back to snapshots of the day, like catching our cake, which Emma near cowped slicing into it with a recklessly brandished knife! There were a few romances kindled at our wedding party, and another of our friends has gone on to marry the girl he met that night.

When Emma told me she was pregnant I was delighted, of course. We hadn't discussed having kids of our own, but this instantly felt so right. We started calling our unborn son – we knew it was a boy after the first scan – Zorro, much to the amusement of family and friends, who weren't quite sure if we were serious.

The morning after Emma was admitted to hospital to be induced, right in the thick of lambing time, I was up early, sorting out problems and feeding up. When Emma wasn't replying to my texts or answering her phone, I started getting worried and decided to cut and run for the hospital. I was still in my lambing clothes, minus the waterproofs, when I got there. It was perfect timing. Emma was already pushing and the baby's head was crowning. I was amazed at how calm and collected Emma was, and massively relieved to have made it.

Things suddenly changed very quickly. One minute the midwife was full of praise for how well Emma was doing, the next she was calling for a doctor. We learned that the baby's heartbeat was decreasing during contractions and he was in distress. He was also turned on his side. We ended up being rushed to theatre and were told we might need a C-section. (I say 'we' – as if I was doing anything!) Emma was wheeled away and I was sent to a room to strip off and don some scrubs. When I came into the theatre it was full of people. Our doctor began talking us through all the risks a caesarean entailed, but we had no time to think it through, and besides, in that situation we were always going to be guided by what-ever the experts thought best. It was terrifying. We had gone in a matter of minutes from me holding Emma's hand and the baby seemingly about to make an appearance, with little assistance, to a scenario where I might lose both my wife and baby if something went wrong.

The doctor and consultant made three attempts between them to turn the baby using forceps so that he could be born naturally. Poor Emma was being hauled up and down the table. I kid you not! When that didn't work they resorted to cutting her open. Even then it was a struggle to free Len. I can still see our doctor stressing and sweating, a knee braced against the table and his hands grasping the legs of our son, whose head was deeply engaged in Emma's pelvis. It was traumatic to watch, and not too different from some of the farmyard birth scenes I've witnessed, bar the twenty or so people involved. But despite his rough start – with his poor head bruised and squished – Len found his voice and was crying and mouthing when he was passed to me to cuddle in one arm, while I continued to hold Emma's hand with the other. She was struggling to stay awake as they stitched her up.

I guess dads the world over feel that unbelievable surge of love for their partner and their baby in these moments, if they are lucky enough to be there at the birth. I certainly did. I'm super-grateful to all the people who were there that day to help us.

I had worried about how my older two, Finn and Jessica, who I have for a day most weeks, would be with Len, imagining some jealousy. Pretty fat-headed, I know, but I feel we have such a good life here, and are so happy in our little family unit, that they might have felt less than welcome somehow. I needn't have been concerned. They are both really sweet with Len. The first time they met him they had made cards and picked out some of their favourite toys from when they were younger to give him. Jess looks out for Len and takes time to play and engage with him, reading stories and drawing pictures with him. Len adores the pair of them and follows his older brother Finn around, watching over his shoulder when he is helping mend things or getting his twenty minutes of *Farming Simulator*, a video game where the player takes on the role of the farmer. They love bouncing on the trampoline together, and it fills me with joy to hear their unbridled laughter.

It is so sweet to see my older pair each holding one of Len's hands when we walk up to the lochan to swim and play in the canoe and kayaks.

I really love the life that Emma and I have at Fallowlees, even more so with Len now part of the crew. I love that Emma is her own boss and admire how successful she is. I can appreciate the dedication and hard work she has put in to get to where she is today. I began to harbour the ambition to strike out with her – to find our way in the world without my other job drawing me away. Ideally, a farm big enough for us both to run without needing other employment.

It's always been a privilege for me to serve my community and help people in their time of need. My parents brought up my two sisters and me to have great respect for the public sector, and I knew how proud they had been when I was successful in the recruitment process for the fire service. But a wee bit of me was longing to be working out in nature once more.

I thought back to my first-ever job – helping out on the farm near my family home. Was I about to come full circle?

40

This Farming Life

I probably shouldn't have entered the English National in 2019. In fact, there's no 'probably' about it. I definitely shouldn't have. I was still adjusting to becoming a mother; and, quite frankly, the dogs were not up to scratch.

With trialling, as with any sport, you can't just turn up on the day without putting some major work in behind the scenes. At that particular time in my life, polishing up the trial work of my dogs came bottom of a very long list of priorities. Both Jamie and Joff, my best dogs, needed practice, and it was an even bigger step for Joff, who had yet to compete in such a major competition.

But with only one National a year, and a dog maybe having six or seven shots at it in a lifetime, I couldn't see any harm in giving it a bash. What's the worst that could happen, I pondered? A bit of humiliation, perhaps? Well, I could cope with that.

But this year, any humiliation would not just be in the trial field – it would be humiliation on a national scale. Ewan and I were being filmed for a television programme.

It all began when I received a phone call one day in the early summer of 2019 from my cousin Darren, son of Uncle Toffa (he of the nine lives). Darren was the coordinator for Northumberland Young Farmers and had been asked if he knew of any young families in the county who would be interested in taking part in a new series of the BBC programme *This Farming Life*. There had been three series of the programme already, so far set wholly in Scotland, but this year the producers had a new remit and were looking for farms south of the border as well.

I have always felt that *This Farming Life* is an important programme, achieving that rare feat of being popular with farmers as well as with the general viewing public. I was a big fan of it, anyway. It showed proper farming, un-sanitised and real. You saw the ups and downs of farming life, not just a rosy picture designed to make city dwellers ooh and aah over country living. I had always thought it gave the public a true taste of the realities of family farming.

I didn't hesitate. 'Definitely give them my number,' I said to Darren.

Shortly after that conversation I had a telephone interview with Kate, the casting agent. I was keen to be involved and didn't hold back on how exciting our daily lives were, though I did wonder, when I put the phone down, if I had overdone it a bit. A few weeks later Kate arrived at Fallowlees, camera in hand, to film a recce video. We were but one on a long list of candidates, and Kate had many more people to visit, even a couple more that same day. Because of that, even though I enjoyed the filming and felt it had gone well, I didn't set too much store by it. Television is very fickle, I told Ewan. I had been let down in the past and had learned not to get my hopes up.

But this time it was different. Not long after Kate's visit, the BBC rang and told us we had been successful. In fact, they wanted to send a crew right away to capture the upcoming National.

I was elated. But then my stomach sank. Ah, yes – the National. I remembered waxing lyrical about it on the phone to Kate, but really, I'd have been happier to give it a miss this year. I couldn't help thinking that it wasn't a good National to be capturing.

That week the BBC sent the producer and crew to Fallowlees to discuss formalities.

'There will be a small fee for having us film,' Fiona, the producer, said over coffee in the farmhouse kitchen.

Damn it, I thought, but I suppose it's only to be expected. The BBC were sending a lot of people and kit, after all.

'Oh, OK. How much would that be, and when do you need us to pay it?'

Fiona looked at me blankly.

'We pay you the fee,' she said. 'Just to cover you for the extra time you might have to spend explaining things to us.'

'Oh, I see!' I beamed, relieved.

Ewan slapped his head in exasperation. 'Honestly, you can't take her anywhere,' he chuckled.

The film crew, Kate and Steven, were a boyfriend and girl-friend of similar ages to Ewan and me. We got on with them like a house on fire. We had similar outlooks on life, and right from the word go they were fun to have around. I'm not going to lie and say they never got in the way or slowed things down, but their company certainly made the days more enjoyable and go faster.

The National took place in Lancashire in August. It was one of the hottest days of the year when I walked the course the day before the main trials began. The grass cracked as I followed the lines of the course beneath my feet. Marquees had been erected housing craft stalls and trade stands. In another area of the grounds there were rides for children. There were going to be smaller events for dog lovers, too – a pet dog show and obedience workshops.

But I could feel the pressure in the air – there was a storm brewing.

What followed were three days of truly horrendous weather. The car parks turned to bogs and, gradually, the spectators were driven away. They had all but disappeared by the time I ran.

Joff was running on day one, Jamie on day two. I had come down on my own as Ewan had stayed at home to look after Len, as well as his bitch Rita – a daughter of Brenna and Jamie – who was due to whelp that weekend.

I was very aware of the crew shadowing my every move. It felt strange, unnatural. I felt awkward for another reason, too: the sheepdog community would be expecting great things of me and my ensemble – I mean, I had brought a bloody camera crew with me! I was really feeling the strain from the start.

Joff and I fluffed it right away. It was all too much for his shallow trial experience. He had missed out on lambing completely that year because I had just had Len, and it showed.

I told the camera crew that I was more confident about Jamie, due to run the next day. He was the more experienced of the pair, I assured them, and would fare better. But deep down I knew I was woefully unprepared.

The next day the weather worsened. There were no spectators at all. The wind picked up tents and blew them across the fields. The TV crew looked fed up. Even Jamie looked fed up.

They strapped an enormous contraption to my chest to try to capture some of our run and I set Jamie off, hoping to regain that feeling of optimism I so often felt when he was running. But when he arrived at the top of the field on his outrun, the sheep took one look at him and ran as hard as they could back to where they had been let out. This wasn't a normal occurrence for Jamie – he never spooked the sheep. He regained control, took charge of his little packet and began to bring them towards me. I could see now that he was nowhere near as fit as he usually was and that he was struggling to outpace his woolly charges. About halfway down the fetch I could tell that he had stopped trying. I whistled with all my might to try to speed him up, but he continued to do the bare minimum and didn't respond to my whistles in his usual way.

Of course I knew the reason for it – he hadn't had my time and attention the way he had in previous years. Nor did he have the fitness a long lambing season would have given him. He just wasn't on the button.

I knew I shouldn't have come, I thought, as I retired. I should take more notice of my instincts in future.

I felt bad for the crew. It hadn't been the most thrilling start to our filming. But then, this was what it was all about – showing the good times and the bad. All the same, I hoped they weren't too disappointed. I hoped too that I wouldn't look too much of a fool when the programme aired. (I needn't have worried as, when the time came, they dealt with it carefully and sympathetically.)

Another lesson learned, I thought, as I drove home. In fact, wasn't my life proving to be a series of lessons, each one teaching me something new. I would never get everything right, but then life would be very dull if I did! I cheered up considerably when I got back in time to see Ewan, with Len in a sling, helping Rita with the last of her pups. What's more, the crew were still with us, filming, and able to capture this miracle of nature. You might expect me to have become blasé about newborn pups, having seen hundreds in my lifetime. But I'm not. Every birth puts a big smile on my face. Puppies – like human babies – are good for the soul! Every new pup is the cutest thing I have ever seen. They are what it's all about. And to cap it all, a little lilac pup slipped out as if on cue – the only one I have ever seen – a rare case of a dilution gene working on a redcoat, giving the pup an almost purple tinge.

I was still smarting from the debacle at the National when a disappointing letter landed on our doormat. It declared that Forestry England would not be renewing our lease on the land we rented from them.

That was it. After eight years we got two lines and no explanation. Most of our land is rented from the National Trust, but twenty-five acres is leased from Forestry England. The land adjoins Fallowlees and has always been included with the farm; it wouldn't make sense for anyone else to rent it. The ground is poor, for sure, but additional land on a marginal farm like ours can make all the difference.

I immediately rang Arthur, my agricultural adviser and one of the partners in the business with John and Rosalind Murray.

It wasn't good news. He said that if the loss of the land meant I was unable to fulfil my obligation to the higher-level environmental scheme, then I was at risk of having to pay back what I had earned on the land as well as warranting a hefty penalty.

We both agreed that the most likely reason for the ending of the lease was that the organisation wanted to plant more trees. Many farmers had been thrown off their land in recent years to make way for landlords cashing in on generous government initiatives to do so.

There was nothing I could do, except explain my predicament to the agent at Forestry England and throw myself on his mercy.

I suddenly felt vulnerable and insecure. Someone who had never clapped eyes on the land surrounding my house had the authority to take it away. That is a tenant farmer's lot. It smacked of the Highland Clearances, which began in the 1750s, and saw Scottish tenants evicted from their land in the Highlands and Islands. Whereas then landlords were looking to increase their income by throwing out the crofters in order to populate the hills with sheep, now sheep were being cast aside for another more lucrative cash crop.

41

Jonjo

Jonjo, the bull we had bought to service our growing herd of cows, had lived a contented life at Fallowlees. But now his own daughters would be coming into the herd, and although there is a certain amount of line breeding in Whitebreds, father and daughter was most certainly too close. Jonjo would have to be sold.

We decided that there was plenty of life left in Jonjo, and that he could continue passing on his genes at another farm. With that in mind, we asked the vet to put a ring in his nose, a procedure that is carried out so that bulls – being potentially dangerous animals – are easier to handle. We then put Jonjo in the polytunnel so that we could pamper him over the winter before entering him for the sale at Carlisle in the new year.

As we had the crew following us, and were aware of the need to provide a good spectacle for the cameras, I suggested to Ewan that we have a go at halter-breaking Jonjo. Yup, I thought, another chance for the great British public to see us making fools of ourselves.

Almost all young bulls are sold haltered in the ring; this proves they are quiet-natured enough to be handled. A halter goes over their head in the same way it would a horse. With a bull, though, a rope is clipped onto the ring through their nose for added security and greater control. Some bulls can weigh up to a ton, and if they start getting feisty the handler isn't going to be able to hold them through sheer brute force.

I had never halter-trained a bull, and nor had Ewan, but hell, we were game.

Jonjo had been used to being handled right from the start, and he quickly grew accustomed to having us around, feeding him and scratching his back. We practised putting a halter on him while he was eating so that he was distracted. I say 'we', but I confess that it was Ewan who undertook this job. Jonjo may have been mild-mannered for one of his species, but he was still a bull.

'Just chuck it on,' I said, from where I stood safely on the other side of the barrier, Len watching from his sling.

I'm not sure what Ewan's reply was to that. It was probably best I didn't hear.

Jonjo tossed his powerful head and tried to shake it off.

Ewan kept a decent distance from Jonjo at first so that he would have time to make a run for it should Jonjo decide to turn on him, gradually getting closer when he had some control. As I watched, I reflected that my fears that I might have overcooked our lives in the hope of being selected for *This*

Farming Life were all unfounded. Every new day on the farm was full of drama – both expected and otherwise.

The next stage was tying Jonjo to the front of the tractor. I drove at a snail's pace and Ewan walked patiently alongside him, holding his halter, day after day. We reached the stage where Ewan could lead him round the field quite effectively. The following year, we hoped, he would be doing the same with him in the ring at Carlisle. Jonjo grew more and more used to Ewan. He particularly enjoyed the shampoo Ewan gave him every week or so to keep his beautiful skin in good condition and his hair whiter than white.

The sale catalogue came and showed a whopping eight entries for bulls, way more than we had expected. There are often few buyers for bulls at the best of times, so this wasn't great, but with a well-trained bull like Jonjo, we were still optimistic.

The day of the sale dawned, with Jonjo in a foul mood. Mum was looking after Len for the day, so that was one less thing to worry about.

The early start didn't help any of us, and was made worse by the additional pressure of the crew filming it all. Jonjo made it clear from the off that he was not going to cooperate. He was a nightmare to load, and by the time we had him in the trailer he was as mad as a cut snake. His twisting and turning all the way to the mart didn't do anything for our nerves as we made our way down the narrow country roads.

Unless he calmed down on our arrival, I couldn't see how Ewan was going to be able to lead him in the ring. I was disappointed for Ewan. All those hours he had spent handling Jonjo, gaining his trust, getting him to cooperate, to be quiet and acquiescent. We knew he could be obstinate, and grumpy at times, but we had never seen this side of his nature. It looked as if all of Ewan's efforts had been for nothing.

When we arrived at the mart we saw that Jonjo's nose was bleeding. He must have caught his nose ring on something while he was getting so worked up. As he emerged onto the unloading bay, his appearance was more that of a Spanish fighting bull than a Whitebred Shorthorn, which is known for its docile nature. He was furious.

'You can't lead him like that,' I told Ewan. 'We'll just have to sell him unled.'

'I'm going to give it a go,' Ewan said.

I went to ready his pen while Ewan tried to put a halter on him and give him a wash. His constant spinning had left long silver go-faster stripes on each flank.

As I put the straw down in his pen, Jonjo's namesake appeared beside me.

'I'd put that bull back in the trailer, if I were you,' Jonjo Pattinson, the farmer who had sold us Longface and Shortface, told me. 'He's just tried to flatten Ewan. He's gone crazy.'

'Oh, Christ!'

I started running up the corridor and met Ewan coming towards me, leading a furious, freshly washed Jonjo down the long alleyway. I could tell by the look on Ewan's face and from the tension in his arm what an effort it was to keep the bull from tearing out of his grasp.

By some superhuman effort Ewan got him into the pen and tied him up.

The show for the Whitebred bulls was about to start.

Ewan looked at me and gave a wry smile. 'I think we should sit the show out.'

Damn right, I thought. I wanted my husband in one piece.

I hoped the time spent standing in the pen would calm Jonjo down. This was his chance to go to a new home as a breeding bull rather than end up as someone's dinner.

C'mon, Jonjo, I willed him, behave. Show them what a nice lad you really are.

As the oldest bull in the sale, Jonjo was first in the ring. We made a last-minute decision to sell him unhaltered. Let's face it, there was no way anyone could have walked round the ring with him and stayed in one piece.

I looked at the foaming, enraged creature in front of me. He was nothing like the docile animal who enjoyed having his back scratched in the polytunnel, or being shampooed by Ewan in the yard. The excitement had clearly been too much for him.

Perhaps a little run round the ring would quieten him down, I hoped, while knowing I was clutching at straws.

Of course, the run around the ring did nothing to help. If anything, he got angrier.

'Just a little excitable!' the auctioneer shouted, pleading for bids.

The crowd weren't buying that. And they weren't buying Jonjo. There were other bulls to follow and they were going to wait for them. It wasn't our day, and it certainly wasn't Jonjo's. He galloped out of the ring unsold, and we took him home to Fallowlees.

He sadly sealed his fate that day. The following week he loaded like a lamb into the trailer that took him away to be sold for burgers. I was disappointed the cameras were there to capture this episode in our life, with its less than happy outcome. But I guess it's all part of our farming life.

42

Megan

Megan had been bought to boost the Fallowlees female numbers. Up to that point we had become quite dog-heavy, not helped by my preference for males. I had been speaking to our friend Lynn Morland, who told me she had kept back three bitch pups from a litter and they were becoming rather a handful at eight months old. Lynn showed me a video of them all. Megan stood out for me straight away. She was a very dark dog with lots of mottles all over her white patches; she also had terrible ears. When choosing a sheepdog, handlers like a dog's ears to be set upright and high on its head, as this makes it easier for them to hear the handler's commands and also lends the dog greater presence when they need to move difficult sheep. Meg's hung down like those of a Labrador, which was far from ideal.

And yet there was something about her that spoke to me, that I just liked, even from viewing a video.

'I'll take her,' I said to Lynn, and we agreed a price.

Now Meg was certainly not the easiest dog to train or have around. She was very driven and could get hyperactive if she wasn't worked enough. People sometimes ask me if collies make good pets, and in reality, some do. If the right line is chosen and the dog gets enough stimulation, a collie can make a very good pet. There are plenty of happy, relaxed pet collies out there to prove it. Meg, however, was not one of those dogs – she was born to work. Had she ended up as a pet, I'm almost certain she would have been a car-chasing, toddler-biting nuisance and her next move would have been to a rehoming centre – or worse.

When Len was born in April 2019, she was top of the transfer list for sale because I could see she was the one suffering the most from the lack of regular training. However, in the end I kept her.

By the time I got out and about with the dogs again, I would aim to make Meg my priority as she needed the training the most. By the time summer came, I was out with her every day, with Len in a sling.

We quickly developed a good relationship. Despite her odd ears, Meg had plenty of positive features as well as a lot of talent. It wasn't long before I realised she had the makings of a very good trial dog.

By the time the nursery season started in November, it had become apparent that Meg really liked competing. I was delighted to be back at the post. We won numerous trials together. Thanks to her I retained both the championship trophy Nessie had won me the year before as well as the

overall Northumberland League nursery title I had won
with Joff.

But I knew I had really bought Meg to sell, and that was
always at the back of my mind, even when she was winning.
I had enough talent in Jamie, Joff and Nessie already, as well
as a rapidly growing pup pack for next year.

I think if it hadn't been for *This Farming Life* I would have
sold Meg privately and that would have been that. But as
it was, I had already pitched the idea of selling a dog at
Skipton to them when we auditioned for the show. The producers hadn't featured a dog auction in any of the previous
series, and I think the idea probably helped to get us on the
programme.

I duly entered Meg for the Skipton sale of February 2020,
and shared a video demonstrating her extensive range of
experience online. The response was spectacular. After a
week or so I reckoned I had three Americans lined up as
potential buyers. They were all competent handlers who only
wanted the best.

About ten days before the sale, a pregnant Nessie – in pup
to Joff – had a squabble with Meg. They had always got along
well; both were daughters of the same dog, so I suppose they
were half-sisters. But for some reason the exuberant Meg
must have annoyed a hormonal Nessie and Meg ended up
with a sore-ish bite on her paw. It wasn't terrible and she
wasn't lame, but with the sale so close it was poor timing. I
sprayed the foot and rested her.

Three days before the auction, one of the Americans offered
me ten thousand pounds for Megan. It was a great offer. But

he added, 'It's this or nothing. If you turn it down and take her to auction, I won't be bidding.'

I didn't know what to do. Ten thousand pounds was a lot of money. She might not make that much at the auction. But I felt I was committed to going to Skipton now. The two other buyers were strong contenders, and I owed it to them to take her. I also felt the crew would be disappointed to miss out on the drama of an auction I had promised them. I remembered the buzz of the previous year's auction when I had sold Brenna. It would have made great television if we'd had the cameras then. So I thanked my potential buyer for his offer but declined politely.

The next day Meg was lame, hopping lame. She couldn't even put her foot to the floor. Ewan and I didn't know what to do. It looked as if we would have to scratch her from the sale. The film crew were supposed to be filming us getting ready for the auction; instead they tagged along as we took her to the vet to get a prognosis.

'I'll give you a fifty-fifty chance of her going to the sale,' Stuart the vet said. 'I've given her some painkillers and some antibiotics. You'll just have to rest her and see.'

I was kicking myself. 'I knew I should have taken the ten thousand,' I wailed to Ewan.

There wasn't another sale for months, and I had a feeling that if I waited and took her to a later one the hubbub would have died down and she wouldn't generate the same interest.

'What's done is done. We'll just have to wait and see,' said Ewan, as calm as ever.

The next day Meg was almost sound, and the day after that, auction day, you couldn't even tell she had been lame.

It was a wet morning as the crew and I travelled down to Skipton. It felt as if it had been raining for months. Ewan was on night shift and was going to drive down to meet us there after work.

I was hopelessly nervous, and this time was worse than the last because of the TV crew. I felt like a real show-off, having a camera and sound team following me round. I could see people thinking, 'Who the hell does she think she is, swaggering about like that?' I felt unworthy of the attention. I remembered how the crew had accompanied me to the National and seen me flop badly. I didn't want it to happen all over again. More national humiliation could be on the cards, I thought.

I reassured myself that I didn't mind taking Megan home if the sale did flop. She was a cracking bitch, after all. But even so, the sum I had turned down was burning in my head.

Where was Ewan? I was relying on him more and more these days to calm me down when I was feeling stressed. I suppose the training for his job helped. Strangely, though, he couldn't watch programmes depicting medical emergencies on TV – he found them too distressing as they brought back memories of that day with Timmy. Yet he was always as cool as a cucumber when he was under pressure.

I kept looking at my watch and thinking he should have been here by now. He arrived on his bike in the nick of time.

'Have you eaten anything?' he asked me.

I shook my head.

'Honestly, Emma.'

I didn't have much appetite but managed to finish my banana and take a few swigs of a Lucozade. Our turn was fast approaching.

'Go get 'em,' said Ewan, giving me a hug and Meg a few gentle slaps on her side.

I went to stand next to the auctioneer. The previous dog was being escorted off the field for disrespecting one of the sheep.

'Do you get nervous?' I asked Steven, the director of *This Farming Life*, who was standing beside me, camera on his shoulder.

'Do you know,' he said, 'I'm kind of feeling nervous for you right now!'

'That makes two of us, I guess.' I managed to laugh but it felt forced.

Ewan gave me a thumbs up from his vantage point. He was live-streaming the sale to one of the potential American bidders.

Meg and I made our way to the post. The atmosphere seemed a little flat compared to last time; the driving rain meant that only the very dedicated were intrepid enough to be ringside.

Of course, I might have known it wouldn't go to plan. Everyone up until now had been given four sheep, but when the door opened, four sheep came out followed by a very dirty and unhappy fifth sheep. I found out later that this was the sheep that had suffered the over-enthusiastic attentions of the previous dog. It had jumped in with my packet after being chased across the field and rolled in the mud before the dog had been removed from the field for bad behaviour.

My heart sank. I could see that it was going to be very difficult to keep this ewe with the others. She was clearly upset and didn't want to join their little group.

Nonetheless, as in trialling, you work with the cards you are dealt, and at a word I sent Meg to gather the mismatched assortment. It took us a little while of careful handling to get the packet moving the way it should, and by that time I realised the bidding had started. I tried to listen this time; I didn't want to miss all the drama as I had done with Brenna.

I angled my head in the direction of the driving wind. Was that eight thousand I heard? It must have been, for the next thing I knew it was nine thousand, and then it had crept up to nine thousand five hundred. A sudden gust blew my hat off my head. I tried not to let it distract me. The bidding had stalled now. Nine thousand five hundred, I heard again. Well, that was fine. I was a little disappointed, of course, bearing in mind the earlier offer, but perhaps it was another lesson. Maybe when I was an old lady in my eighties I would have it all figured out! I picked up my now filthy hat and crushed it back onto my head.

I called Meg to me, to make our walk down the field to the rostrum, happy we hadn't made fools of ourselves, when the bidding restarted. Up it went.

Twelve thousand. Thirteen. It was flying now.

Fifteen thousand. Sixteen. Seventeen.

Surely not.

And then – eighteen thousand.

'And for the last time – eighteen thousand,' said the auctioneer. The hammer fell.

It was a new world record, and yet there was none of the cheering or applause that we had got when I sold Brenna – everyone was too wet and cold to manage that level of enthusiasm. Everyone apart from Ewan, who was beaming from ear to ear. He gave me a big hug. What a lot of money that was. And for a dog that I had trained. I was proud – and totally stunned. Steven, holding the camera, asked me for my reaction. I'm not sure what I said. I could hardly make sense of what had just happened.

'Eighteen thousand guineas, Megan! You're a record-breaker.' Her turn for a hug. What a good girl she was.

'You've broken your own record,' said Ewan.

I hadn't thought of it like that, but it was true. A year ago Brenna had been the most expensive sheepdog bitch to be sold. Now Megan had broken that record, while at the same time becoming the most expensive sheepdog of either sex.

The press had covered Brenna's sale, but there was even more publicity this time. We were featured on both the BBC and ITV news, as well as in several of the biggest newspapers. I think this story helped the general public to realise for the first time just how valuable a well-trained dog is to a farmer, as well as the importance of good bloodlines.

Meg was sold to a big cattle and sheep rancher in Oklahoma who had seen some of my videos on Facebook and had followed Megan's progress throughout the season. As I felt a random raindrop drip off my nose, I reflected that she was off to a better climate.

I bought her half a chicken from Marks & Spencer and she slept right beside me, on my pillow, in the guest house where I was staying as we were en route to a trial. I realised that Megan had just helped me tick another box on the dream list I'd written all those years ago.

43

Coronavirus

Meg set off for the US in March, two weeks before lockdown came fully into force. I was more upset to see her go than I thought I would be. A couple of weeks later I received a photo of her, sitting in a well-worn but handsome leather armchair in a room that looked every inch that of the millionaire American ranch owner. She had clearly found a new throne, and a new kingdom to rule over.

Ewan and I were preparing for lambing and our days were spent at Healey Mill, feeding the expectant ewes and building pens ready for the influx of new arrivals. We still ran four hundred ewes there: two hundred of the partnership ewes and two hundred of our own. The breed of sheep we ran on our own side of the farm had changed since the early days. At the beginning we had mainly Blackfaced ewes, which we put to a Bluefaced Leicester, but as time wore on – and with the addition of all the female lambs resulting from these unions – our flock now consisted mostly of Mule ewes with some Texel crosses, as well as those cursed Suffolks I bought before Len was born, the ones who had forced me to take a back seat for the previous year's lambing. I was pretty confident that the abortions would be a distant memory this year; at least I hoped so.

At Fallowlees, my latest Blue Greys had grown into remarkable little heifers and this year we would be buying our first Angus bull to breed with them. Chalky, my favourite of the cows raised on Penny, was now on her third calf. She has only ever given us heifer calves, all of whom I have kept, so I now have Tippex, Powder and Snowy, who will each enter the herd when they come of age. We still have Shortface and Longface, the pedigree Whitebred Shorthorns, and have added a range of their daughters to the herd over the years.

Beef gets a bad press these days, along with the cattle that produce it, who are blamed for the part they play in producing greenhouse gases. But I am cautiously optimistic that the demand for good-quality red meat is not going to disappear. If other farmers are cutting down on their cattle numbers, then perhaps it is a good time for us to up ours. Only time will tell.

All was well and we were happy with our growing farm when it became clear that a virus that originated in China and that no one had heard of six months earlier was going to start affecting our everyday lives, as it had the lives of our continental neighbours. On Monday 23 March, the world as we knew it came to a halt and Britain entered official lockdown thanks to Covid-19, the respiratory disease caused by a coronavirus.

Coronavirus meant that Len, now just under a year old, could no longer go to the childminder two days a week. With

Ewan still working full-time as a firefighter, and therefore a key worker, I just had to get on with things and take Len with me to work each day. Before the virus I would have thought it irresponsible to have him around when I was working, but now there was no alternative.

Farming is one of the most dangerous professions, I know that. I know farmers who are missing arms or legs, or have had near misses – well, just look at Uncle Toffa! But I hadn't seen danger in so many places until I had Len by my side. Suddenly I saw death or a potential maiming round every corner. That water trough standing innocently in the field was just the right height for a small child to fall into and drown in. Farmyard machinery took on the appearance of medieval torture instruments, in which arms, legs and heads could easily become trapped. The wheels of the tractor had never looked so big and dangerous! Every animal from the biggest to the smallest looked capable of delivering a crippling kick. I found I was anxious all the time, and jobs were taking twice as long to perform as they used to.

As soon as Len started walking I had to be even more vigilant. Len is already showing a penchant for the animals, which is both a blessing and a curse. He is far too familiar with the dogs, and is regularly chasing them round or catching them and opening their mouths to giggle at their teeth! Most of them have easy-going natures and are incredibly tolerant of him – they seem to have accepted him as a rather annoying new member of the pack. But I do worry that one day he'll grab an unfamiliar dog in the same way and get a sharp nip or worse for his efforts.

Our cat, Salem, is also a fond favourite of Len's. During the weeks of lockdown, Salem was even more indulgent with him than usual. I think Salem was missing the camera crew, whom he always managed to seek out and put on a performance for. He liked to crawl up the director's legs when he was busy filming.

Len's love for and attitude to animals reminds me of myself as a child, which makes me think Len could really benefit from a pony ...

Once I began to accept the fact that jobs were going to take longer with Len at my side, I started to enjoy having him around and spending the extra time with him, as did Ewan on the days when he was at home. He was (and still is) a real daddy's boy and loved to copy everything Ewan did, from the way he ate his cereal in the morning to trying to climb up and help him drive the quad bike. We watched proudly as he learned to pull himself up and take his first steps. I realised his first words wouldn't be far away either. I do worry, though, that some of his first will be along the lines of 'That'll do!' or 'Quiet!', the ones I use most often at three in the morning when our resident hedgehog is teasing the dogs again, snuffling around outside their kennels.

As the world shut down, the weather improved. It had been a long, wet winter, but suddenly, as if to make up for it, the sun shone down every day. Ewan and I enjoyed the best lambing we had ever had. The rays warmed the stone byres – usually such chill places – and cheerful wild flowers put in an early appearance in unexpected corners of the farmyard. The world was in turmoil, but life was still sweet and we went about our jobs with smiles on our faces. The newborn lambs thrived. 'The film crew would have loved this!' we found ourselves saying at regular intervals. Filming for *This Farming Life* had inevitably been cut short and we missed the craic and having them around.

My sister Caroline, having been forced to shut her dog-grooming parlour in Kelso in the Scottish Borders, came down to look after Len for us while we were in the thick of lambing. In return I gave her Coquet.

I loved that horse as much as I had loved his gentle mother, but I no longer felt I could give him the time and attention he needed. I had such a lot going on in my life that exercising a horse inevitably came low on my list of priorities. I felt sad to see him go, and with him the reminder of the lovely Delphi. At about the same time, I gave the mischievous Mr Tumnus to a friend. Having a free-range goat was getting more difficult as I was becoming more farm-proud. One day he stripped the tops off a whole row of saplings I had been nurturing. When a friend asked on Facebook if anyone had a goat looking for a home, I knew instantly that was the answer to my problem. Dear old Mr Tumnus – we had been together a long time. It felt like the end of an era.

Despite the despondency we felt because of the virus, everything we had been working towards was finally coming together. We were a happy family unit. Our cows were looking good, our sheep were healthy and the dogs were, well, the cherry on top. I felt the planets were aligning for us. There was talk of filming for *This Farming Life* resuming later in the year.

One day Lisa, my friend from Bute, phoned. There was a

massive farm coming up to let on the island, and they were looking specifically for a young couple. She knew Plan Farm well as she had worked there before she and Ian got together. It was one of multiple livestock farms on the island under the management umbrella of the Mount Stuart Trust, a trust set up to manage the Bute Estate on behalf of the current Marquess. The tenancy was a rarely seen twenty-year duration, real security, a once-in-a-lifetime opportunity

Was this what we had been waiting for? Could this be the farm to tempt us to leave Fallowlees?

Fallowlees was my baby. Ewan loved it too, of course, but we now needed somewhere that worked for us as a couple and as a family. We had already discussed the possibility of moving. We wanted – needed – somewhere that was big enough to employ both of us. It was hard for Ewan to juggle his work, his two older kids and the farm work I needed him to help me with. I was also becoming aware that although in some ways Fallowlees was an idyllic environment for a child to be raised in, there were drawbacks, too. In a few years, Len would start school and make friends of his own. He might want to attend after-school clubs or join the football or cricket team. None of this was going to be easy if we were living at Fallowlees. I didn't want him to be known as the boy who lived in the house in the forest, the one that nobody's parents wanted to drive to for risk of getting a puncture. I thought back to my own childhood. It had been wonderful most of the time, but more difficult in my teenage years, being stuck on the farm, reliant on lifts into town, and I was a mere fifteen minutes away.

Plan Farm was advertised in the *Scottish Farmer* the same week that the paper ran a big spread on Ewan and me at Fallowlees. It felt like a good omen. We sent for the particulars and pored over the beauty of it. It was huge! One thousand four hundred and seventy acres of stunning countryside, hills and improved in-bye. It had a broken-down castle, a chapel, even the remains of an ancient village. It covered the entire lower part of the island, and as such included great lengths of coastline. The house was built of stunning whitewashed stone, with lots of adjoining buildings just ripe for kennels.

A few weeks later we set off for the viewing. It was a wild and wet day as we made the three-hour drive to Wemyss Bay, from where we caught the ferry to Rothesay, the main town on the island. The ferry was on amber storm alert and the thirty-five-minute crossing was choppy. Thanks to Covid-19 we had to wear face coverings and stay in our car, and there were signs about handwashing and observing physical distancing everywhere. But we were both in a good mood. We already knew from our visits to Lisa and Ian that we loved the island.

There were thirty parties viewing the farm over two days, and arrivals were staggered so that everyone could be interviewed. Ewan and I were both suited and booted to create a good impression. Just because you are viewing a farm doesn't mean you turn up in your twenty-year-old Barbour and muddy wellies – although that would have been more sensible gear that day. However, as it was blowing a hurricane, much of our effort was wasted – it was all we could do to stay dry and keep our feet on terra firma.

The agents, Harry and Ian, had pulled some garden furniture into one of the living rooms to set up an impromptu interview room. It was supposed to be an informal interview, but actually felt anything but. The questions went into details we hadn't been expecting. Ewan and I sat there in our soaking-wet clothes trying to put our minds to matters of funding, our experience and plans for the future, while I secretly cringed at the boot prints from all those farmers adorning the pale carpets.

We looked at each other, shell-shocked, as we left the room.

'I wasn't expecting that!' was about all I could manage. But at least we could relax now and enjoy seeing the rest of the farm. Having missed the last ferry, we stayed with Ian and Lisa overnight, thankful that my mum was looking after Len.

The next day the weather had done a U-turn, as often happens on islands. The wind and rain had blown off somewhere else and left us with blue sky and sunshine. With her knowledge of the farm, Lisa took us round the parts we hadn't seen. She and Ewan walked ahead. I could see Lisa waving her arms around energetically, pointing out this and that, and sense the enthusiasm in Ewan's replies and questions, even if I couldn't hear exactly what he was saying.

A peregrine falcon shot through the air above us before dropping like a bullet onto some unseen prey and disappearing from view. Below us we could see the coast and a lighthouse. It was sensational. And yet, and yet ... Something was holding me back. I could feel a twinge of – what? Doubt? Fear? Whatever it was, it wasn't the excitement that Ewan was clearly feeling. Perhaps it was the thought of leaving my familiar life at Fallowlees. God, I loved that farm so much! It was my baby, and always would be. But I knew this was an amazing opportunity for Ewan and me, a project we could start together. There was no doubt we were going to give the application our very best shot, but my heart wasn't exactly where I knew it should be.

I remembered having a feeling like this just before I took over Fallowlees. Just cold feet, I suppose, but I could remember clearly that feeling of dread, of terror, when you are about to uproot your life for a whole new one.

'What's up?' asked Lisa, sensing my lack of interest.

Ewan gave me a querying look. 'You OK?'

'Just imagine, we can be neighbours!' said Lisa.

Feeling bad about being such a mood hoover, I forced a smile and made an effort to shake off the apathy that had come over me.

Back at Fallowlees, we had ten days to prepare the business plan. It seemed no time at all when we were potentially planning the rest of our lives. We put our all into it, the same way I had done for Broomhouse and before that, for Fallowlees. But now there were two of us pulling for the same cause and it felt so much easier. I really felt we could get this farm.

So tight was the turnaround that we used an agricultural consultant. Consultants know what agents are looking for in tenancy applications and we felt it was a worthwhile investment. I hoped our sales of dogs in the past few years, coupled with our successes on the trial field, would stand us in good stead, as well as our achievement in building up our herd of cattle and our flock. Perhaps our upcoming TV show would help too.

All the same, I cautioned Ewan against hoping for too much. I knew how I had felt after missing out on Broomhouse. It was disappointing when you invested so much of yourself in something to see it slip out of your hands.

Our application won us an interview on the island in the large Gothic house of Mount Stuart, the ancestral home of the Marquesses of Bute. It was for 8.15 in the morning, and with the ferries operating a limited timetable due to Covid-19, we decided it would be safest to leave Len with Mum again and stay at Lisa and Ian's the night before.

I didn't sleep a wink all night; my anxiety levels were sky-high. I spent the whole time going over our facts and figures until I was word-perfect. It was the height of summer, and I heard the dawn chorus at around 3.30 a.m. Ewan woke up at five, looking refreshed and unflustered, while I staggered out of bed looking as if I hadn't slept for a week. Ewan, thankfully, is a rock in these situations and just takes it all in his stride. His level-headedness helped to calm me.

I tried to work a miracle on my face and hair while Ewan went to have breakfast with our hosts. He brought me up some orange juice and toast.

'We'll be fine,' he said, putting my breakfast down. 'Our figures are sound. Now eat something.'

I looked at my handsome husband. If I had been the chair of the interview panel, I would have given the farm to Ewan there and then. He was surely the personification of what they were looking for: capable, wise, calm under pressure.

In our haste to not be late we were outrageously early, arriving even before the interview panel. I looked at the house, a magnificent mix of Georgian and Victorian architecture. It was hard not to feel daunted by its splendour.

A couple of people walked past us and we wondered whether to pretend we hadn't seen them or to introduce ourselves formally. Oh, why did we have to be so early, I thought, becoming even more nervous.

Then I managed to drop the five files containing our proposal on the gravel. As I scrabbled to pick them up, more of the panel arrived. Classy, Emma, I thought.

When the time finally came we were taken into the bowels of the house to a rather grand room, where four men sat, socially distanced, around a large table.

The opener was brutal.

So, tell us about yourselves?

Straight in, no messing. A question like that, with no parameters, can floor you. I hesitated briefly before launching into my prepared introduction. Did I say prepared? I think I actually made most of it up as I went along.

Afterwards I felt relieved, like people do after a near-miss car accident. The adrenaline was gone. I just felt empty.

We had asked if we could return to the farm for another look round. The panel agreed and said they would be pleased for us to see Plan Farm on such a nice day.

We spent a good few hours going round the farm at our leisure. This was the prize, but did I still want it? I just wasn't sure about my feelings for it; it didn't sing to me the way Fallowlees had done that fateful day ten years ago. But I looked at Ewan and knew that this would be a brilliant future for us as a family. There was a school close by, and the nearest supermarket was only fifteen minutes' drive away. Even though this was a small island, we would have access to the facilities that we didn't have at Fallowlees, the ones that other people take for granted.

The estate was moving very quickly with their search for a new tenant and within a week we received word that we had made it through to the next stage. I heard on the grapevine that our rivals were another young family. I knew them – they were very similar to us, a couple with a young son. The next step was a visit from Harry and Nick, two of the men who had interviewed us, to see Fallowlees and how we farmed it.

Even reading the email set my nerves a-jangling. I had been expecting it, but now it was really happening. They were coming to the farm to judge us.

The next week saw a Herculean effort from everyone involved. Thankfully we had the added assistance of Nusa and Nate, two Slovenians who had been stranded by Covid and had resigned themselves to helping out on farms instead of sightseeing.

It reminded us of the days spent preparing for our wedding party. I topped the long grasses on the fields. We pulled weeds out of the cracks in the concrete and planted flowers, even though I knew the dogs would wreck them in no time at all. We primped and we fluffed. In short, we did all those little jobs that normally don't get done.

I even baked a cake. Yes, me. It was spectacular, if I do

say so myself: a three-tiered Black Forest gateau with fresh cherries on the top. We all eyed it greedily while waiting for our arrivals. You would have thought the Queen was coming for tea.

Just before they were due, Len – who was tottering about practising his new walking skills – managed to pull himself up on the table, smashing our only coffee pot and hitting his head painfully at the same time. Len has a very disconcerting habit of holding his breath when he is hurt. It's as if he gets stuck on that first outward breath and can't inhale again. He goes blue about the lips and passes out before coming round. I've been to the doctor about it and done research of my own, but there is nothing anyone can do – it's just a habit that does no harm and that he will eventually grow out of.

But seeing it is a horrifying experience, and even when it sometimes happens a couple of times a week, it doesn't get any easier to witness. Len was holding his breath and had turned blue when a dust cloud in the distance announced the arrival of our judges.

Len was still very distressed and Ewan was working hard to placate him as we invited Nick and Harry into our home.

'Would you like a tea or a coffee?' I asked, remembering at the last moment that we didn't have any coffee – we had just swept it, glass shards and all, into the bin.

They both opted for tea, and Ewan gave me a sly wink.

I fed them generous slices of my cake. I cut a slice for myself but found I could hardly eat it.

Fed and watered, we took them on a whistle-stop tour of Fallowlees. The clock was ticking as Ewan was on night shift and needed to leave shortly, but I was confident we could cram a lot in.

We showed them the cows and discussed why we liked the Blue Greys so much. We demonstrated one of the dogs working. We showed them our pristine kennels. We took them across to Healey to see the breeding ewes, fat and contented in our managed grassland. Ewan had to leave before the end of the tour, but I finished up at the steading at Healey, feeling a little breathless but pleased with how it had gone.

They met Steven, one of the partners, and Kirstine, daughter of John and Rosalind, who lives on the farm itself. She kindly took Len from me so that I could chat to them more easily.

As we wrapped up, they asked me, 'If you are unsuccessful with your tender for this farm, would you consider another farm on the island?'

I didn't think twice. I was so keen to please them that I answered, 'Yes, of course.'

In the days that followed I cursed my answer to that question, over and over.

A week later we received an email from the agent to tell us we had been unsuccessful in our tender for the farm.

It had happened again.

Although I had been unsure how I would feel should this be the outcome, I found that, like Ewan, I was bitterly disappointed. Despite my misgivings I knew that this farm had been an opportunity for us that wouldn't come around again for a long time.

That night, Ian the agent rang, telling me not to be too

despondent as Nick and Harry were going to contact us about other farming opportunities on the island.

But it wasn't much consolation. Plan Farm had been a rare gem. That bloody question, I thought. I wish I'd said no. I wish I'd said it was that farm or none at all.

44

Nether Ardroscadale

I had time to stop and smell the roses after we lost out. It was high summer, and the days were long. The fields shimmered in the sparkling light. We had a mini heatwave and it was an effort to do anything. Even the dogs sought shelter from the sun and found cool, dark corners to lie in.

I knew that Fallowlees was still a wonderful home and provided the most fabulous life for me and my family.

Then a few weeks later, as promised, we heard from Harry, one of the agents. I was still pretty sore about being turned down for Plan Farm. I felt that they would never be able to offer us anything close to what we were hoping for. I knew in my mind that the next move was going to be our last move, so it had to be the perfect fit. No room for compromise. Bute had now lost some of her lustre for me – she had become entwined with my disappointment. I didn't really want the booby prize, especially when I knew that, deep down, I had even had some doubts about the main prize.

It was Ewan who got the email. I could tell he was excited. He said that Harry and Nick had 'multiple' opportunities on the island they would like to show us.

I kind of pooh-poohed it all. I had a feeling that because we were such a rough little farm at Fallowlees, they probably thought we would be suited to a rough little farm on the island.

'Give it a chance, Emma,' Ewan told me. 'It's surely worth a look at least.'

I knew he was right, but we had invested so much time as well as money in our application for the last farm, and I didn't want to throw away more. I felt that ever since Plan Farm had been advertised we had put our life on hold: waiting, always waiting for the next hurdle to be cleared. After the interview we can relax, we had thought, but then there was another interview, and then one more. It felt as if we had been gearing up to move for months now, and I was actually relieved to have put it to the back of my mind at last.

But I knew Ewan was right. It would be silly not to give it another shot. We loved the island, and, well, it was a day out if nothing else.

So we took the ferry once more and greeted Harry and Nick at Mount Stuart House ('The Big House', as all the tenants called it, for obvious reasons).

It was immediately a less intimidating and far more friendly affair. The pressure was off and I found I wasn't nervous at all. We sat on a picnic bench in the gardens where Nick and Harry laid out maps of the farms they wanted to show us, weighing them down to stop the summer breeze whisking them away.

I gave Ewan a sly surprised look. He gave me a half-smile that said, 'I told you so.'

The maps showed not tiny smallholdings but real farms – *good* farms, large and viable.

Harry and Nick announced that three farms were looking for new tenants. Yes, three! All of them were over six hundred acres in size. They asked if we would like to take a drive to see which one we liked.

At this point I was struggling very hard not to give away how utterly overwhelmed I was. I steadied myself with the thought that they might not be as good as they seemed on paper, but I still couldn't suppress a shiver of excitement.

Ewan and I hopped into the back of Harry's pickup. The boot was on the other foot now, I thought. It hadn't been all that long ago that I had been showing them round Fallowlees and Healey.

It was a stunning August day with no cloud to taint the bright blue sky. We pulled onto a bumpy track, and Harry gestured across to the fields both right and left. I looked at Ewan wide-eyed. He gave an appreciative grin. The maps, laid out between us on the back seat, told us that those fields were part of the farm. Those fields were perfection.

When I look at fields I have a different appreciation to other people. While most farmers will admire the size, the soil and the drainage, at the forefront of my mind is how these fields will benefit a sheepdog's education. And here I had just seen the training field of my dreams. It was a long, large and wide arc, sweeping right down to the sea. Although it was huge, the viewing was excellent. I would be able to see a dog eight

hundred yards away. It also looked like super ground for grazing – yes, I had my farmer's hat on, too.

I nudged Ewan, trying not to draw too much attention from
the front.

'Look at that!' I mouthed, pointing surreptitiously.

'It's amazing!' he mouthed back.

We pulled up onto an immaculate concrete steading while
swallows swooped overhead.

'This is Nether Ardroscadale farm,' said Harry.

'Nether Ardroscadale,' I said, trying out the new name. It
certainly had a ring to it.

The farmer and his wife came out of a dazzling whitewashed
farmhouse. Harry introduced them as Duncan and Janey.

The outgoing tenants were friendly and accommodating.
Duncan said he could hitch up the trailer to the quad and take
us for a tour. Ewan and I accepted the offer with enthusiasm,
as did Harry, who had been managing the estate for less than
a year and hadn't seen the farm yet. Nick, who was already
familiar with it, opted for a coffee in the farmhouse instead.

It was immediately apparent that Duncan and Janey were
excellent farmers. Everything was where it should be, and as
the farm whipped by from our vantage point on the trailer, we
could tell that the land had been seriously well maintained.
The grassland was quality, fertile, weed-free and rush-free,
with no great big wet patches, a stark contrast to what we were
used to working with at Fallowlees.

And then there was the view. As we drew close to the high
point of the farm, we could see all the way down to a little
peninsula jutting out into the sea, where a ruined church and

two abandoned cottages lay. Where the peninsula met the mainland was a long sandy white beach.

'It goes all the way to there?' I consulted the map.

'All the way,' said Duncan.

I kept looking at Ewan to see if my excitement was reflected in him. It was – and more.

This could be ours, I thought. It was too good to be true. I was really falling for the place, no doubt about it. It was like a first date that was going far better than expected. This farm sang to me in a way the other farm hadn't. But dare we get too excited? We had had our hopes dashed before. Surely this was too good for us?

We arrived back in the main steading and were reunited with Janey and Nick to have a look around the farm buildings. The main cattle shed backed onto the house.

'You can check the calvers in your dressing gown,' Janey told us.

The buildings were better than anything I'd ever imagined. In the past the farm had held over two hundred cows, a figure that made our herd of thirty seem puny in comparison.

In the kitchen the kettle boiled on a pristine Aga and Janey served us coffee and some unbelievably short shortbread. While Duncan and Janey were all smiles and answered our questions enthusiastically, I couldn't help wondering how they were feeling inside. I imagined myself leading strangers around Fallowlees, knowing I was leaving. It made me well up just to think about it. Running a farm is like having a rela- tionship, a marriage, even. It is like part of your identity. When I buy sheep at the mart they are knocked down to 'Emma

Fallowlees'. When I am introduced to people, it's always, 'This is Emma from Fallowlees.' No one takes on a farm thinking it will be for the short term; farmers are serial monogamists.

This time it wasn't just my marriage, it was Ewan's, too. But I could tell from the look on his face that the farm was singing to him as much as it was to me.

I was astounded. This was no booby prize. This could be our future.

Harry and Nick took us, as promised, to the other farms that day, but we were already ruined for anywhere else. Nether Ardroscadale was what we wanted.

The next step for us in the weeks that followed was to get Mum and Dad over to see it. I value my parents' opinions, and I was particularly anxious to see what Mum thought, as she helped out so much with Len. She doted on her only grand-child, and I felt whisking him off to a Scottish island would be mean for both him and her. I wanted Mum and Dad to tell me straight what they thought.

We ended up booking a hotel on the island so that we could show my parents round properly. I actually classed it as our first foreign family holiday! We did the whole tourist shebang: open-top bus tour, tea and cake in cafés, aimless wandering round the shops, before Ewan, Len and I took them to meet Duncan and Janey.

Mum and Dad were as sold on the place as we were. However, I could tell that Mum was putting on a brave face. She told me there was no way she could cope with driving the complex roads around Glasgow that had to be negotiated to reach the ferry terminal at Wemyss Bay, so could only ever visit if Dad was able to drive her.

I felt horrible. She had been there to support me through all those difficult times, and now, when things were going well, I was about to up sticks and take her grandson further away. It seemed a cruel thing to do.

Dad went for an early-morning walk the next day and got chatting to someone from the Borders. He brought back to the hotel the news that Mum could, in fact, get a train when she wanted to visit. It wasn't quite door to door, but she could catch one from the Borders all the way to the ferry terminal by making a few changes. The news was a comfort to Mum – at least I hoped it was.

With Mum and Dad's approval we completed another proposal, we tendered a new rent amount and we waited.

Our life was back on hold, only this time I had a feeling we wouldn't be disappointed.

Epilogue: Farewell to Fallowlees

Our proposal was accepted by the Mount Stuart Trust, and just like that, our lives were about to change. We weren't just starting out on a new chapter. This time, Ewan, Len and I were on the first page of a whole new book. Ewan would be able to give up his job – we were in this together.

It's a book we could never have started without Fallowlees. I am so thankful for everything she has given us. There is no doubt in my mind that I am standing where I am today thanks to Fallowlees and the succession of lucky strokes that took me to her. I am an advert for being in the right place at the right time. Like the saying goes: better to be lucky than good.

A few weeks after being granted the tenancy of Fallowlees all those years ago, before I had even moved in, I was at the wedding of one of my cousins. At the reception I ended up in conversation with a well-known property agent, one of the biggest in the area.

'You know that farm is probably the worst farm in the whole

of Northumberland, don't you?' he declared with a sympathetic smile.

I hadn't thought of it like that, but I knew what he meant. From a purely technical point of view Fallowlees was small, unproductive and inhospitable. She was never going to generate a lot of income for her tenant. Perhaps the agent was trying to warn me that I was doomed to fail.

The words stuck with me, though, and I think of them often.

I'd like to show him round the farm now as I prepare to leave. Fallowlees may be small as farms go, she may be wild and remote, but she has a big heart; she has weathered many storms and will go on to weather many more.

This small farm has helped me to grow. Because of her size, I had to think differently in order to support myself. I had to think beyond the land and the number of sheep she could support. The steps I trod luckily led me to the partnership at Healey Mill and everything it offered. Having both farms allowed me to give the dogs the training they needed to become excellent work and trial dogs. I have been so proud of our achievements on the local, national and international stage.

I can't deny there were low times and heartache over the years. That's part of being a farmer – in fact, it's part of life. But each setback – physical, emotional and professional – taught me something and helped me to move on.

When I look back at the twenty-three-year-old who moved in on a chilly January day, I know that even if I don't feel so very different now, I have matured in many ways. And best of all, I have Ewan beside me, someone who loves this farming life as much as I do. I am fortunate indeed.

We are bound together, Fallowlees and I. That will never change; we have too much history, too many memories. Knowing we are about to part makes me take stock of all we have been through together, and how we have both changed.

We are only ever custodians of our farms and of the land. It is part of the cycle of nature that we too will move on and our farms will welcome the generations that come after us. And so it is with me and Fallowlees, who has stood for hundreds of years and will stand for many more.

It will be a wrench to let go of the farm I have called home for the past ten years, but I hope when the day comes I will be able to leave without too much heartache. It will be done with a heavy heart, of course, but I hope I will be happy knowing that the time is right to allow someone else to take custody of her. I hope she will nurture them as she has nurtured me. I am honoured to have been part of her legacy.

I know that if the choice of the next tenant was down to me, I wouldn't choose the one with the big bank balance, or the one with the smooth patter and the superior business plan. I would choose the one with the glint in their eye that told me they had fallen in love with the farm the way I did – the one with the spirit and determination to take her on.

As I look out of the window on to the world that I will soon say goodbye to, I know that in my heart I will always be 'Emma from Fallowlees'.

Acknowledgements

I would like to thank my mum, the first strong woman in my life, and still the best I know, though I know she will deny it.

To Dad, whose quiet support and faith in me has enabled me to trust my gut instincts, and whose advice is always sound.

To my sisters Caroline and Elizabeth, the best friends I could ever have – apart from Lisa and Nikki, who are pretty much sisters in all but name!

To Ewan and Len, for completing my world.

To John and Rosalind Murray, for putting their faith and trust in me and supporting me throughout the years. I will never be able to pay back everything the partnership has afforded me, but will be for ever grateful that they chose me.

To Arthur and Kirstine, for finding me in the first place and putting up with having me around all of the time – sometimes with my grumpy pants on!

I would also like to thank everyone whose support has helped me get to where I am today.

Finally, thanks to Barbara, who now knows more about me than I do myself, to our agent Sallyanne Sweeney at MMB Creative, and to our editors at the Little, Brown Book Group, Rhiannon Smith and Nicola Crane. Thank you also to copy-editor Jenny Page, and to Nithya Rae and all of the rest of the team at Little, Brown, who have helped in different ways.